SEVEN AGES OF BRITAIN

Justin Pollard

SEVEN AGES
OF BRITAIN

Hodder & Stoughton

For my wife
Stephanie
and our daughter
Constance
who arrived on the day that I finished this book
and so opened a new chapter

Contents

Foreword

I remember the length of that journey. Each August, our destination was the vicar's elfin cottage in Whalebone Yard, Wells Next The Sea – half a day's travel across the country. To get there we would brave London and then negotiate the A roads and country lanes that zigzagged their way up to the Norfolk Coast. The tedium was made bearable by the familiar monuments that flashed past, and by vying to see how many new sites we could add to the list. A bombed Hawksmoor Church on the edges of the city, Norman motte and bailey castles, the Roman Road that bypasses Cambridge, and then proof that we were really getting somewhere – Grimes Graves in East Anglia, sheltered by the flat expanse of Thetford Forest.

I didn't ever come to history: it was always there, I grew up in it. Here in Britain, the landscape wraps history around us. We have a country alive with the memories and remnants of millennia of human activity. Sometimes the past is a comforting presence – the saggy armchair that you know will never move from the corner of the kitchen – but often it can be something more challenging and enigmatic: a half open door, a dark story waiting to be told.

Grimes Graves was definitely the latter. A complex of Neolithic flint mines where between around 3000 and 2000 BC, hundreds of shafts were sunk deep into the earth. At ground level Grimes Graves takes the form of a scrubby, bumpy, rather distressed field. But go up in a helicopter and the site shows itself for what it is: a vast, symmetrical, lunar landscape. Each pockmark is an in-filled pit. Here, in its heyday, men, women and children would carefully carve the inky black flint out of the chalky earth with antler pick-axes and precision flint tools. This was a mammoth, organised operation. It has been estimated that 5 million Neolithic axes, made from that distinctive black stone, could have been produced here.

When I first went, there was palpable excitement around the Grimes Graves sites. This, it was thought, was proto-industry – an industrial revolution in a land that had only just embraced farming. But then new evidence emerged and ideas shifted. The beautiful, polished axes and disc-shaped knives made at Grimes Graves weren't turning up in the local area as you would expect, chipped and worn after years of felling trees. Grimes Graves wasn't the efficient production line it first appeared.

Instead the axes surfaced in odd places – traded around the country as prestige gifts or maybe passed from one settlement to another as sacred objects. In the shafts, offerings have been left; strategically buried tools or the flint itself, dragged out of the earth, skilfully knapped and shaped and then buried again, perhaps as a ritual gift.

There are human remains, maybe the casualties of a pit accident, but just as likely, bodies placed there after death or the living offered the greatest honour – chosen to be sacrificed to the gods in the earth. This landscape inhabited by the early British was bristling with gods. It seems that the sweat and imagination that went into realising this vast project was as much an exercise in mystery and spirituality as it was in engineering. Grimes Graves carries a health warning for all of us – the past may hold out its hand to you but just because it does, don't presume you can describe its face.

This evolving, unique and surprising land, populated by men

and women who have often been forgotten or misrepresented by history, is the Britain that Justin Pollard has written about and which our television series illustrates. This is not the official version: we don't just offer tablets of stone but try to be transparent about the sources that allow us to embark on historical and archaeological analysis – the bones, the pottery, the arrowheads, the poems, the letters, the hoards of cash. There are gaps as well as facts, questions as well as certainties – but these are the meat and drink of the historian. This story of the country emerges from the landscape; it uses physical evidence to posit how the population kept body and soul together. It tells of a fluid past created, enjoyed and endured by the ordinary people who live here.

When we started work on one of those seething, dusty, late summer days we hoped that as we travelled through the twenty-first century British landscape we might be able to people it with the men and women who were once its inhabitants. Certainly, picking our way through the Neolithic waste at Grimes Graves and clambering down into one of the renovated mines to touch the neat little holes gouged out by a Stone Age child, the shadows of the past felt very close.

We also wanted to tell the nation's story via those who have helped make history, but haven't necessarily made the history headlines. As a historian it is easy to cherish the men and women who leave behind rich goods and a convenient paper trail. But, it can be more thrilling to find clues to the lives of those who have been written out of history – or in a pre-literate society, have never had the chance to write their own. The history game can be even more rewarding when its characters fight back, play their cards close to their chest and guard their secrets.

We travelled the length and breadth of the country on the

trail of these elusive, modest Britons. Often motorways would dwindle to B roads which in turn would turn into dirt tracks as we went back to try and find the spot where coal was first shipped out to Europe or an innocent Anglo Saxon woman had been hanged. We thanked the gods for pub loos and cursed the man who invented roadworks. The archaeological evidence we used as our pointers had often survived by chance – the bits and pieces of people's lives that had been ditched or dropped, buried or burnt – unconscious time capsules that allowed us to make some sense of their world. The most ephemeral of activities can leave surprisingly substantial clues. As we walked across fields and through suburban streets, we wondered what other stories lay lost, waiting to be told.

We started at the moment we became an island, in 6000 BC when tiny fragments of charred food around hearths give us an idea of what (during long nights that must have been filled with fire-light and stories) Mesolithic families ate – bog-beans, knotweed, bullrush roots and sweet sticky birch syrup tapped straight from the tree. Outside, elks, brown bear, the flightless great auks and those giant, irascible wild-cows – aurochs, who stood over two metres high, and have left hoof prints the size of steering wheels – prowled and crashed their way through the surrounding forests.

In the labyrinthine interior of the British Museum, one of the curators carefully lifted black indigenous pots and imported terracotta-red Roman cups form their storage boxes to talk about social climbing and the emergence of a class system in the first century BC. These smart Iron Age dinner-services were used by influential men and women as visible proof that their proud owners were powerful enough to access goods from all over the Mediterranean world. But they were also status symbols – owning them said you were a cut above the rest. Communal eating from the shared, roughly worked pots of the generation before was for yesterday's people – this was to be a world where individual ambition came ahead of the needs of the group.

As historians and archaeologists across the country helped the *Seven Ages of Britain* team to gather material, it became clear we were following a nation's journey. Not from A to B, because history doesn't work like that, but from A to B via XYZ, a Palmyrian script, A minus and a couple of mathematical equations. There are the giant steps you might expect, such as when we decide to live in communities rather than isolated groups; when the outside world identifies us as a nation; when Julius Caesar first starts to make notes about the island – a man with the power to record, positioning his people to take power. An ideology of education is born in the Dark Ages and during the medieval period; the monopoly that church and state have over individual enterprise is broken by the chutzpah of the guild movement; in the seventeenth century there are revolutions of every kind, religious, political, local, nationwide, cultural and scientific.

But there are also smaller, quieter passages that say just as much about the country's character – the emergence of feisty English women after the Black Death had eradicated half the male population; the Norman consolidation of our passion for lists and for writing things down; the confidence of the individual, as reflected in Shakespeare's soliloquies; the advent of tea and its appropriation by workers in the late seventeenth century – men eager to create their own rituals, to show that they had standing in the world, that they were worth a tea-break.

We end where we began, with people travelling around the island and across the seas that surround it. Although by the seventeenth century, men and women are beginning to re-locate to work for new masters, to follow new dreams, to found colonies in new continents rather than simply moving with the tides and the seasons, in a repeating rhythm, as their Mesolithic ancestors had done.

Of course so much had changed over the millennia – but there are surprising continuities. In the 1690s, one Sir Humphrey Mackworth owned coal mines near Neath in Wales. Like the flint of pre-history, his raw material coal would fuel a techno-logical and economic revolution. A devotee of Mackworth's business practice was a man called William Waller. Mackworth and Waller were early capitalists and their ambitions seem very modern. In honour of Mackworth, Waller wrote what must be one of the earliest management consultant documents. Read between its lines, and you get the feeling these men inhabited an emotional sphere not so far removed from those early flint miners at Grimes Graves.

Who [writes Waller] can admire that mines are sometimes un-successful when men presume to ship out the very bowels of the earth, enter into the secrets of the deep, and rifle the choicest cabinet of nature, without so much as consecrating the least part thereof to pious and charitable uses.

Drawing constant parallels between our own lives and those in history is a specious exercise, but neither should we presume we are all isolated from each other. There is much that separ-ates Waller and a Stone Age child, but there are some things that connect them. As well as shared experiences, the thoughts and deeds of the past inform the present – our lives are in part a creation of our ancestors. As islanders of Britain, we are relatively blessed in our history and in the documents and artefacts that have survived to tell us about it. We have the inspiration and industry, the application and endurance, the pleasure-seeking and suffering of ordinary Britons to thank for that fortunate position, knowledge which should make us not just proud, but humble.

Bettany Hughes, June 2003

Prologue

The idea behind this book and the television series it accompanies is to tell some of the stories of the 'ordinary' inhabitants of Britain at different stages in our history. It is designed as a counterpoint to the headline histories with their kings, queens, laws and wars, concentrating instead on the experience of everyday life against which the tales of those more famous characters and events were played out.

Rather than being a march through the history of Britain this is more of a stroll through the lives of a selection of people who inhabited this land before us. It is the story of those people whose names never reached the history books but whose lives have been recorded nonetheless in the archaeology and fragmentary records of each period. They are people we don't often hear about, but that doesn't mean they weren't there or make them any less important in their way than the great names of the past.

Over the years their stories have been painstakingly teased out by many academic historians and archaeologists and, having had the privilege of talking to many of them about their work during the making of this series, this is an attempt to weave them together into a narrative. It is a stroll with an admittedly inexpert guide, but one who has at least had a glimpse at the maps. Along the way I hope you'll get some snapshots of old ways of life – traditions, fashions, beliefs and fears – in seven eras that were all startlingly different from our own.

Prologue

During this wander we will travel across most of Britain, by which I mean Scotland, England and Wales, but I have not tried to talk about every part of the country at every period. The stories chosen are those that I think best exemplify some of the experiences of life in each age, or sometimes, particularly in deep prehistory, they are simply set in the only place where a story survives or has so far been uncovered.

This book, like the TV series, is divided into seven chapters – seven ages. The 'Seven Ages' I have chosen are not the only ages of Britain, nor are they definitively self-contained, but they are a way of cutting an otherwise unfeasibly large 'cake' and each age shares a theme that I think unites more than it divides. Other turning-points could have been chosen to begin and end chapters, but these are mine and I hope they don't seem too artificial.

This is a journey to meet history's silent majority and catch a glimpse of their experience of life in each age against the backdrop of the grander events of that time. It is the story of those who never had the privilege of making history but to whom it happened nonetheless, who lived with it, and survived or died with its consequences. I, for one, think they're all worth meeting.

Justin Pollard
Surrey, May 2003

I

Making the Land

What seest thou else
In the dark backward and abysm of time?
        William Shakespeare, *The Tempest*

Nine and a half thousand years ago a small group of humans made the long climb up the slopes of the Vale of Pickering to the hills above. They were in every way a modern people – biologically identical to ourselves, physically and mentally as adept as any human of today, with every capacity and faculty we now possess. As they walked, they spoke to each other in an ancient language, now unknown and unknowable, and as they talked, they perhaps wondered what they might see when they reached the top.

These were not the first people to inhabit the land we now call Britain. Since before the last Ice Age people had been coming to this damp corner of northern Europe, perhaps to fish or gather plants, or follow the game with the changing seasons. The earliest remains of these humans, including a skull from Swanscombe in Kent and some teeth from Boxgrove in West Sussex, date from well over a quarter of a million years ago and evidence of their stone tools dates back even further. Their remains, buried beneath several metres of glacial rubble, are from another time and another world where long-extinct animals still roamed, and atlases, if they had existed, would have marked out very different coastlines.

But those were not the people whom we might have seen on their weary trek up the Vale of Pickering. For them, around

7500 BC, a new story was beginning. They might have been descended from the Swanscombe and Boxgrove folk but since the last Ice Age had ended a crucial difference had begun to emerge. They were about to become something their ancestors had never been: islanders.

As they reached the top of the hills overlooking the Vale perhaps they stopped and rested. Sitting on the stony outcrops along the ridge they might have looked east with the last rays of the setting spring sun on their backs. Somewhere over there the world was changing, not so fast as to be visible, but relentlessly. As far as the eye could see a dank, flat, marshy plain extended. In fact had they known it, or dared to cross it, they would have found that it reached right across to Germany and Scandinavia. Perhaps even then as the sun set, those people could see fires springing to life across the plain where other groups of hunters were settling for the night. It was a grandstand view of a dying way of life.

We can never know if those people had any idea of the changes that were taking place. This was a pre-literate society, or at least one from which no evidence of writing has been found. Their history was not fixed like ours – anchored with dates and events – but floated. The history of the group was only as long as its eldest member's memory of what a former eldest member told him or her as a child. Beyond that, assuming we can make this parallel with more recent non-literate societies, lay the realm of legend. As such, the group, or tribe, never grew any older but simply retained a knowledge of what had happened for the past five or six generations, drifting in a sea of myth.

If one of the group had chosen to tell a story that night, they might have told of a different time, when the vast plain stretching out to the east was drier, firmer, without the dangers of marsh, bog and quicksand. But since the end of the last Ice Age, the world – well, Britain at least – had been getting warmer and wetter as the ice melted and the sea-level rose. The plain that the group overlooked was getting a little wetter every year, increasingly impassable. Soon the inundations of salty water would kill off the plants and trees and as the water continued to rise the landscape slowly disappeared. The group was watching the birth of the North Sea – which probably marked the loss of hunting and foraging grounds but also marked a profound change in who these people were.

Rising sea-levels were not just affecting the future North Sea. Far to the south, at Hengistbury Head in Dorset, other groups met and, over generations, perhaps wondered at a similar process taking hold of their world. The chalk valley between the South Downs and what is now the region of Paris, in France, was filling with water, becoming year by year a little less land and a little more lagoon. As the tides rose higher with each flood, the chalk faces of the hills eroded and those groups of hunters had a new marvel to gaze at: the nascent White Cliffs of Dover. Soon the waters no longer retreated, and the people at Hengistbury Head were looking out across the English Channel.

From the perspective of our two groups, these events must have been inconvenient, although they occurred so slowly that they were barely noticeable. But they made a great difference to how we view these people today. Before then, the people who came here wandered freely across a vast Eurasian land-mass. With the formation of the English Channel and the North Sea, those wanderings had ended for anyone caught on this side of the water. Britain had become an island and the groups in the Vale of Pickering and at Hengistbury Head had become the first true Britons.

The evidence we have for the lives of these first Britons is scant and often hard, if not impossible, to interpret. What we know of them we have deduced from the things they left behind, their bones, their tools, the remnants of their meals and the faint scars of their fires and shelters. Although we cannot talk about specific dates or individuals we can glimpse moments in their lives. We cannot give a date on which a group of people climbed high above the Vale of Pickering, or name them, or know if they had realised that they were becoming islanders. But we do know that they were there – that one day, at some time in the distant past, someone stood on those hills and cast away, or lost, a stone tool, which lay for nearly ten thousand years before it was discovered again. That loss only took a moment, but it left an echo of this unimaginably ancient time that has rung down to us through a hundred centuries.

So, what was this early Britain like? At the time it became an island, it was still covered in primeval forest, which in fact hadn't been there very long, and wouldn't survive for much longer. The trees were invaders and, like most invaders, it seems that they were unwelcome. After the end of the last Ice Age the climate warmed, the ice melted and the tree cover moved north rapidly. Pollen samples taken from ancient buried soils show that oaks from Spain and Italy, and limes from the Balkans converged in a sort of pincer movement on a Britain that was then still attached to Europe. By the time the rising seas finally cut off Britain, it was already a forested land.

Today you might look askance at anyone who claimed to be intimidated by trees. They are not, of themselves, dangerous, unless one is about to fall on you. But for the ancient peoples of northern Europe, they were threatening. As anyone who has ventured too far into woodland a little late in the evening will tell you, forests are easy to get lost in. Visibility is limited to a few metres, there are no convenient landmarks by which to orientate yourself and, there's also plenty of cover for anything that might want to attack you. At this date forests contained predators that might make a meal of an unwary human, notably wolves. The thick cover also made it harder to find the animals you might want to hunt compared to the days when much of Europe was an open plain. For the people who lived with it the primeval forest was a new and dangerous inconvenience, which forced them to live a life not in the heart of Britain but on its periphery.

Today the Vale of Pickering is a gentle valley lined with arable farms and dotted with small coppices, but nine and a half millennia ago it was different. At that time the valley was filled with a large, shallow lake, fed by warm underground springs, and those small clumps of trees formed a string of little islands in the water. Around the lake lay dense stands of rushes and reeds, giving way to an open shoreline. Set back some way from this a forest of birch, hazel and pine began and, in that open space between wood and water, we might see the human inhabitants of this rich, new world.

These are the people of what archaeologists call the 'Meso-lithic' period or Middle Stone Age, which lasted from the end of the last Ice Age until the arrival of farming in Britain some time around 4000 BC. It is tempting to see this as a primitive world in which farming and even pottery were unknown, but that is to underestimate our ancestors. A hundred years from now people will probably look back to the early twenty-first century and marvel at how gruelling and inconvenient life must have been without this or that invention, but as we don't have it we can't miss it. The Victorians didn't have television, but they almost certainly enjoyed their evenings as much as we do.

Nor should we be beguiled into thinking that in these days before farming, life was necessarily harder or more unpredictable. It was long held as a fact that farming was a safer and more sophisticated way of making a living than that practised by our Mesolithic forebears. They were 'hunter-gatherers': they hunted game, fish and birds, and gathered fruit, vegetables and roots. To do this they moved around their landscape, not settling in one location but living in more temporary lodgings, at times and places where they knew food would be available. This seems today a laborious and somewhat tenuous means of existence, but we don't have the mind or skills of our Mesolithic ancestors.

In fact, hunter-gathering is a successful, productive and even secure way of life. Well into the twentieth century a small number of groups still practised it, most famously the Kalahari Bushmen of southern Africa. Many archaeologists believe that these peoples hold a clue as to how our ancestors had lived and have studied and interviewed them intensively. There are dangers in using a modern tribe as an analogy for how we all used to live. The Kalahari Bushmen may not be typical of previous hunter-gatherers – after all, it's unusual enough that they've survived with this way of life for so long and, furthermore, the Kalahari desert is not overly similar to the Vale of Pickering. The Bushmen, however, provided some eye-opening insights for archaeologists, which might also have held true for Mesolithic people. The first surprise was that hunter-gatherers knew all about seeds and how, if you planted, watered and tended them, they grew into new plants that you could eat. The Bushmen were asked why they hadn't become farmers. This they found hilarious. The main difference between being a hunter-gatherer and a subsistence farmer in sub-Saharan

Africa was the amount of work you had to do. Where farmers had to work at least six days a week, hunter-gatherers could collect all they needed for the week in two or three days. Would you rather work the whole week or half of it? The Bushmen also thought that farming sounded risky. While they had a large number of food animals and plants to choose from in each season, farmers had one or two, and if anything happened to their crops they had nothing to eat until the next year. So, this apparently primitive way of life was highly successful and sophisticated – it sustained our ancestors for over 99 per cent of the time humans have walked the earth.

If we were to have walked down into the Vale of Pickering at that time, what would we have seen? Clues to this come from one of the most extraordinary early Mesolithic sites found in Britain, Star Carr: which lies in the valley bottom on the edge of that long-vanished lake. In the sloping field that now marks the ancient shoreline, it's still possible to find, in the ploughed soil, the flakes of flint left by a Mesolithic tool-maker. Nine and a half thousand years ago someone sat on what was then a beach with a nodule of black flint, took another stone and struck the two together to produce blades. The flint itself was not local and must have been brought into the area, perhaps by the person who worked it, or perhaps even traded for. Either way, the evidence of their labour is still scattered in the earth today. We know exactly how those people worked because archaeologists have collected these waste flakes. By painstakingly reassembling them, like a complex 3D jigsaw, it has been possible to reconstruct the raw flint blocks to get a glimpse into the mind of the stone worker as they sat on the beach wondering how to strike the most useable tools from that precious nodule.

The Mesolithic people made many different tools for many

different purposes. Scrapers were used for cleaning animal hides for clothing, blades for skinning and cutting meat, and tiny flint points for the tips and barbs of arrows. Nor was flint the only material they worked. Most of the materials available in the Mesolithic period were organic – wood, leather, sinew and fibres – and generally these have rotted over the intervening centuries. But at Star Carr the waterlogged conditions of the soil on the ancient lake bed preserved some organic artefacts – bone pins, perhaps for fastening clothes, harpoon points, and other, stranger insights into the world at the lake's edge. Two finds from Star Carr show us that something more than the fight for life was going on. Shale beads hint at the importance of personal adornment – perhaps they were believed to have magical properties, or displayed status, or perhaps they were the first pieces of jewellery in British history, worn simply for the owner's delight in their beauty. More unusual were the 'antler frontlets': they consisted of the top piece of a deer's skull, with the antlers still attached, and two holes bored through the bone. Since they were discovered there has been much argument over what they were for. It was suggested that they were an aid to hunting, allowing their owners to creep up on their prey, but many a modern hunter has raised an eyebrow at that idea – it's difficult to creep around with antlers strapped to your head and even the most short-sighted deer would notice that you're not one of them.

More likely, perhaps, these are the first evidence we have of the spiritual beliefs of these distant people. There are dangers in ascribing anything we don't understand to the realm of religion and archaeologists have often used the label 'ritual object' to mean 'I don't know what it is'. However, the finding of several of these items in one specific area of the site may point to an ancient ceremony.

Deer were important to these people, as our flint-knapper sitting on the beach would have known. They did not randomly hunt deer, they managed them in a way that was only a few steps short of farming. Excavations of the ancient shoreline have revealed traces of reed pollen mixed with tiny flecks of charcoal, which may indicate that areas of reed were deliberately and regularly burned; it seems that people here did this to encourage the growth of new shoots. They didn't want these for themselves, but to attract the herds of wild deer to the water's edge. For the unwary deer falling into this trap lunch was to be, as it were, on them.

If we look further down the coastline we might see more evidence of this complex interaction between people and their prey. One of the first – possibly *the* first – domesticated animals in British history stalked through the reeds. It was not a sheep, cow or any other food animal, but a dog, one of four found around the lake and the earliest known domesticated canine in Europe. Long before farmers began to rear livestock, humans and dogs had realised the advantages of working together in the hunt. Man's best friend is also his oldest, and that partnership might have managed the deer population around Star Carr long before anyone thought of fencing them in. Indeed, the close relationship between the people, dogs and deer at Star Carr might have been livestock farming in all but name. Perhaps a marrowbone from that day's kill tossed to the dog by the flint-knapper fulfilled the human side of the bargain, before he returned to knapping the blades and scrapers that would be used to divide up the meat among the humans.

Perhaps when he looked up from his work, through the smoke rising from the burning reeds, he saw another of their group on a wooden platform on the foreshore – a distant, shadowy form – with the body of a man but the antlers of a deer, lost in the rites and rituals of asking whatever gods inhabited that place to grant them success in the next hunt.

The lakeside was not a permanent home for our Mesolithic group. The wilderness of the Vale of Pickering could not sustain a large static population for long and the whole surrounding area supported perhaps no more than around a hundred people. Evidence from the excavation of deer remains around the lake suggests that the site was only used from around March to June or July. With the lengthening summer days, the group moved off to another, as yet unknown place.

With the sea so close, perhaps they went to the coast of the new North Sea where the availability of shellfish made for a plentiful supply of summer food. Certainly, coastal areas were important to our Mesolithic ancestors. On the little island of Oronsay in the Inner Hebrides the grass-covered dunes behind the coast still bear witness to the lives of other family groups from this time. Three campsites have been found here: three moments from this distant past when a family group of perhaps twenty people gathered around a fire, a rest from their endless seasonal travels around the islands in search of food. That they were remarkably successful in this quest is still evident today from the piles of hazelnut shells that have been found around these camps. Just beyond them, larger monuments to their way of life survive in the form of sandy hills, called middens. From a distance these might be dunes thrown up by the winter storms but excavations have revealed that they are man-made dumps. It seems that the groups moving around these islands were particular about where they left their rubbish – mainly limpet shells and fish bones – and over many years these dumps grew to form great heaps, which have survived to this day. Buried among the debris archaeologists even found evidence of their builders in the form of part of a human hand and two human teeth, although just what they were doing in the rubbish remains a mystery.

The teeth offer another glimpse into the Mesolithic world. In days long before cakes and confectionery they were free of cavities, but their worn, polished surfaces indicate a diet that required considerable chewing. As well as eating game and fish, these people gathered foods from the forest's edge. In the absence of modern staples, such as potatoes, rice and wheat, finding local sources of starch and carbohydrate was an essential counterpart to hunting. This would have required not only a comprehensive knowledge of local plant life and the seasons, but also how to cook otherwise unappetising or inedible foods and how to avoid potential poisons. Nor are all the sources of food obvious to us today: in place of the potato, our Mesolithic ancestors might have dug up the rhizomes of bulrushes and charred them in the fire, then sucked the starch from the fibrous interior. Something almost guaranteed to put some polish on your teeth.

As the night wore on and the temperatures dropped, the family groups did not simply huddle closer to the fire. Although the camps were temporary they were hardly living rough. Had we been able to stand on their midden and look down on them at night, we would have seen a little group of shelters set back from the fire, of a type known as 'bender dwellings'. Our knowledge of Mesolithic 'housing' is limited, but we know that the shelters were constructed of organic materials. The only clue we have of what they looked like comes from post-holes – marks left in the ground where the timbers for these shelters were stood – by which it has been possible to calculate the width of the timbers used and the angle at which they were driven into the ground. This has enabled archaeologists to reconstruct some of Britain's earliest homes. They were sturdy structures, built by bending a series of flexible tree saplings, often hazel, into arcs to form a dome. This was covered with whatever insulating material could be found locally – grass, heather or lichen. Inside, a central fire would have kept the half-dozen or so occupants warm. At one Irish site there is even evidence that a wooden 'fireguard' was put around the central hearth, perhaps to keep the small hands and feet of the newest generation of hunter-gatherers away from the dangers of the fire.

Children, of course, were the most valuable investment in Mesolithic society: their protection ensured they would grow up to become the next generation of hunter-gatherers, who might not only continue the family line but also care for their elders in later life when they proved less able to hunt and gather for themselves. Discovering anything about children's lives at this period is extremely difficult. Learning about family groups usually involves studying human remains from burials. Osteoarchaeologists – bone specialists – can deduce huge amounts about people from looking at their physical remains, from their age and sex to their diet and the diseases they suffered from. But few human remains have been found from the Mesolithic period and the children's bones, which are particularly fragile, have rarely survived.

But it is still possible to glimpse Mesolithic children and their families. During this time the shoreline at Formby, just north of Liverpool, was protected by a group of 'barrier' islands in the bay, which sheltered a shallow lagoon from the sea. Mesolithic men, women and children once walked along in soft mud banks and, incredibly, their preserved footsteps can still be seen there. The process that left these ancient footprints intact is remarkable in itself and brings us as close as it is now possible to get to the first true Britons.

While the barrier islands of that ancient lagoon survived, the footprints laid down each day in the mud were dried by the sun, slowly filled with windblown sand, then covered by the rising tide and sealed with a fresh layer of silt. Since the barrier islands disappeared, however, about two thousand years ago, the process has been running in reverse. Each tide that sweeps up the beach at Formby now removes another layer of hardened mud and, as the waters scour away the sand from the freshly uncovered depressions, the footprints of our Mesolithic and Neolithic ancestors reappear, like some ancient Polaroid. For a few hours a moment in time – a single day – from six thousand years ago is revealed, before the tide returns and the footprints are washed away forever.

Thanks to a scientific technique known as quartz-luminescent dating, it has been established that the footprints are between five and six thousand years old, but a study of their patterns, size and shape has revealed much more. To begin with, we know now that, as at Star Carr, the people hunted deer: a series of hoofprints from red and fallow deer skid through the mud, closely followed by the large, deep imprints of a man's running feet. Other tracks belong to a heavily pregnant woman, as shown by her slower, heavy gait, rolling on the balls of her feet. But one other set of prints gives us a yet more immediate feeling of connection with this deep past. To either side of the distinctive straight track of a woman's feet lie a scatter of much smaller prints, passing in circles around the woman's. If you want to know what this represents, look across the Formby beach today at the parents ambling along the seashore while their children scamper around them. To walk along Formby beach today as the tide recedes is to walk hand-in-hand with the first families of Britain.

The fate of these families and their descendants is one of

the great mysteries of archaeology. The hunter-gathering life-style supported perhaps a hundred thousand people across Britain from the Scottish islands of the far north to the south coast of England. Across all that range and more than four thousand years we know of only about fifteen hundred sites where these people lived, which puts them among the most elusive group of our prehistory. What we do know is that by around five and a half thousand years ago this way of life had ended.

The change that brought about its demise was one of the greatest upheavals ever to hit the British Isles: the introduction of farming. Archaeological debate has raged over the origins of agriculture and its spread across the world ever since archaeology emerged as an academic discipline. Old models of the diffusion of civilisation (including agriculture, building in stone, and writing) from the Middle East have been vigorously countered in more recent times with suggestions that many such developments occurred independently in several places at different times. Agriculture is first known of in the Middle East around ten thousand years ago, and over the subsequent millennia its practice moved north and west until it arrived in Britain around 5500 years ago.

The principal question that remains unanswered is whether it was brought here by a new people as they moved across Europe or whether farming was slowly taken up by the indigenous Mesolithic population. Perhaps the descendants of the deer-herders at Star Carr might have told us that they had successfully invented a form of farming – livestock rearing – themselves, and didn't need the help of foreign people or ideas. That part of farming may have a uniquely British heritage.

The answer probably lies in a combination of all these, although recent genetic studies have suggested that between 20 and 40 per cent of the genetic make-up of modern Britons owes its ancestry to Middle Eastern blood lines. That people could have crossed to Britain at this early date from Europe is not as surprising as it sounds. In recent centuries we have become used to viewing the sea that surrounds us as a barrier, protecting us from invaders. The truth, of course, is that the sea has been an effective highway, too, for transporting people and ideas. People have taken to the water from the earliest times: even at Star Carr we might have seen our Mesolithic friends paddling dugout canoes to the islands in the lake.

By 3500 BC the Mesolithic hunters standing on Hengistbury Head – as the flint flakes found there suggest they did – looking south across the Channel, might have seen boats arriving. Whether or not they brought an invasion of people, they certainly carried ideas: farming and the technologies that went with it were about to revolutionise the way of life in these islands and change our relationship with the landscape around us for ever. But whether those Mesolithic people simply moved off into the more inaccessible corners of Britain or welcomed the new world order remains a mystery. Recently a study of a type of DNA only passed through the maternal line (and as such resistant to change as we all basically inherit a version identical to our mother's) has shown that the native modern population around the Cheddar Gorge in Somerset has nearly identical sequences to that taken from a Mesolithic skeleton of a man recovered from a nearby cave and dating to before 7000 BC. This would suggest that the people who hunted and gathered there nine thousand years ago stayed put, took up farming and were the ancestors of the modern population rather than having been displaced by foreign farmers. More prosaically, the presence of Mesolithic finds on so many early farming sites across Britain suggests that old and new managed to get along together, and that even the most tenacious of old-guard hunters eventually settled down.

Whatever the fate of the small Mesolithic population of Britain, the first farmers who began to tend the land brought with them a whole new way of life. Farming required new materials, new technologies and new tools. Many of the things we consider indigenous to Britain were imported at this time, including primitive forms of wheat and barley, as well as cattle and sheep. The tools for farming were also being introduced: the flint sickle, the first ploughs and, most important of all, the axe.

The stone axe was the tool most responsible for the shaping of the countryside we see around us today, even though it fell out of use over a thousand years before the birth of Christ. The first farmers in Britain found themselves in a land well suited to growing crops and raising animals, with its temperate climate and regular rainfall, but there was one major problem: it was covered with trees. The great work of the Neolithic period, or the New Stone Age, was to clear them.

We often imagine that, until relatively recent times, the British landscape was in a pristine state – that Robin Hood holed up in primeval forests that had stood since the last ice sheets melted away, that the wild wastelands of the high moors stood bleakly above the land in which hunter-gatherers once wandered. Neither is true. During the Neolithic period the countryside underwent the greatest transformation it saw until the modern era: vast tracts of ancient forest were cleared from the lowlands and valleys and the great moorlands were created. When farming first arrived in the West Country, Dartmoor, Exmoor and Bodmin were still covered with forest. Today's open moorland is not a 'natural' landscape at all. Likewise, the woods and forest we imagine to be ancient are almost all remnants of managed Saxon and medieval woods, grown deliberately as crops.

The scale of the task awaiting those first farmers was immense. It has been estimated that five generations of a family working for a century might have cleared half a square mile of tree cover using the technologies available at the time. Yet generation by generation, mile by mile, this was exactly what they did. It is perhaps not surprising that some of the most exquisite artefacts to survive from this time are ground and polished axe heads, made in rare, but functionally useless, stones such as imported jadeite from Brittany – eulogies to the magnificent tool that was creating this new world.

The transformation brought about by these farmers and their axes was colossal. Farming could support a far larger population on a given area of land – more hands to man the axes – and it required a different way of life. Perhaps the greatest change of all was that, for the first time, people had to settle in one place. Rearing animals or raising crops meant that farmers had to be around all year to tend them. Britain was settling down and seasonal shelters gave way to permanent homes.

Today it is difficult to find homes from the earliest days of farming. Ever since those first settlements, land has been used and reused. Old buildings have fallen out of use, been demolished and replaced. Wood and thatch have rotted, and new buildings now stand on ancient foundations. There is, however, one site where we can still walk into the homes of the first farmers.

In 1850 a freak storm hit the Orkney Islands and in an evening tore away a series of huge sand dunes from the coast at Skara Brae. Beneath them lay a time-capsule, a near perfectly preserved village dating from around 3000 BC.

The complex at Skara Brae consists of seven almost identical stone houses, each believed to have been the home of a family unit, and all interconnected by deep stone passages designed to baffle the often wild Orkney weather. This extraordinary survival owes much to the fact that nearly everything in the village was made of stone, a readily available building material on an island devoid of woodland where the only wood available was driftwood. But these are not 'man-made caves', primitive hovels for farmers eking out a poor living in a desolate land. They are homes, offering many of what we might consider the conveniences of modern life.

Had we walked into one of these houses some time around 3000 BC we would have found a world much further removed from the immediate Mesolithic past than it is different from our own. Stumbling down the dark, enclosed stone passages between the houses we would have noticed the wind drop as the walls' gentle curve deflected the bitter gale from a doorway. Ahead lay a lockable door – clearly these people prized their privacy – and beyond this a single room with high stone walls and probably a thatched roof. Inside, the space was lit by a huge fire burning in the central hearth.

On walking into this room we might have found a family enjoying a meal around a fire that burned seaweed and bone (in a land that was then without wood or peat). The food resources available in Orkney in the Stone Age, when the weather was a degree or two warmer, were excellent, and the people's diet might even be considered luxurious by some modern standards. The first farmers to arrive on Orkney had brought deer with them to hunt, and also cattle and sheep to tend, so this family might have been eating roast beef, lamb chops or venison. From the shore, there were sea-bird eggs, and the sea yielded lobster, crab, whale, dolphin and other huge fish – the remains of a cod weighing seventy-five pounds – at the limit of the modern world line-fishing record – have been found here.

Through the flames of the fire we would see on the wall behind it a great stone 'dresser', a series of shelves and cupboards where, judging from its position opposite the door, the most important things in this family's life were kept. Perhaps they held the food for the evening, or the family's treasures. Perhaps objects venerating now long-forgotten gods lurked in the niches. Strange carved stones found here might have had religious significance, although equally they might have been playing pieces for ancient games of 'jacks' and dice designed to while away the long northern winter nights. Anthropologists studying modern tribal societies have suggested that other spiral carvings found here might have been the work of this society's 'shamen' – spiritual leaders, who used hyperventilation or psychotropic drugs to work themselves into an altered state in which they could communicate with the spirits. Some Scottish sites of about this period have produced residues of what experiments have suggested was a rather foul-tasting barley beer, which certainly would have made the drinker's head spin. If these swirling carvings are indeed evidence of the hallucinations common to all humans in such states, then the British have been 'turning on', 'tuning in' and 'dropping out' for at least five thousand years longer than anyone who remembers the sixties might have us believe.

But if we could have sat that evening by their fireside, what might we have seen? First, there were querns on the floor – sets of stones, perhaps for grinding cereals to make unleavened bread (no yeast was used in bread-making at this time) or perhaps for grinding fishbones to make fishmeal as a winter feed for cattle. Beside them, stone tanks contained seawater and weed to conceal a haul of limpets – live bait being softened up for the next day's fishing trip. To the right stood a great stone bed, piled high with heather, fleeces and duck down, supporting a canopy, like that of a four-poster bed, on stone pillars. The animal skins suspended from the pillars helped to keep out draughts and perhaps caught the drips from a leaky thatch. Opposite, on the left, there was a smaller, canopied bed, and in the wall behind we might just spot the glimmer of a fish-oil lamp in a niche that might have served as a bedside table.

In recent years it has been argued that the smaller bed represents the female side of the house, and the larger one the male. This is based on evidence from the eighteenth- and nineteenth-century Western Isles where such divisions were still apparently in use. Perhaps that would explain the two necklaces of carved bone and killer whale teeth in the niche above the female bed – the prized possessions of the mistress of the house.

Not far from the bed stood another doorway and beyond it a small cell with a hole in the floor leading to a series of drains. Although it is difficult for modern archaeologists to be certain, this might have been an *en-suite* toilet – perhaps more of an essential than a luxury on a cold, dark Orkney winter night.

It is, of course, dangerous to draw too many parallels between what we might use things for today and what they were used for then. This was a society that left no written record to tell us that the stone cell was a toilet or that what looks to us like shelving was a dresser. Just because we think an object might have been used for a particular purpose does not mean that it was. For all the apparent modernity of Skara Brae, its inhabitants lived in a very different world from ours, one in which what we might think of as unimaginable was everyday to them.

Trying to look into the minds of the first farmers is also risky. Unpicking the threads of their motivation and the meaning of what they left behind is fraught with difficulty. What we can do is look at the monuments they left and attempt to examine what they might have meant. And it's not just the types of monument that were new at this time, but the monuments themselves.

During the semi-itinerant Mesolithic period there was little need to make bold, permanent statements on the landscape because it was something you moved *through* rather than lived *on*. With farming, all that changed. To farm an area success-fully requires long-term investment of time and labour to clear the tree cover, plough the fields, remove stones, sow and rear crops and livestock, harvest and store them. When you've made that sort of investment you'd be annoyed if your neighbour wandered through your fields eating whatever they fancied.

Suddenly it was important to own land – to lay claim to the area that you and your family would tend, and prevent others moving in. This wholesale modification and division of the landscape required a system of signals to indicate who was where and what belonged to whom – physical marks that asserted the presence of a group or family. Monuments weren't something farmers built in their spare time: they were an essen-tial part of farming itself. Britain now belonged to someone and people staked their early claims with some of the greatest monuments of British prehistory.

Around 3000 BC long barrows began to appear on the land-scape. They consist of a long underground passage, sometimes with a series of side-chambers and usually one entrance. Most of these huge monuments, so prominent even in the modern landscape, were excavated early in the history of archaeology so much of the detail of what happened here might have been lost in the diggings of over-eager antiquarians, and landowners with a taste for treasure. What is clear, though, is that human remains were found in these structures so, to some degree, they were tombs. But they were much more than that.

Long barrows were not simply convenient burial grounds for the local dead, they were an integral part of the world of the early farmer. At West Kennet long barrow in Wiltshire we can perhaps gain a hazy picture of what these places might have meant five thousand years ago. All those millennia ago West Kennet was undoubtedly a wonder. It was a vast structure, built from stones weighing as much as five tons that would have had to be dragged up the hill, arranged into a corridor with side compartments, roofed over, then covered with thousands of tons of earth. It was clearly the work of a closely knit group who were able to co-operate on a large scale to achieve such an impressive result. But it was more than just an architectural stunt. We don't know if these barrows were generally open, or if their interiors were reserved for a select few people or times, or both. But if we had walked into the gloomy interior of West Kennet shortly after its construction, we would have been confronted with a surprising scene.

Certainly we would have seen human remains – parts of over fifty individuals were found in West Kennet while other barrows, like Isbister on Orkney, held over three hundred – perhaps arranged in groups or lineages. Many of the artefacts of daily life were placed around them – flint tools, the remains of animals and, another recent invention, pottery, representing all aspects of life in the early farmers' world. The rituals or rites that took place are lost now, but there is evidence that the bones and artefacts were moved and re-ordered from time to time. This was not a sealed vault where the dead awaited eternity but a living statement in which the local farming community associated itself with, and laid claim to, the land around it; in which the dead had an active role to play in the world of the living.

The barrow spoke to the people who saw it: it spoke of ownership (although not necessarily in the way in which we think of it), of a connection with the land, and of the line of ancestors whose foundation myth formed the basis of the current claims of the living. No doubt the body parts inside the barrow had religious significance, but they also laid out a lineage and stated the rights of the people who lived there. They were, in effect, a title deed, in a world where no division could be drawn between the sacred and the profane, the religious and the secular. Using human remains to lay claim to a territory may seem gruesome to us today, but it is only a step beyond the modern world's infatuation with family history and tracing our roots.

Of course, not every member of every community ended up (whole or in part) in a long barrow. Farming had changed the entire landscape with ritual and meaning, and the sights and sounds of a walk through the Neolithic countryside would have been different from what we experience today.

In 3000 BC, if we had walked past the edge of the fields — recently marked out in relation to the barrow — we would have seen the new crops, barley and wheat, with thinner, smaller ears than those of modern varieties. There is even a little evidence that grapevines were grown. Almost certainly more important at this date than fruit and cereals, however, was livestock — some sheep, more like the wild Mouflon than modern breeds, and small cattle. Animals provided many of the raw materials of life in the Neolithic period apart from meat. Recent studies of minute quantities of residue inside Neolithic pottery have revealed traces of milk fat, suggesting that milk had been a food source, probably in its fresh and preserved forms – cheese and butter – since at least 4500 BC, probably before the introduction of cereal farming. These animals also provided the skins, tendons and bones that went to make many of the tools, clothes and shelters of the period. They even played their part in the great forest clearance, stripping tree bark and preventing forests from re-establishing themselves. So far we might have been walking through a primitive Ambridge. However, had we looked up to the brow of the hill, that illusion would have been shattered. Here was a place strewn with the rotting remnants of innumerable people. This was Hambledon Hill in Dorset, one of the largest prehistoric enclosures in Europe.

Walking across Hambledon in the Neolithic we would have had to tread carefully. Around us we might have seen dogs and carrion birds picking over the often dismembered human remains. Looking more closely there might be corpses of men, women and children, some whole, some in pieces, in various states of decay. The site looked like a battlefield, but it was in fact, at least in part, a burial ground. This was a causewayed enclosure – a ring of oval hollows separated by pathways into the circle's interior. But the question on the lips of any passing stranger must have been – 'what is this place for?'

This was already an important place when the causewayed enclosure was begun around 3800 BC: archaeologists uncovered Mesolithic post-holes there, that dated from perhaps 7000 BC. Just what these posts were for remains a mystery, as does the true function of the enclosure that superseded it some three thousand years later. Perhaps the first monuments in British prehistory, the enclosures seem to have been built on the edges rather than in the centre of farming areas and might have been meeting-places, neutral no man's lands, where farmers could come together to trade, solve disputes, perhaps arrange marriages. There is even evidence that they were fought over. The discovery of the body of a young man lying face down in a ditch with his hand over his head speaks of a sudden, violent death. A flint arrowhead was recovered from among his ribs, indicating that he had been shot from behind with an arrow that pierced his lungs. He must subsequently have drowned in his own blood and been hastily buried.

The evidence does not reveal whether he was a victim of warfare, execution or even murder, but the enclosures were clearly places of death, as the remains of more than a hundred and twenty bodies at Hambledon show. Most had not died violently on the hill, but were exposed as corpses here or interred in shallow trenches. At the causewayed enclosure at Etton in Cambridgeshire it has been suggested that each hollow in the circular enclosure may have represented the private burial ground of one family or clan. The positioning of a number of domestic items in a trench marked at one end by the inverted skull of a fox might perhaps thus have represented the burial place of the 'fox clan'. But the grave was only half the story. Across on the other side of the enclosure evidence of feasting and the presence of animals suggest that the living had a role here too. Perhaps the mourners at a fox clan funeral moved across to the 'living' side of the enclosure to celebrate the life of the man or woman to whom they had just said goodbye and toasted their departure to the next world.

Just who ended up buried in a hollow, who was left exposed on the hill and who, or which bits of who ended up in a long barrow remains obscure. It is possible that some parts of some bodies went through many stages, being exposed then buried then dug up again and moved. Some also had a more unusual fate. A few bones recovered from Hambledon show the distinctive signs of butchery where stone tools have been used to cut away flesh. It may be that the meat was removed as part of some ritual for the dead or for use in some form of magical medicine but there is always, at the back of our minds, the thought that perhaps this is evidence of cannibalism.

The idea of cannibalism has haunted our imaginings of ancient or primitive societies ever since western explorers first brought back stories of head-hunters and savages who preyed on human flesh. In fact, there is precious little evidence for cannibalism in any society and where it has been attested it has been as part of a ritual that related to taking on the powers of a deceased family or group member rather than looking out for a tasty snack. The Fore of Papua New Guinea reportedly ate the brains of their dead relatives for this reason, but even in this relatively recent and most celebrated case, the frequency of such acts and their true meaning remains obscure.

What beliefs drove early farmers to haul huge stones up hills to build long barrows, or to leave loved ones exposed on a barren hillside, may now be impossible to know. Perhaps having the bones of close family on that hilltop, or secure in a subterranean niche, provided the living with justification for why they were there. This was where their ancestors had lived, and the whole landscape around them, the soil, the animals and plants and even the air, was infused with their presence.

The society that built the long barrows was not static, and if we had returned to West Kennet around 2500 BC we would have found a very different place. The entrance to the long barrow where we had walked some five hundred years earlier would have gone, sealed with a gargantuan flat stone: it seems that the bones of the ancestors no longer spoke to their descendants.

Why this ancient religion – or, at least, this manifestation of ancient religion should have fallen out of favour is hotly debated. It has been suggested that some climatic or biological disaster befell the people – perhaps famine or a plague – in which people turned away from the gods who had protected them for so long. Equally, all religions evolve, and it might be that the beliefs of the Neolithic farmers survived but were now expressed differently. Whether new religion or new expression one thing was certain, the new forms of worship were everywhere and they were expressed in the simple but powerful geometry of circles.

The purpose of stone circles is even more obscure than that of the long barrows or causewayed enclosures. What is clear is that this was a very different experience of religion from that found in the claustrophobic niches of a barrow. Stone circles dominate the countryside openly, grand theatre in an increasingly man-made landscape. They were also very popular: nearly a thousand survive in Britain, and that is just in the north and west where they were made of stone. Many more earth or wooden sites might have been erased by centuries of ploughing in the south and east. In their day, they might have been almost as common as parish churches. Furthermore they were peculiarly British. While there are standing stones, menhirs and stone alignments in continental Europe, the circle seems to be almost uniquely British.

What we don't know, of course, is why they were all needed. Almost certainly if you had stood among some at dawn on the summer (or winter) solstice you would have witnessed an ancient rite, but it is doubtful that the circles, many of which have been altered since they were erected by farmers or well-meaning antiquaries, were complex astronomical computers. That is not to say we shouldn't credit the ancient builders with the engineering skills to construct these often vast monuments, the mathematical skill to arrange them and the astronomical know-how to make at least a few deliberate alignments. After all, the Neolithic night sky was clear of the yellow smear of the street-lamps that cloud our view today, and the passing of the hours, days and seasons would have been the clock beating out the rhythm of every farmer's life.

What is clear is that the circular shape of the monuments of this era was important to their builders, and it wasn't just the monuments that were circular. While the earliest houses, back at Skara Brae, were oblong, the later ones were round and sat in a landscape of round buildings, from the stone circles at the Ring of Brodgar and the Stones of Stennes to the awesome burial mound at Maes Howe. That the homes of the living and the dead had this in common is perhaps not surprising and might give a clue to the purpose of the circles. In fact, there might have been a progression of building types of similar forms but very different functions on one site relating to the family who lived and worked there. A round house of one generation might have been memorialised inside a ring of stones by a later generation, then become a tomb after that. This was a connected landscape, where the homes of the living and the dead were intimately related, and where the living of one generation walked among the stones and tombs that commemorated those who came before them. We may call this 'prehistory', but walking through this world was an act of memory to the people who lived here, an historical narrative that told them who they were, where they had come from, and why they were there.

Later in the Neolithic other types of monument also begin to appear. Henges (which take their name from the most famous, Stonehenge) consist of a continuous circular ditch, with just one or two entrances and often a bank outside the ditch. These range in size from a few metres across, which a small group might have knocked up over a summer, to the Wiltshire super-henge at Durrington Walls, which has a diameter of nearly half a kilometre. They cannot have been intended as defences because the earth bank was usually placed outside the ditch, so attackers would have been able to get a really good shot at those inside, but the purpose of what lay inside many of these structures is still much debated. We all know what lies inside Stonehenge, and others contain circles of standing stones, or stains in the soil where circles of wooden posts once stood. Of course, Stonehenge was not built all at once and in its original form, which dates to around 3000 BC, the circular banked ditch simply enclosed a ring of fifty-six mysterious pits. They might have served a different purpose from the later stone monument, where users might have been unaware of their ancestors' intentions.

Excavations have shown that different things seem to have been done in the centres of henges. At the extraordinary Sea-henge, on the coast at Holme in Norfolk, a wooden henge had an inverted oak trunk in its centre which its excavator claims might have represented a connection to the 'other world', which in their cosmology wasn't them in the heavens (as in the Christian tradition) but beneath the ground. The appropriately named 'woodhenge', seems to have been a place where large numbers of people gathered for feasts – mainly of pork judging from the quantity of pig bones found there. Stonehenge, how-ever, is devoid of such remains. It has been suggested that the wooden henges were thus places for the living, built of a living material, while Stonehenge, a 'fossilised' version, built in dead stone, was for the dead. On that theory the stones themselves, of course, remain silent.

We may never know what this burst of building activity actually meant, but if you had walked across Salisbury Plain at the end of the third millennium BC you would have been aware that you were walking in a changed and changing landscape, whose significance was expressed through virtuoso, interconnected monument-building – a world of stone and wooden circles connected by lines of posts, stones and ditches. As we walked past the small round barrows that huddled a short way from Stonehenge we might have begun to see the reasons for the changes. Individual tombs were generally new at this time – although some earlier examples survive from the time of the long barrows. These round barrows often contained just one central burial, sometimes accompanied by precious grave goods such as daggers and ornaments of the latest and best technology to reach Britain: metal-working.

The move from Stone Age to Bronze Age was not sudden. No Neolithic farmer sat over the specifications for a bronze smithy, slapped his head in disbelief that he hadn't thought of it himself, then sent off the coupon for a make-your-own-bronze kit. 'Bronze Age' is just a convenient term used by archaeologists to slice up the yawning stretches of prehistoric time. That the advent of bronze technology eventually changed the way we live is certain, but it was not a revolution. Were we to meet a Bronze Age farmer as we stood by a barrow on Salisbury Plain, we would almost certainly find that he still carried a sophisticated range of stone tools, from axes and knives to exquisite flint arrowheads with perfectly flaked barbs and a central tang for fixing to the wooden arrow shaft. The significance of the bronze items deposited in the nearby barrow lay elsewhere.

For many years archaeologists thought that the Bronze Age was marked by the invasion of a new people from Europe. These people were thus credited with the changes in the land-scape – the sealing of long barrows, the advent of bronze working, and the introduction of the item that gave them their name, a pottery mug, sometimes highly decorated, with or without a handle. It was called a 'beaker' so these Bronze Age invaders became known as the 'Beaker People'.

Naming a whole people after a piece of crockery might possibly be considered offensive today. In fact archaeologists are now questioning whether such people ever existed. After all, pots are not people, and anyone digging up a British home in the distant future would be wrong to assume that the large quantity of Japanese electronics found inside it implied that there had been a Japanese invasion and that the people of Britain were therefore now of Japanese descent. Certainly, around the time that the beakers began to appear, new burial practices emerged in which individuals were buried alone, often accompanied by a pottery beaker. But this does not necessarily mean that the Neolithic farmers were swept away and replaced by invaders: ideas and objects can travel without the need for mass folk movement. The beaker might have been the mobile phone of its day, the latest must-have accessory for every up-and-coming farmer.

That they were 'up-and-coming' may be where the true change lies. What was changing, regardless of whether it was brought about by foreign invaders or native fashion, was the role of the individual. People who for centuries had looked to communal graveyards now apparently wanted to be seen as individuals. And with their single burials something else was emerging: wealth.

If we walk away from Stonehenge, some five kilometres

south-east, we arrive on Boscombe Down. Here we might have witnessed a burial taking place in this new world some time around 2300 BC. One day, in a forgotten month of a forgotten year around that time, a man's body was lowered into a deep, timber-lined pit and laid gently on its left side, with the legs bent up. He was not what we would today call old, perhaps thirty-five or forty. Placed around him were the things he had known in life – slate wrist-guards to protect his forearms from the recoil of a bowstring, carefully crafted flint arrowheads, boars' tusks, perhaps from the animals he had hunted, five beakers, a whetstone, and, most impressive of all, a collection of copper and copper-alloy knives, and gold earrings. More than a hundred items went into his grave. It may not seem like a particularly rich haul of goods, but for its date it was extraordinary. To have been buried alone was still relatively unusual, but to have been buried with what look like personal prestigious items was novel. Known today as the Amesbury Archer, this man had a status and wealth that marked him out from his fellow men and women – and that was new.

A surprising amount can be deduced from the things with which the Amesbury Archer was buried, and the remains of his body. Tests on his bones have shown that he was a foreigner, a traveller from Europe, probably from the vicinity of the Swiss Alps. Another body, found in a grave next to his, has many similarities in both its appearance and date, and was possibly his son: tests show that he was brought up in the Bristol region, so perhaps the Amesbury Archer came to Britain and had a family. The Archer's bones tell a more cruel story too: in life this stocky man limped – his withered left leg had lost its kneecap through some traumatic injury, and a terrible smell would have emanated from the infection that still raged within.

But he was no outcast: he was a collector, and a magician.

Although he is referred to now as an archer, because of the two hunting kits with which he was buried, it is unlikely that this partly crippled man made his living from hunting alone. Clues to his real value in society lie in the distinctively decorated beakers, some of which have stylistic links with Scotland, and the copper knives and gold ornaments – the earliest metal items known from British prehistory. More important still, and almost unique in Britain at this time, is an unimposing smooth stone: it is a 'cushion stone', the tool of a goldsmith; perhaps the stone on which he had made the curls of decorated gold sheets that he and his son wore in their hair. This man was a metal worker and that was a wonderful, magical new skill, which he might have been one of the first to bring to Britain from Europe. It was a skill that clearly made a difference: he was not buried in a communal site, or cremated, but placed in his own grave in a key position in the then most elaborate ritual landscape in Britain: at a bend in the river Avon, in line with a processional avenue that ended just out of sight, over the hill at Stonehenge.

If there was social differentiation in the Neolithic period, archaeologists have been unable to uncover it. The Amesbury Archer, who stands at the beginning of the Bronze Age, was different: the people gathered around the pit on Boscombe Down that day were mourning the passing of someone 'important', one of the first 'important' people in British archaeology, and the herald of a new age.

2
Home

Most of the inland inhabitants do not sow corn, but live on milk and flesh, and are clad with skins. All the Britons, indeed, dye themselves with woad, which occasions a bluish colour, and thereby have a more terrible appearance in fight. They wear their hair long, and have every part of their body shaved except their head and upper lip.

Julius Caesar

Dartmoor, 3500 years ago: to stand in the small settlement of Grimspound one summer's day was to stand in the middle of one of Britain's great success stories. At the end of the Mesolithic period this vast granite plateau had been covered in dense, impenetrable woodland, but now, some two thousand years later, the view was magnificent. From the low wall that surrounded the settlement, huddled in the saddle between two hills back in the mid-Bronze Age, we might have witnessed an extraordinary scene.

Looking across what was then a small village we might have seen a group of roundhouses, each with its doorway to the south and each forming half of a pair: one was a house for living in, the other for craft and work. Ten or eleven of these small groups stood inside Grimspound's wall. Beyond the wall lay a little cemetery, not the site of a communal long barrow but a modest field of individual burials.

So far this might not seem very impressive. The smoke rising through the chimneyless thatch was not from the earliest hearth, or even a hearth that was different from those at Skara

Brae. So few artefacts were found here when the site was excavated that it is difficult to know if this was a permanent village or just a summer settlement. What was extraordinary about this place was the view. Everywhere, for as far as could be seen, was fields. Not the heather and heath, peat and gorse of Dartmoor today, but rolling farmland, divided neatly by a thousand low stone walls. And there, people planted crops, drove sheep and cattle to pasture. Scattered across the horizon, columns of smoke would have risen from the hearths of over 1500 other settlements. Dartmoor in 1500 BC was the pinnacle of the early farmers' achievement. Over countless generations this huge granite plateau had been cleared of trees and was now divided into productive field systems supporting a burgeoning human population. Now agriculture reached from the shoreline to the hilltops.

We know little about how the society at Grimspound, or anywhere else, was organised. Clearly, looking at the vast system of field boundaries radiating from the settlements, there was some central order and the community had found ways of working together to achieve results far greater than any individual could hope for. What is difficult to determine is whether this was the work of an egalitarian society or of a few powerful individuals who 'ordered' the work and controlled the land. Since the days of the Amesbury Archer, however, some eight hundred years before, there had been signs of differences in wealth between individuals – clearly visible in the artefacts with which they were buried. Single burials with prestigious grave-goods, including bronze daggers, hint that this was not perhaps the communal idyll we might imagine and that perhaps the nascent ambitions of individuals were marked out in the stone walls that marched across the hillsides.

What we do know is that this agricultural success story did not have a simple happy ending. Just three hundred years later, at Grimspound, the wall around the settlement was tumble-down and the settlement had been abandoned long enough for decay to set in – the thatching on the roofs had fallen through the rafters, the beams were rotting. All of the hearths were cold, and only rainwater now gathered in the stones where the former occupants once ground their flour.

And not only had the people gone, the whole landscape had changed. No cereals grew in sheltered fields, no livestock grazed on the high pasture. Not a single column of smoke rose from where so many other settlements had stood. In places, the old stone walls were still visible, but the fields between them had become clogged with peat. This once productive land was reduced to a blasted, empty wilderness.

What happened at Grimspound was not unique. All over Britain high farming ground was turning to moorland, the monuments of the old agricultural world were falling out of use and a new age was dawning. Not everywhere saw catastrophic change, but nowhere escaped it altogether and certainly not Dartmoor.

Since the end of the Neolithic period many changes had already taken place in Britain. The earliest metalwork of the Bronze Age, such as the pieces owned by the Amesbury Archer, were probably more for show than practical use, but since then the technology had improved rapidly. Making bronze was a skilled and difficult process, requiring not just the techniques to build up the temperatures to create the alloy and cast objects, but the trading connections to bring together the copper and tin that formed it, both of which only occurred naturally in a few disparate areas. Despite these challenges, though, bronze production had taken off in Britain, and by around 2000 BC the last flint tools were falling out of use. For those who seized the opportunities of this brave new world a new future awaited, while those who shunned them, such as the farmers at Skara Brae on Orkney, would quickly be left behind. By the mid-second millennium BC large-scale trading in bronze seems to have been taking place, as witnessed by the discovery of submerged hoards of axes – the lost cargoes of ancient shipwrecks – and the recovery of an entire Bronze Age boat (currently the oldest known sea-going vessel on earth) from Dover in 1992. Large vessels like this (the Dover boat may have been up to 18 metres long and 2.5 metres wide) were probably conducting a cross-Channel trade in finished goods and scrap bronze, and might also have carried the raw materials for bronze production, such as copper ore from the mines at Great Orme in North Wales. The extensive mines there, which we know were worked from at least 2500 BC, are esti-mated to have produced enough copper for up to ten million axes during their active life. This huge output had been put to good use in shaping the agricultural landscape of Britain but now, in the latter half of the second millennium BC, something was going wrong and nowhere more so than at Grimspound.

The fate of the people of Grimspound is one of the great mysteries of British prehistory. Many theories have been put forward to explain the abandonment of the huge tracts of land, and much has been done to link this to changes in the ritual landscape that also occurred at this time.

A clue may possibly lie in the peat that buried many moor-land areas. The high humic acid content of peat and its low oxygen levels 'pickle' submerged organic material. In Ireland this process has preserved a series of ancient oak trees, whose growth rings suggest at least one cause for the catastrophe of the mid-Bronze Age. Trees put on growth rings each year, usually consisting of a wide summer band and a narrower winter one. For a long time archaeologists have been using this handy fact to date archaeological sites by counting tree rings and comparing the result to larger calibrated charts to date the wood. But other information is hidden within the rings. By not just counting the rings but measuring them, it is possible to map the life of a tree and discover how it fared each year depending on the weather. In good years trees put on wide rings, in bad years narrow ones. The Irish bog oaks from around the time Grimspound was abandoned tell a stark tale. Until 1159 BC they show wide summer growth rings each year. Then for the next eighteen, almost no new wood was put on and the trees barely grew. What had happened?

Many suggestions have been put forward for this 'climatic catastrophe', from volcanic eruptions to a dimming of the sun in the dust from a comet's tail. At around this time there was also a collapse in Greek culture in the Mediterranean, and a major dynasty change in China which might hint at some spectacular cause. In truth, though, it might have been no single calamitous event that precipitated the end. The land of the high moor was always 'marginal' and, with increasing populations, it would have taken only a minor change in climate to start an irreversible trend. We like to think of the ancient farmers as careful guardians of the soil, but they were as prone as we are to over-exploit their land: increasingly heavy demands on thin, exposed soils was likely to strain a delicate ecosystem, and perhaps only a gentle push sent it over the edge.

Whether by sudden cataclysm or through imperceptibly small steps, the climate seems to have been changing, slowly getting wetter, and even this subtle difference might have been enough to force the people of Grimspound away from what would soon become the moor.

But the retreat from the moors – indeed the formation of the moors – was not the only sign of change in the later Bronze Age: it affected the more protected lowland valleys too. Stonehenge was no longer a hive of activity, and no funeral parties stood around the barrows in the Amesbury Archer's field. The henges, stone circles and standing stones were silent, and the children playing around them probably had as little idea of their original purpose as we do today. Even before the moors were abandoned, the people had long given up building great open-air monuments to concentrate on dividing up ever more of the landscape with man-made boundaries. The age of the henge was giving way to the age of the hedge. The old gods, or at least the ways in which people had communicated with them, had gone, and the new deities of this wetter age looked up from beneath the waters.

Finding the gods of this new age is far harder than locating their ancestors. The beliefs of the middle Bronze Age and before may be obscure in their meaning but they are easy to see because they are written in stone across the landscape. But their decline, whether it represented a wholesale change in religion or, more likely, a prehistoric 'Reformation', certainly did not mean that all the gods were dead.

To catch a glimpse of these deities we must travel to just outside Peterborough in Cambridgeshire, and back in time over three thousand years. If the climate was indeed getting wetter, due not only to rainfall but also to rising sea-levels, there can have been few places that were more affected by this than the Fens. This was a water-world where the difference between dry land and sea was never more than a couple of feet; a world where water not only controlled the cycle of life but acted as a conduit to the ritual world beyond. This was where the new gods dwelt.

Today the area around Flag Fen to the south-east of Peterborough is a typically flat fenland landscape, where the industrial suburbs of Peterborough slowly give way to the enormous arable fields of agribusiness. Over the whole scene stands a monument to the modern world: a vast power station. Had we paused at that vantage-point three thousand years earlier, we would have witnessed a different but perhaps no less impressive sight.

We would have been standing on a marshy inlet with land to the south and west but only sea to the north. To the east, there was more open fen, edged with reed, rush and flag iris, then another piece of land, Northey Island, just a few feet above the water. It was not a wild landscape, though: wherever there was dry land there were farms, and between them lay an elaborate system of field boundaries. Across the open fen over on Northey Island there were a few roundhouses, each separated from its neighbour by a droveway and surrounded by its own system of fields. They were not grouped in what we might think of as villages but scattered across the landscape, each house the centre of its own small farming world. In the fields, a farmer might have herded his livestock with the aid of a dog – a descendant of the first one skulking among the reeds at Star Carr more than seven thousand years earlier. It was, perhaps, a disparate and lonely existence, spread over the vast, flat plain of the fen, and might also have seemed a godless place, devoid of the field monuments of previous ages. However, at the marshy inlet between this point and Northey Island, connecting the land with the island more than a kilometre away, via a strange artificial island, stood one of the greatest engineering achievements of British prehistory: a huge trackway of sixty thousand wooden posts, driven into the silt of the marsh and bridging the gulf of open fen. It was the Golden Gate Bridge of the Bronze Age.

Had not this landscape, like the moors, been covered with a protective layer of peat, we would know nothing of this wooden wonder. The monuments of earlier ages built in stone have survived much better than organic ones, but sites like this might have been the successors to the circles and standing stones, and Britain might once have been home to many thousands of them. The survival of this monument gives us a glimpse into this new and strange world.

To understand what the great line of posts, over seven metres wide in places, is for, we must walk down to the water's edge to see it close up. Initially the posts look like nothing more than a bridge across the open water of the fen between the farmlands of what is now Fengate and those on Northey Island. Even if that were so it would still have been an extraordinary engineering feat, but if we take a tentative step on to the trackway and look down into the waters beside it, it soon becomes clear that this is far more than a bridge. As we crunch across the white sand that dusts the surface to prevent us slipping, we might peer into the shallow waters below and see the glint of metal and the soft glow of quartz pebbles, mixed with the shadowy outlines of hundreds of man-made shapes. Were we to reach in, we might pull out some of the rarest, most valuable objects of the day: bronze rapiers and daggers, black shale bracelets, flesh hooks for pulling meat from boiling cauldrons, a set of bronze shears still in their wooden case, a wooden wheel (the first we know of in Britain). But these are not simply items lost while crossing the fen: in a world where bronze is rare and valuable, someone losing a dagger would retrieve it. Nor are all these items scattered randomly beneath the posts: most lie on the landward side of the alignment making loss unlikely.

If we look at one of the bronze swords other things might strike us as unusual: the blade has been repeatedly hit against a hard corner, ruining the edge. Others have been bent or even snapped. But these are not old tools – some seem to have been hardly used before they were broken.

To understand, we must step back from the water's edge and watch a small group from Northey Island as they head towards us over the trackway. Among the forest of oak posts, which tower three metres above them, the group has stopped in an area of track that has been partitioned off, almost like an open-air room. Words of their long-dead language now drift to us across the fen. Among them a man takes a bronze sword – a beautifully crafted object with a blade like gold and a polished wooden handle – seizes the blade and bends it over his knee. There is a short awe-struck silence before he kneels and places the now useless weapon in the still waters. He produces another: a tiny tin wheel, made over a thousand miles away in the Alps. It slips beneath the water and is lost.

We have, perhaps, witnessed one of the major rites of this watery religion: some of the most valuable objects from the human world have been deliberately 'killed' and placed in the water. The post alignment is not simply a bridge between places but between worlds: between land and water, life and death, heaven and hell. It was at these waterside places that the ceremonies of the new age took place, not perhaps on the scale of the open-air theatre possible at stone circles and henges, but more intimate communications across a boundary both everyday and mysterious – the water's silvery surface.

It is perhaps too much to ask what such rituals might have meant. What we do know is that the objects consigned to the waters had often been transported over long distances and certainly commanded a high price, however it was paid. These people were not throwing pennies into a fountain but the equivalent of diamond rings and sports cars.

Perhaps the offerings, and even the trackway itself were a ritual attempt to control the rising waters that threatened the local farmland more with each passing year. Perhaps the trackway marked out the boundaries of ownership in an increasingly 'pressed' society; a Bronze Age Canute, holding back the water, or the tide of people whom the rising seas were slowly displacing. It might have served more prosaic social functions too: it was the biggest landmark for miles around, and possibly a place where the disparate communities of the Bronze Age fen could meet up to find husbands or wives and exchange livestock, thereby keeping healthy the bloodlines of both humans and animals. Either way, at Flag Fen another type of worship had replaced that associated with the old monuments and would continue to do so for centuries to come.

The obsession with placing valuable objects in water out of reach of human world continued into the Iron Age and beyond. At Llyn Fawr in south Wales a vast treasure was recovered from a mountain lake during the Second World War: items that had been deposited over a thousand-year period. In London today, extraordinary things are occasionally dredged from the Thames, including two of the most iconic British Iron Age items: the Battersea Shield and the Waterloo Helmet. Both are far too elaborate to have been of any practical use, and their discovery, whole, on the bed of the Thames suggests that they had been placed there deliberately in a ceremony perhaps not dissimilar from the one we witnessed at Flag Fen all those years before.

In fact, it has been argued that, in many ways, the water cult of the later Bronze Age has never left us. The hand rising from the lake with King Arthur's sword Excalibur has an eerie overtone of the scene at Flag Fen. And every time we throw a coin into a wishing well we are, in a way, making an offering to some distant, half-remembered god.

The changes in Bronze Age life were not confined to the water's edge. In a world where the everyday and the divine were almost certainly not strictly separated as they are today, the changes in life and belief spread into and throughout the home. The roundhouse of prehistory presents a cosy image of life – a home of mud and wood with the smoke from a central hearth rising through the thatch, a simple Asterix-style world of hard work and honest values, no different in its way from the rural cottages of later centuries. But it is a mistake to see this emerging world as simply a more primitive form of later times. To walk into a late Bronze Age British home would be to walk into another world. At Cladh Hallan on South Uist in the Outer Hebrides a remarkable archaeological site allows us to do just that. Although the structures of the seven houses that once stood there in a little 'terrace' are long gone, painstaking excavation has revealed much about how they were laid out and what they meant to the people who lived in them. If we could have clambered over the dunes towards the seven conical, turf-covered roofs of the hamlet we would have found that, for the people of Cladh Hallan, their home was not just a retreat from the outside world, it *was* their world and, more than that, their entire cosmos.

To step across the threshold of one of those homes would have been to walk into not just a home but a sort of ritual planetarium – a model of the universe as the occupants saw it. The space was not divided up simply for convenience. Inside there were areas of day and night, places of light and darkness, even life and death, and they survived through six hundred years of building and rebuilding on the site. To step over the threshold is to step into the Bronze Age mind.

The journey round a roundhouse was a model of many larger journeys, from day to night and from life to death. Ahead, there was the central hearth, the middle point of the house that provided light and warmth – a miniature sun. Turning first to the left we would find ourselves in the daytime, living part of the house, travelling clockwise or 'sunwise', mimicking the path of the sun as it crossed the sky. The first zone here, in the south-east quadrant, was for preparing food and was filled with cooking pots, grinding stones and bone utensils; it was located where the light was best. Although it was not a distinct 'room', it was perhaps the first kitchen in Britain. Continuing clockwise, we would have come to the south-west quadrant, a storage and working area with a deep cellar where foodstuffs were kept. Here we might have made out a figure hunched over some leatherwork, piercing a hide with a bone awl, surrounded by other tools strewn on the floor. Moving on we would have passed to the night side of the house and, in the north-west quadrant, we'd find the bed: a pile of cut turf and soft sand, probably covered with animal skins and perhaps heather on which all the family would have slept.

But the internal divisions of this house run deeper than simply day and night, light and darkness. The final, north-eastern quadrant was the darkest area, and its gloom cloaked the building's greatest secrets. In this area there were no everyday items: it was where the domestic gave way to the divine. Although there was nothing to see on the surface, if we had looked beneath the floor we would have found the decapitated body of a dog, a whole sheep, and, deep in the foundation deposits, human remains.

A number of human bodies have been found under the floors in the north-east areas of these houses, including those of a teenage girl, a three-year-old toddler, an adult man and woman. They were not simply older burials over which the house had been accidentally built: the builders had placed the bodies there. And the burial of two of them was only the last phase in an already long and bizarre history. When the bodies of the adult man and woman were excavated and sent for routine carbon14 dating, an extraordinary fact came to light: neither body had been buried within days, months or even years of death. In fact, the male had already been dead for six hundred years when he was buried and the female had waited some three hundred years for her last rites, which begs the question what happened to them in the meantime?

The answer seems to have been that they were preserved above ground as mummies. Had this been Egypt, parts of South America or China, the idea of finding mummies at an archaeo-logical site might not seem unusual, but this was the Outer Hebrides. It seems that the two bodies were preserved by having been temporarily submerged in peat bogs, then bound tightly, knees to chest, and allowed to dry. What purpose they served is hard to say, but in the settlement that immediately preceded the houses at Cladh Hallan it would seem that visitors might have been greeted by the dead as well as the living. Perhaps these bodies were the ancient ancestors around whose myth-ology the Bronze Age inhabitants of the Outer Hebrides had built their rights to the land. As such they might have been kept on show in the home. Perhaps, as in some more recent cultures, they were only brought out to share with their descendants in the great rites of passage or to act as mediators

1. *The Vale of Pickering, Yorkshire. At the time when Britain was becoming an island the view from here would have been across a warm, shallow lake. Around the edges we might just have caught a glimpse of the men and women of the Mesolithic era – the first island Britons.*

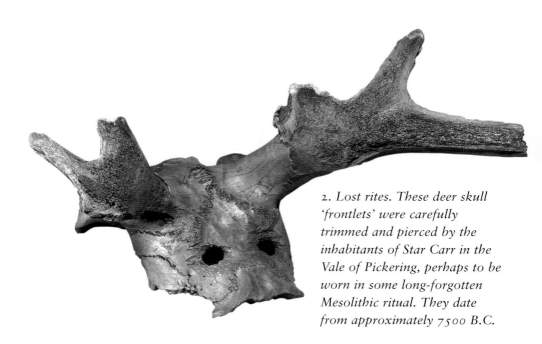

2. Lost rites. These deer skull 'frontlets' were carefully trimmed and pierced by the inhabitants of Star Carr in the Vale of Pickering, perhaps to be worn in some long-forgotten Mesolithic ritual. They date from approximately 7500 B.C.

3. This reconstruction of a Mesolithic 'bender dwelling' at Bentley Wildfowl and Motor Museum in East Sussex gives some idea of the sort of temporary shelters that hunter-gathering Britons probably called home.

4. *A walk in the past. Preserved in layer upon layer
of mud on Formby Point beach in Lancashire are the
footprints of the inhabitants of Mesolithic and
Neolithic Britain. This Neolithic set belonged to a
young man, estimated to be about 5'3" tall, walking
from right to left towards us. In the foreground his
tracks are crossed by those of an older man walking
from right to left. The scattering of roe deer tracks in
the same stratum gives a clue as to what brought
these two men to the beach.*

5. *The tool that changed Britain. Without the stone axes of Neolithic farmers, Britain today would still be a forested land. To celebrate the extraordinary power of this tool they carved examples in rare but functionally useless stones, such as this example in jadeite.*

6. *Island life. Dating back to around 3000 B.C., the settlement at Skara Brae on Orkney was one of the most sophisticated in Neolithic Europe. Each of the seven almost identical houses was carefully laid out around a central hearth with beds against the walls, an indoor 'toilet' and a 'dresser' taking pride of place opposite the doorway. These familiar items would find a place in nearly every country cottage for the next five thousand years.*

7. The home of the ancestors. The long barrow at West Kennet in Wiltshire once held the bones of the first farmers of this region. Building it involved dragging boulders of up to five tons uphill and arranging them to form a covered passage, which was then earthed over. It must have taken the co-ordinated resources of the entire local community.

8. The path to the next world. When the West Kennet long barrow was built the doorway was left open, allowing the people of the area access to the bones of their ancestors – which, it seems, they occasionally felt the need to re-arrange. By the Bronze Age the bones may have lost their power as the entrance was sealed.

9. *The landscape of memory. A recent theory suggests that this stone circle on Orkney – known today as the Ring of Brodgar – may once have memorialised the location of the home of an early island settler. As such it formed part of a readable history of the prehistoric people of Orkney, written in stone across their land.*

10. *The epitome of prehistory. Stonehenge on Salisbury Plain lies at the centre of the most famous complex of Neolithic monuments in Britain. It was into this sophisticated ritual landscape that the body of one of the pioneers of the Bronze Age, the 'Amesbury Archer', was placed.*

11. *The end of an era. The discovery of these beautifully flaked stone arrowheads in an early bronze Age grave have led to their owner being called the 'Amesbury Archer'. In fact he probably did not make his living from hunting, and these tools represented to him an old stone technology that he had begun to replace.*

12. *A new beginning. These corroded copper knife blades, also from the grave of the Amesbury Archer, were the most sophisticated objects of their day and may well be the earliest metal objects in British history. Both the metal and their owner had come to Britain from continental Europe.*

13. *Lost worlds. Lying today in ruins on a blasted moor, the settlement of Grimspound on Dartmoor once stood at the centre of a patchwork of carefully tended farmland. By 1000 B.C., however, this whole landscape was becoming choked with peat as the 'wild' moorlands of modern Dartmoor formed. Today the area is still uninhabitable.*

between the living and the dead. Either way, in the early and middle Bronze Age it looks as though it wasn't difficult on the Hebrides to 'meet the ancestors'.

But at the time the Cladh Hallan houses were built, these ancient super-ancestors were finally buried. It was around 1000 BC and, as at Grimspound hundreds of miles to the south, it seems that trouble was brewing. There is a chance that the builders at Cladh Hallan were invaders who had taken the bodies – the powerful cult object of the people they had dis-placed – and disposed of them, but their careful burial inside houses seems to contradict this. Alternatively, in a world of change, it might be that in troubled times the people of the Outer Hebrides no longer believed in the bodies' power to intercede for them. They were, perhaps, idols of an old and now discredited religion, the victims of a Bronze Age Reformation.

In this new age there was no use for mummified bodies but the dead fulfilled a role by being buried in the homes of the living. The body of the teenage girl was not mummified before burial; she had died at the time the houses were built. How her body got there remains unknown. A tragic family loss? A deliberate sacrifice? The reasons behind her presence there remains as dim and dark as the place where she lay buried, but it was no accident, and clearly the people who lived there wanted her body beneath the floor. She was an essential part of their Bronze Age home.

To a visitor of the time, all of these symbolic references in the Cladh Hallan houses would have been readable. They were more than houses: they were a self-contained world, a circular physical structure that paralleled the circling days, years and lives of its inhabitants. Although the stone circles had fallen out of use it seems their meaning might have been taken into the home, where a more private and intimate relationship with the gods was taking over from the public displays of the monumental landscape. Perhaps the old gods had not simply died or gone away, but had moved in with the living and now crouched in those dark north-eastern recesses.

Nor was it only the relationship with the gods that was changing. As the Bronze Age went on, relationships between the people of Britain evolved. The problem for us in discovering how the world was changing is that from this period and until the Roman invasion, archaeology is missing one of its main clues: the bodies of the dead. The Outer Hebrides are unusual in producing human remains from this time: we only have around forty skeletons from the whole of the late Bronze Age in Britain. In the centuries after that the problem, if anything, becomes worse. What happened to the dead remains mysterious. It has been suggested that they were exposed to be eaten by wild animals, as had happened in earlier times, or cremated, or even offered to the water with their possessions in a final funerary rite. While the number of identified living sites from this time increases dramatically, the evidence of the people living there dwindles. There are plenty of doors to knock on, but hardly anyone is at home.

What we do know from the living sites is that this was a society of small groupings that were coming more and more into contact with each other. As the population increased so people were forced together and individual farmsteads gave way to larger communities. While this might even be seen as the origins of British village society, the arrival of 'neighbours' came at a considerable cost. Even the tiny settlement of seven houses at Cladh Hallan was a veritable conurbation compared to the disparate settlements of earlier ages, and more people on the land must have created more dispute and more opportunity for the differences to be displayed. The rising tensions are perhaps best exemplified in a revolutionary tool that originated at this time.

Since the Neolithic the standard British toolkit had included arrows, knives, axes and sickles, but the later Bronze Age saw the invention of a far more specialised implement: the rapier. The development of a tool whose only purpose was to kill other humans marks a deadly turn in British history, demonstrating not necessarily an escalation in violence but certainly an escalation in the overt threat of it. It has been argued that the appearance of what archaeologists call 'rapiers' and then swords in this period show that society had discovered war. This is probably too simplistic as you don't need a specialised tool to kill someone – just about anything applied with enough vigour to the right place can do the job. What it does mark out, though, is a change in belief. A slashing sword was the shock weapon of its day and had a singular purpose. As we walked through the causewayed enclosure at Hambledon Hill or among the houses of Skara Brae, we might have come across people carrying objects that could be used as weapons, but they did not advertise an overt threat as the new sword did.

From the later Bronze Age people began to carry specific weapons and, however elaborately decorated or apparently 'ceremonial' they appeared, their message was 'Don't argue with me!' Modern city gun culture may be more about showing off ownership of a gun than using it, but behind the display the implication is still that it might be used, and the occasional carrying through of the threat reinforces the message. If we could ask the people of Cladh Hallan what their main export was, we should not perhaps be surprised to learn that, beyond farming, archaeological evidence suggests they were major arms dealers.

With this more militaristic display, we find other changes in the landscape and a reflected feeling that while we may not have just left Eden, we have certainly come to a world which feels more dangerous. Other technological changes were taking place which accelerated these distinctions. Around the seventh century BC iron began to be used in Britain. Although the earliest artefacts might have been purely for show, as was early bronze before it, this technology quickly established its practical use. Iron ore is far more commonly available than copper and tin, and there is no need for a complicated alloying process. Also, iron holds a sharper edge for longer. It was one of a series of slow shifts that were bringing Britain to a unique break-point. Iron tools were easier and cheaper to manufacture than bronze ones so more people could use them, which meant greater farming efficiency. For the first time an acre of land could feed more people than were required to tend it. Britain was in profit.

How you see profit affecting people depends on your politics. What is clear, however, is that in Iron Age society profit allowed people to show their difference, based on their ability to acquire prestigious items. By the Iron Age many could afford such things and a society was emerging with that sort of prestige as its currency.

As you walk out of the large supermarket on the edge of Winchester in Hampshire, weighed down with the week's shopping, it is hard to imagine how our ancestors displayed their social standing in a world without money. In the car park, as people load up their cars, it's easy to see the differences today – some drive Ford Fiestas, others drive Range Rovers; some eat beans on toast, others eat olive tapenade on ciabatta. Yet as you pull out of the car park, could you drive back two thousand three hundred years you might find exactly these types of social display, just beginning.

The roundabout outside the supermarket on Winnal Down was a very different place in the Iron Age, as you might expect, but one where the sort of social considerations that we face today were not unknown. Could we have pulled up there (and then) we'd have found two small rows of roundhouses similar to the Bronze Age homes at Cladh Hallan, in which several, probably related, families lived. They still made a living from intensively farming the surrounding area. Around each central hearth we would have found the extended family enjoying the fruits of their labour – milk, butter and cheese from their cows and goats, mutton, lamb and wool from their sheep, bread and beer made from the barley and wheat grown in the fields. Add to that some fruit and vegetables, and they had a fairly balanced diet. Noticeable for its absence, however, was wild game – deer, birds and even fish, which these people seemed to shun, perhaps because they were wild and not farmed. Fish, whose remains are almost never found in rubbish dumps of this era, might even have represented inhabitants of that other world beyond the mirror of the water's surface. Instead, they might have tucked into a joint of horse or dog without a qualm.

But the most interesting thing we know about the Iron Age inhabitants of Winnal is that one night they threw a party, in which conspicuous consumption was the order of the day. We know what happened on that day 2300 years ago, thanks to a series of pits found in the ground around the houses when the site was excavated by archaeologists in the 1980s. Traditionally, prehistoric pits have been seen as one of two things: either a place to store food (usually grain) or to dump rubbish. In most cases the received wisdom was that when the pit was no longer of use for the first purpose it was used for the second. But a careful examination showed that something odd had happened here. What initially looked like rubbish was in fact a very carefully selected group of objects placed in the ground in a very particular order, everything from household items to entire animal carcasses. These rubbish pits meant something, and it related back to that party.

On that night, as the sun set, the little community started to buzz. A large number of animals was corralled within the compound, including horses, cattle, sheep, pigs and dogs, and the inhabitants prepared a vast quantity of food. In front of the entrance to a house on the outskirts of the row an old grain pit had been opened and emptied, its walls still a tangle of germinated seed, like a bad haircut. Perhaps as many as three hundred people arrived for the festivities from the local area and beyond. Later the animals were slaughtered – perhaps as many as twelve cows just for starters which equated to a very large quantity of steak. This huge group of people intended to eat and the inhabitants of the Winnal Down settlement wanted to make sure they ate well. The meat was butchered and thrown into huge simmering cauldrons. From time to time an attendant plunged a flesh-hook into the pot and drew out a chunk of meat to see if it was done. There were copious amounts of barley beer to drink, which might have loosened a few tongues. Perhaps a song or two rose up from the crowd to accompany the raucous sound of horns. Although this was a world without literature the people lived in a landscape filled with stories, and sights on the journey here tonight might have reminded some of the tales that they recounted around the fire. Others met and greeted rarely seen neighbours or planned marriages for sons and daughters. Some complained over the distribution of meat – who had the best cuts and who was served first. Perhaps local politics were discussed, and certainly everyone compared the gathering to previous ones, while the hosts hoped nervously that their comparison was a positive one.

The reason for the gathering is lost to us – perhaps it celebrated some rite of passage such as a marriage or a birth, or maybe it was just this group's turn to throw a party. The important thing, though, was the conspicuous consumption: there had to be food and drink in such enormous quantities not only to impress the guests but also to thank the gods for the profitability of the land.

At some point in the festivities a group might have broken away from the crowd. Remembering those gods who had provided the feast was important to these people, and around that disused grain pit the deities who ruled the place received their share of the largesse. First whole pots, like those being handed round for the feast, were thrown into the pit to smash on the floor – perhaps for the same reason that the people at Flag Fen bent their sword before offering it to the waters. Then a thick layer of bones went in – horse, pig, cow, dog and sheep. The meat had been previously cut away and cooked for the crowd. Next, a man was lowered into the two-metre deep pit to cover the fresh bones with daub – a mix of clay and straw used to cover the walls of Iron Age houses. Then basketloads of chalk came down and others joined the man in the pit to trample it into a dazzling white dome. At this point all except the first man were hauled up and a skinned pig carcass, whole except for one leg, was lowered in and arranged by the attendant on the chalk where its startling bloody surface must have stood out against the pure white backdrop. Then a dog carcass, similarly treated, was placed next to the pig. Finally the man was pulled out and the pit sealed. The gods had received their share. It must have been a night to remember. Such an event might not have happened again for another twenty years and in the Iron

Age, when life expectancy was not much above twenty-five, that was a lifetime away.

Just what this huge party meant to those who organised it and those who enjoyed it is hard to say. Certainly it had a religious element, but it was a social gathering too. In fact, in a world where the secular and religious were not clearly divided, the feast probably served all functions. What was important was the bringing together of so many people and the planning. The Winnal Down settlement probably only ever supported five or ten cattle and perhaps forty sheep so the huge amount of food for one night of feasting must have been prepared over weeks and months, if not years. The farmers at Winnal Down were keen to impress and, even in a society without money, they knew how to do it. The party showed they could afford to throw one – a big one at that. It meant they were doing well, which made them important. It also meant that the people who enjoyed their hospitality now 'owed them one' and, in an increasingly competitive society, it was always good to be owed favours. Those farmers were determined to make their way up the greasy pole, and went about it in a way little different from some of our fellow shoppers in the car park some twenty two centuries later, loading their cars with expensive foods for dinner parties and barbecues at which to impress their neighbours.

Gatherings like that one were having a profound effect on society. Large-scale meetings encouraged large-scale trading patterns, large-scale allegiances and hence larger-scale societies. In a Britain with a rising population and an increasing level of social interaction, this might have encouraged bigger groups to band together to protect mutual interests – probably land and livestock. The party at Winnal Down brought together a group with a common interest, but it also marked out who

54

was not in it. In a society where status derived from overt displays of wealth and the most popular prestige item was the sword, it was important to know who was 'in' and who was 'out'. Behind the niceties of social interaction lay the clear threat of force.

It has often been said that the rising tensions of the Iron Age can be seen in the landscape even today. In the last millennium BC new structures began to appear – settlements and sites that seemed to be highly defended, as though the emerging tribes were digging in for a difficult and dangerous future. In Scotland, stone tower-houses, known as 'brochs', were erected, while man-made islands of timber and stone in lochs housed lonely 'crannog' dwellings. Stranger still were the sites whose stone and earth ramparts were laced with timber and fired to such high temperatures that the stone fused into a glassy mass, forming what are known as 'vitrified forts'. In the west of England whole promontories were cut off from their hinterlands with deep trenches, while in the south the great hillforts appeared. If the invention of the sword had marked the beginning of a British arms race, perhaps these new, defended settlements were the bunkers of a nascent cold war.

In fact, had we been able to visit an Iron Age hillfort around, say, 400 BC it might have been a lot harder to tell what its purpose was. The great hillfort at Danebury, in Hampshire, lies atop the highest land for miles around and commands 360-degree views of the plains below – plains that presumably the builders of the hillfort controlled. Climbing towards the main east gate we pass a Bronze Age barrow – this was an important place long before the hillfort was built. Ahead of us now is a sight that looks frankly military to modern eyes: a huge series of curving ramparts, their walls packed with dazzling white chalk some ten metres high and topped with a wooden palisade, sweep around the entrance gate. It is a blinding, awe-inspiring scene. The entire top of the hill has been circumscribed with this massive complex of banks and ditches, representing the movement by hand of hundreds of thousands of tons of earth and chalk. As we pass through the outer defences the ramparts force us to turn to the left, exposing our unshielded right side to the bowmen and slingsmen peering at us through the palisade. They could stop us with ease: we're standing in what military architects call a 'killing zone'. Perhaps with a little less confidence now, we can continue to the main gate – a huge set of wooden doors beneath a tower from which more defenders look down at us suspiciously. So far, so frightening.

The wooden doors swing open to reveal, not a barracks as we might have suspected, but a surprisingly peaceful scene. To left and right there are lines of roundhouses, enough for three or four hundred people, huddled beneath the ramparts and strung out along a circular road that runs round the interior. Ahead, other paths are lined with small square granaries and, at the highest point, there is what appears to be a shrine. As we wander down one of the roads we pass livestock, penned to either side – cattle and sheep – and craft workshops, where blacksmiths, weavers, leatherworkers and basketmakers ply their trade. The scene would seem almost idyllically rural,were it not for the slingsman eyeing us from his place behind the gate, his hand hovering over a huge ammunition dump of smooth river pebbles.

So what were these places for? The high ramparts, the palisade, the ammunition dumps and the gate all suggest this was a defended place, but that does not make it a fort. Nor are all the defences necessarily practical. Many a medieval city was ringed with walls that said more about the civic pride of the inhabitants than the dangers they believed lurked without. Inside the rampart the shrine suggests that this was a religious site, a high place whose position has given it some mystical value. From the houses around the edge it might have been a small town, or perhaps, from the granaries and animal pens, it was a market. In fact, it could have been all these things, like villages, towns and cities today.

It was clear to everyone from miles around, though, that this was a central place at which large numbers of people could come together, for religion, for socialising, for trade or for defence. It was not perhaps the first 'town' in British history, as these people were still intimately tied to the land around them, making their living directly from it, but it might have served many of the functions of a town. With its commanding view of the farmland below, it certainly dominated the area and might have controlled it. It was an obvious location for trading, and for storing the main wealth of a community – its food. But we should perhaps be careful not to draw too many of its teeth. If we could have climbed on to the ramparts and joined the defenders looking over the palisade we would have seen other, similar places in the landscape, perhaps competing for the same resources. This was a competitive society – and competition can get out of hand. The defenders on the walls could have told us of attacks by other groups – of the time when even the great wooden gate was burned down. Many of the men standing there might have borne the scars of battle. The few human remains recovered by archaeologists from this site have shown that this could be a bruising and bloody place – pelvises with slashing cuts from swords, and skulls with elliptical puncture-marks that only an Iron Age spear could have made. But it was successful too, and population and productivity were increasing, so if this was a land of endemic petty warfare, then war was working.

Of course, the few human remains that survive from this period cannot tell us whether this was a society in which only the occasional vendetta was settled violently or which was permanently at war. Perhaps the truth lay somewhere in between. In a land without large-scale central authorities, a police force and a formal legal framework, there was always scope for violence, but perhaps not the organisational capacity for large-scale war. Your neighbours might have worn their swords mainly for show but there can be little doubt that they were sometimes tempted to use them. Just as with hillforts, if we could step into the stone keep of a Scottish broch we would probably not find ourselves in a 'castle' in the defensive sense, but the important family living there would undoubtedly appreciate the value of the threat their imposing home implied, and might have been grateful for the protection of its thick stone walls. As larger and larger groups of people found common cause, larger-scale differences emerged over anything from ownership of land and political allegiance to cattle-rustling. These were frontier times and the hillforts and brochs were how this part of the west was won.

Leaving Danebury hillfort we might cast a backward glance at the central shrine. To understand it might be to get into the minds of the people who lived there but, like those of their Bronze Age forebears, the beliefs of these people are hard to fathom. We might find them depositing valuable treasures in watery places, and we have seen the care with which food and other offerings were placed in the ground at Winnal Down. But without their dead bodies, or perhaps more importantly the grave goods deposited with them, they remain harder to understand than people who died a thousand years beforehand.

But in one case we can come face-to-face with an Iron Age man. He is the only prehistoric Briton we can still look in the eye, and his story offers dark insights into our ancestors' souls.

Were you to meet Lindow Man in a pub you probably wouldn't take much notice of him. In modern clothing he would look no more exotic than the rest of us. At about five foot six you wouldn't say he was tall but he looks well built and tanned, as though he spends a lot of time outdoors. You probably wouldn't think he was a workman – his dark hair is cut quite short and his beard and moustache have been neatly trimmed. His fingernails are neatly manicured and his hands are smooth. Looking into his blue-grey eyes you might guess his age at about twenty-five and not be far wrong. But if he might not attract a second glance in the modern world, in the late Iron Age he was something special – as his grisly story demonstrates.

We know so much about the appearance of Lindow Man because we have his body – a unique survival from British prehistory, naturally mummified in the peat of a Cheshire bog. Since his death in Lindow Moss around two thousand years ago, the highly acidic peat has pickled his body, tanning the skin and preventing microbes breaking down his flesh. He lay there until 1985 when a commercial peat-cutting machine uncovered part of him.

Two thousand years earlier Lindow Moss was a bog, a watery, dangerous place where a false step could prove fatal, but this man had not stumbled to his death. Had we stood next to him on his last day, some time in the first century AD, we would have come as close, perhaps, as it is possible to get to the beliefs of Iron Age people, and they would have seemed utterly alien to us.

When he died, Lindow Man had recently eaten a light meal of unleavened bread made from wheat and barley and cooked on a heather fire at the edge of the bog. He had washed it down with a drink that contained mistletoe pollen and moss. Afterwards he stood naked, save for a single thin armband of fox fur, at the edge of the bog and awaited his fate. Had we been able to look into those greyish blue eyes that day we might have detected a look of fear.

What happened next we only know about from the marks left on his body. Someone, possibly one of the mysterious caste of priests whom the Romans called druids, led him forward into the bog and there dealt two savage blows to the back of his skull with a blunt instrument. His knees sagged and he fell to the ground. A thin string was passed around his neck and tightened. With the final twist, it broke his neck and he died. The noose still tight, a knife was dug into his throat, severing the jugular vein. As blood gouted from the wound, he was placed face down in the bog that was to be his final resting-place.

His terrible injuries bear witness to a sacrifice, but what it meant to those performing it, to its victim and society beyond, we may never know. We do not know if Lindow Man was a priest, an aristocrat or even a prisoner chosen for sacrifice. The sheer amount of 'overkill' involved in his death might preclude an execution – although hanging, drawing and quartering in the Middle Ages was perhaps such a 'triple execution' – but his silent lips cannot give us clues as to whether he went quietly and willingly to his death or if his screams echoed across Lindow Moss. Neither can we be sure why he died – if in response to some specific event or if this was a usual, if macabre, part of the prehistoric ritual year. We do know, though, that some events in Iron Age society called for a sacrifice that went beyond the cattle and pigs or swords and spears found in earth and water. There were times when the gods demanded the ultimate sacrifice of human life – and it was an obligation that the people of prehistoric Britain were prepared to fulfil.

The world in which Lindow Man had lived lay on the edge of prehistory, a tantalising but murky world where individuals and peoples almost emerge into history only to fade back into the preliterate past. His world was one of increasing complexity, now far removed from the disparate farming communities of the Bronze Age, but not yet really 'British'. Britain in the last century BC was not yet a single place. Since perhaps the Neolithic period, people had been tending to form into larger and more complex groups, and certainly that process seems to have accelerated in the Iron Age, but Britain remained a collection of localities, of regions, and was not yet a nation. In recent centuries we have seen the great dividing line between Britain and the rest of the world as our coast, a line within which everything is familiar and friendly and beyond which everything is alien and dangerous. But in the Iron Age Britain was riddled with political and cultural fault-lines, where crossing a hill could take you from the familiar to the foreign.

How these territories were marked out is unclear. Indeed, without later writers it would be almost impossible to locate the various political and social groupings that now vied for control of land. It may be that the hillforts of southern and western England marked the centres (or perhaps the edges) of these territories, from where powerful families ruled small but acquisitive 'kingdoms'. Certainly an Iron Age farmer in the last century BC would have identified himself with a larger grouping of people – what the Romans would refer to as tribes. Had we spoken to one in the Vale of Uffington in Oxfordshire they might have gone further and pointed up the hill to a unique feature in the landscape – one that said everything about who they were and, of course, who they were not.

The White Horse at Uffington, a stylised figure cut into the side of a hill at the point where three 'tribal' territories met, is probably the earliest chalk figure in Britain and as such is the first uniquely British art in our history. It was not a new feature of the landscape in the Iron Age. In fact, archaeological research has shown that a thousand years might already have passed since Bronze Age farmers had cut deep trenches into the hillside in the shape of a horse before they began the laborious task of removing white chalk from another hill (the bedrock on Uffington Hill was not white enough) and carrying it in baskets to pack into the trenches. A millennium later this figure still stood out on the hillside, still retained its meaning and might have gained more over the centuries. The meaning of the horse image in prehistory has often been debated. A Bronze Age find, dating back to about the time when the White Horse was cut, from Trundholm in Denmark, shows a horse hitched to a chariot carrying the sun so perhaps horses had a similar religious significance in the Vale. Certainly the role of the horse in society was changing: it was no longer restricted to chariot pulling but ridden as well.

But the significance of the Uffington White Horse has probably as much to do with the land into which it is carved as the people who lived on it. Perhaps the horse had a meaning for a small group of local farmers in the Bronze Age but by the late Iron Age had come to represent larger, more sophisticated groups. By the time the first coinage appears in this region there was only one choice for the symbol the coins should bear: the horse at Uffington had become the logo of the 'people of the horse'.

Growing regional identity had its price, of course. Bringing together large groups of people, persuading them of their common cause and organising their defence against other groups with equal ambition required leadership. There might have been kings in the Bronze Age, but they have proved impossible to identify, and even if they existed their influence can only have been localised. But as regional identities emerged in the last centuries BC more powerful rulers stepped on to the British stage; people who called themselves kings. Of course, we don't know whether a desire or need to organise in larger groups forced the people to elect rulers, or if powerful families used their own ambition to force others into larger groups, but either way, the culture of gift exchange and hospitality – which we saw in the 'barbecue' at Winnal Down – was now driving the development of one of Britain's most famous institutions – the class system.

All men and women of the Iron Age were not born equal, and how those social differences developed is not clear-cut. Since the days of the Amesbury Archer there had been stark differences in relative wealth between individuals, but there is evidence that this was not a one-way street. If we had collected up the crockery the day after the Winnal Down party one thing would immediately be clear: it was communal pottery. There were no individual items, no plates for one person's portion, no individuals' drinking cups. The sharing of food and drink that night might have been indicative of a society more communal than that of a thousand years earlier. But if the earlier Iron Age had witnessed a new egalitarianism, it was not to last. Ironically it might have been lavish gift-giving and large-scale partying that started the pendulum of difference swinging again. At the base of society, Britain was still a wholly agrarian land, a patchwork of small farms providing for the needs of their local area. But higher up the scale of profitability of these local economies provided a surplus for those who could control an area to trade. Wealth meant status, and status was displayed, then as today, in a show of conspicuous consumption. In late Iron Age society, rulers as well as farmers had to participate in gift exchange and party-throwing, but rulers' gifts and parties were on a larger, more exotic scale. It was this that drove the people of Britain to look to the dangerous world outside.

As we ambled along the Solent coast around 100 BC towards Hengistbury Head we might have come face to face with the extraordinary machinery of this world. Rounding the headland, we would have been confronted with not just a few farms and fields but an international port. Since the Mesolithic period, the Channel had been as much a highway as a barrier between Britain and continental Europe, and a walk through the cosmopolitan port of Hengistbury would have shown that prehistoric Britain was anything but 'insular' except in its geography. But Hengistbury was about more than the booze-cruise of cross-Channel trade. Across the sea lay the world of classical antiquity, a literate, highly cultured world with trading connections that reached from Spain to India, a grand bazaar of the rare and unusual items that ever aspiring Briton craved. Hengistbury was the entrepôt for the world.

Excavations here have shown the surprisingly 'classical' taste of the ruling élites of Iron Age society and the amazing degree to which they were connected with a trading empire that covered half of the globe. For the wealthy, the meat and drink of everyday life was supplemented with Mediterranean figs and spices from the Far East eaten off fine tableware and washed down with Roman wine in rooms filled with the scent of North African incense. Life at least for the few, was far removed from the image of barbarian savagery that prehistoric Britain still evokes.

Of course, in a world of trade everything has a price, and that price was paid less by the novelty-loving élites as it was by the people they controlled. While the rulers of southern Britain were introducing money in imitation of their sophisticated continental counterparts, the underside of that glittering coin was poverty and worse. For every overlord, there were underdogs who paid for their rulers with more than money. Trade with Europe required exports from Britain to pay for the little luxuries that some were getting rather used to, but what did Britain have to offer in exchange?

In the port of Hengistbury we might have found an unsettling answer. Along the shingle strand, we might have seen rows of Gaulish ships from the coast of Amorica, modern-day Brittany, each with a stall beside it selling its wares. Britons from as far way as Devon and Cornwall might be here bartering metals for vividly coloured lumps of raw glass, while local people offered grain and other foodstuffs. Perhaps there was a fairground atmosphere – a cacophony of Celtic dialects, arguments, songs, drinking, eating and fights. But among all the small-scale trading, a more sinister trade was taking place. High-value wine and spices were offloaded from Armorican ships and handed over to ostentatiously dressed and wealth individuals. In return, their empty holds were filled with a very British cargo: slaves. The Greek geographer Strabo lists slaves as one of Britain's major exports – indeed, many of the 'barbarian' tribes in northern Europe, Gaul and Britain seem to have run a thriving slave trade. Britain had people in abundance and her rulers didn't value them highly. On the continent slaves were the labour-saving device of the ancient world, and the backbone of the Roman Empire. For each slave loaded on to a ship at Hengistbury, a Roman wine jar or similar was given in return, and no one, except the slave, felt they were getting a bad deal.

Where Britain's slaves came from remains uncertain. It may be that in a land still criss-crossed with territorial boundaries they were prisoners-of-war from other tribes, taken during raids; indeed, the numbers of slaves provided by Gaul according to Roman sources (perhaps thirty thousand a year) might suggest that raiding other groups to capture slaves might have been a business in itself. Equally they might have been criminals who were enslaved as a penalty, although this could hardly have provided the numbers needed to keep the ruling élites in wine. It has even been suggested that Strabo made it up to show the world how barbarous the people of Britain were, but the happy acceptance of slavery in the Roman world and the discovery of a pair of iron slave manacles in the lake deposit at Llyn Fawr suggest that the poor of Britain were indeed being used to pay for the rich.

Of course, the fascination of the ruling élites of Britain with the classical world was bound to be reciprocated. Just as Britain began to look beyond her shores, so continental Europe gazed acquisitively at Britain. By the mid-first century BC the people of southern England would have heard of the Roman Empire and probably of the man who was, apparently single-handedly, sweeping before him all of the peoples of Europe: Julius Caesar. Had we returned to Hengistbury in the fifties BC we might have noticed a new type of arrival alongside the Roman wine and Roman pottery: the refugee fleeing from the Roman conquest of Gaul. By the summer of 55 BC that threat was closer to home. On the French coast Julius Caesar was scanning the horizon for the dazzling white cliffs of Dover. The ancient and disparate collection of island peoples across the water were about to step into history and, perhaps for the first time, hear a single name given to their country: 'Britannia'.

When Julius Caesar set sail for Britain in 55 BC he was not intend on invading, although the people of Britain, who waited on the Dover cliffs as the ships with his ten thousand troops approached, could not have known that. The stories of what had happened in Gaul must have spread like wildfire among them and provoked terror. But all was not as it might seem. Among the Romanised élites of the south coast some would have seen they had everything to gain from a more robust Roman influence in their land. They might not only have expected but wanted it, and perhaps even helped to plan it. For the poor the idea of one ruling class replacing another might have seemed irrelevant. Further to the north and west, the concerns of the southern people would have been of little interest. The Romans might have looked on Britain as a single entity, but the people who lived there certainly did not. In years to come each part of Britain would have to look after itself.

This was of little comfort to those who lined the cliffs that summer day and rained stones and spears on the Roman ships as soon as they came in range. They couldn't have known that the expedition to Britain was little more than a publicity stunt, enacted not for the British, the Roman army or the good of the Empire but for the folks back home. In the Roman mind Britain was a uniquely distant and dangerous land, lying, as it did, not in an enclosed sea but in the apparently endless ocean 'at the very edge of the world', as the Romans were fond of putting it. For a Roman army to go there was the first century

BC equivalent of a moonshot – daring, audacious and not without danger. For Julius Caesar, it was almost the definition of fame and, as a man of limitless ambition, fame was his currency.

The expedition of 55 BC resulted in something of a victory for the people of southern England. The Roman army had been in Britain for just under a week when a sudden storm badly damaged its ships and they were forced to retreat to Gaul for the winter. It must have seemed that they had met their match, but any Briton thinking that during the winter of 55 BC was in for a rude awakening the next spring: 54 BC saw Caesar's return with nearly twice the manpower and the intention of making a longer tour. Over eight hundred Roman ships appeared on the horizon, bringing upwards of twenty-five thousand troops. Only two larger forces would ever cross the Channel: one was the Claudian invasion a century later and the other would head in the opposite direction some two thousand years later on D-Day in 1944. Over six months in 54 BC many of the leaders of southern Britain came face to face with the producers of the little luxuries they had been importing for the last half-century or so, and their meetings were by no means always on the best of terms.

By the autumn of that year, however, the Roman legions were gathering again on the south coast ready to cross back to Gaul before the winter storms made the Channel impassable. Caesar would leave behind new friends as well as enemies, but he would not be back to remake their acquaintance, or bring Britain into the Empire, although he would change it in a fundamental way. The written account he left of this land and its people is the first historical snapshot of an island race emerging from over eight thousands years of prehistory. As they walked blinking into the half-light of their first historical era, they can barely have been aware that the countdown to the end of their independence had begun. In just under a century the Romans would be back, this time to stay.

3
Under the Eagle

The island of Britain lies virtually at the end of the World.

Gildas

In the spring of AD 42 Lucius Vitellius Tancinus boarded a heavy wooden barge moored in the French port of Gesoriacum – modern Boulogne. He was an ordinary soldier, setting out on the last leg of an extraordinary adventure that had begun some nine years earlier outside Salamanca in his native Spain.

He had been born into a native Spanish tribe – the Vettone – but his ambitions lay beyond the traditional horizons of his family's land. Spain was part of something much bigger than any tribe or clan: it was part of the Roman Empire, and around AD 34 the young Tancinus had thrown in his lot with his rulers. As a native of Roman Spain he was not automatically a Roman citizen, with all the legal and social benefits that that brought, but there was a way in which he could become one. By joining one of the auxiliary regiments of the Roman army he could look forward to regular pay, good working conditions and, most importantly, after twenty-five years' service, a retirement package that gave him either land, money or both and, most prized of all, Roman citizenship for himself and his heirs.

The allure of the old adage 'Join the army and see the world' was as strong then as it is now. Tancinus had done the first part in Salamanca some eight years previously. He was now about to achieve the second, and the part of the world he was going to see was called Britannia. And he was not going alone.

From his barge he would have seen a port teeming with life: some forty thousand troops from four legions and a host of auxiliary regiments from across the Roman world were embarking. But if the sight of so many troops provided some comfort for Tancinus it could not have left him entirely happy. This was not an army of unbounded confidence – indeed, only days before, the soldiers had been refusing to embark at all. The Emperor had even been forced to send one of his own staff to attempt to persuade them. Nor was this the first time that Roman troops had massed on the French coast only to melt away before setting foot on ship: a rather confused and half-hearted expedition had been planned by the Emperor Caligula just a few years earlier; it ended, so the chroniclers say, in the troops collecting shells on the French beach.

The reason for their concern lay just a few miles away across the English Channel at their destination. In the Roman mind Britain was not simply another country. It lay beyond the comfortable confines of the Mediterranean world, in what the Roman author Avienus called the 'wide ocean's monster-haunted waters'. These images, and the drizzly rain blowing across the decks of the barges, were enough to sow the seeds of doubt in any self-respecting Spaniard, and Tancinus could have been no different from the rest.

Far across the Channel on the south coast of Britain another group of people were gazing nervously at the horizon. Since the Mesolithic period, the Channel had been more of a highway than a barrier and news of the massing Roman forces just across the water must have reached the tribes of southern Britain fairly quickly. The Roman soldiers were concerned about encountering these people, who were perhaps not as alien as Roman authors would have had their public believe.

Just under a hundred years had passed since Julius Caesar

took his two Roman holidays in Britain, and a great deal had changed since then. Far from being a wild tribal society cut off from civilisation, Britain, or southern Britain at least, was heavily engaged in trading with the Roman world, and many aspects of the Roman way of life were familiar, at least to the higher strata of society.

Since as early as the first century BC constant contact with Roman Gaul had had a profound effect on British society. Throughout the Iron Age, status in British society had been demonstrated by displays of overt wealth, from the throwing of huge parties to the carrying of elaborate swords and shields or the wearing of the massive gold neck torques beloved of the East Anglian Iceni tribe. Contact with the classical world had opened up a new way to 'keep up with the Joneses'. For those who could afford it, luxury was the name of the game, and in the south, ruling families vied for status with the help of continental imports. And it was not just the objects that were new: the whole way of doing things in Britain was changing. Had the auxiliary soldiers massing at Boulogne been coming over for dinner rather than to invade they might have found a surprisingly familiar world.

An Anglo-Roman dinner party on the eve of the invasion offered entertainments more novel to the people of Britain than to the Roman invaders. The invitation to dinner was new, and new foods and drink would have been offered. The food might have included imported items, such as dried figs, and be flavoured with exotic spices from the Far East. Instead of beer, Italian and Spanish wine might have been available – which would have made Tancinus feel at home. It would have been served differently too. There was no sharing of meat and drink here. Instead individual portions of food on imported plates – the first tableware in British history – and drink in Italian cups or perhaps Egyptian glasses. The people sitting in the chieftain's house might have sported new jewellery that they could adjust with neatly manicured fingers. Their unwanted facial hair would have been plucked in the Roman manner, ensuring that they were certainly not 'hairy barbarians', and the traditional smell of sweat and livestock would have been replaced with the scent of Persian perfumes. Such was the reception we might have expected in the houses of some of the first-named leaders of pre-conquest Britain such as Cunobelinus – Shakespeare's Cymbeline – and his tumultuous son Caractacus.

A scene like this would have been familiar to Tancinus from his journey across Roman Gaul to Boulogne, but he would hardly have expected to see it in Britain. However, this way of life was probably confined to southern Britain and the lucky few who commanded the resources to pay for such luxury – but it was available, to those who would welcome the Romans with open arms and those who were about to oppose them.

Of course, the forty thousand Romans setting sail from Boulogne were coming for more than dinner and those Britons watching from the white cliffs as the dark stain of four hundred troop barges oozed over the horizon knew it. Their invitation to the classical world was not being brought by sweet-talking diplomats but by the iron fist of such feared institutions as the Second Augustan Legion, under the command of men like Vespasian, a Roman whose ruthless ambition would eventually place him on the imperial throne. We can never know what went through the minds of the ordinary men and women of late Iron Age Britain as the Roman army approached because, in an illiterate society, their thoughts were never written down. Undoubtedly some were expected to fight while others would be required by their pro-Roman leaders to offer assistance to the alien invaders. Either way, it must have seemed that the cosy world of British prehistory was about to change for ever. The question was, would it?

For the short answer we need only look around us today. The huge stumps of Roman town walls still straddle many modern cities, whose museums are filled with Roman mosaics and classical inscriptions. Every schoolchild learns that the Romans brought us central heating, proper plumbing, indoor toilets, baths and even corners for our buildings. Ordnance Survey maps are still filled with 'villa sites', 'Roman roads' and 'Roman forts'. Clearly Tancinus and his friends won, but the plethora of Roman remains we see today hides a more complicated story in which the experience of Roman rule for the ordinary people of Britain is often forgotten.

When the Emperor Claudius rode into Colchester accompanied by fanfares and elephants – brought to impress the locals – he was celebrating not just a series of military victories over those Iron Age leaders foolish enough to oppose him but a more subtle victory over the minds of a few important people. Colchester was to be the capital of his new province of Britannia, a colony of retired Roman soldiers in a 'model city' centred on the great temple to the 'Divine Claudius'. It was a bold and typically Roman statement but it was not the true foundation of the province. That was being laid far to the south on the coast at Fishbourne in Sussex, where gangs of conscript workmen were levelling a sloping field with thousands of buckets of gravel and clay.

At the time of its construction, the Fishbourne villa complex was the largest Roman palace north of the Alps – a ridiculously large Roman statement in a small Iron Age world. There was not a hint of the old Iron Age about it – it was a high-tech super-house, a Roman show-home, advertising the benefits of

Roman rule. But it also held a clue to how the conquest happened and who it happened to.

This was not a palace for Claudius – he certainly didn't intend to stay in Britain: for him the invasion had been the fulfilling of a Roman dream, a great victory that would play well to the audience in Rome and help to secure his rather shaky hold on the imperial throne. He had only recently inherited it from his nephew Gaius (known to his friends, of whom he can have had very few, as Caligula) following his death at the hands of his bodyguard. Nor does the palace appear to have been for the governor Claudius intended to run the new province. While no inscription survives to tell us the name of the owner of Fishbourne, the most likely answer is that he wasn't a Roman but a British tribal leader who had sided with the invading army, a man called Togidubnus.

To say that Togidubnus was a fan of the Roman system would be an understatement. Since long before the invasion he had had close contacts with the Roman world and knew exactly which way to jump when it came to an invasion. This was not, of course, unusual among the leaders of southern Britain in the late Iron Age. Many had dealings with Rome, asked for Roman support in resolving disputes and even sent their sons to Rome to receive a classical education in much the same way that the sons of Indian princes during the Raj were educated at Eton. Togidubnus seems to have been among the forefront of these 'Romanophiles' and might even have been educated in Rome. He changed his name to Tiberius Claudius Togidubnus, which indicates he had been granted Roman citizenship, and took on the grand (and wholly inappropriate) title Great King of Britain. His reward for unswerving support during the invasion might have been the grand palace of Fishbourne. In conquering the mind of one man, the Romans had saved themselves the bother of conquering a whole tribe. Tacitus pithily described the policy:

Certain of the tribes were given to Togidubnus as king. The latter survived, ever most loyal, to within our own memory. This was in accordance with the long-accepted Roman habit of making even kings instruments for the imposition of servitude.

Life for the pro-Roman chieftains in places like Fishbourne underwent a wholesale change from what they had known before and must also have had a profound effect on the people they ruled. No British visitor to Fishbourne would have seen anything like it: the scale of the palace, the size of its rooms, and the vivid, colourful decoration, after the muted colour schemes of the Iron Age, was revolutionary. It was designed to impress, but even for the lucky occupant of this monument to Roman mod cons there was a price to pay, and palace life was not always an improvement on what had gone before. Abandoning the warm roundhouses of the Iron Age for the square stone and plaster rooms of the palace brought its own problems. The colonnaded gardens, built on a Mediterranean model, were of limited use in cooler, wetter Britain. The huge, echoing rooms were difficult to heat even with the new 'hypocaust' technology. To make matters worse, the wonderful mosaics, executed by the finest Roman craftsmen, meant cold feet on winter mornings. So cold, in fact, that braziers were placed on the delicate floors to warm the place, which scorched and warped the mosaics. Despite these drawbacks, though, Togidubnus was now undoubtedly a Roman. But what about his people?

The Roman invasion had had surprisingly little impact on the countryside where most of the people of late Iron Age Britain lived. Britain did not fill with Italians who forced the native population into the sea. There was an army, which included some Italian legionaries among Spaniards, Romanians, North Africans, Belgians and just about every other European people, but it was relatively small. While the official governors were from abroad (not just from Italy – Britain had Spanish, Gaulish and several North African governors in later centuries), the Romans didn't intend to come over in thousands and rule Britain directly. They wanted the old aristocracy – people like Togidubnus – to do it for them. In the century leading up to the invasion the farmers of southern Britain had probably been paying tax to the likes of Togidubnus and his allied leaders; now they would continue to pay, with a little more, to Togidubnus who, in return, would pass on some of this harvest to his Roman masters. While Claudius and the eleven 'kings' who submitted to him at Colchester (according to the monumental arch he built to celebrate the fact in Rome) were drawing up the 'Pax Britannica', for most of the population this amounted to little more than a 'Tax Britannica'.

But the Roman invaders were not welcomed everywhere in Britain. Scotland, despite many attempts, never fell to the Romans, and neither did Ireland, while in the uplands of Wales their hold was never more than tenuous. In the south not every tribal leader was a Togidubnus, and the West Country and even the Isle of Wight were dogged in their resistance to their new overlords. In a land of small-scale tribal groupings, these areas of Britain were conquered one hillfort at a time. At Maiden Castle in Dorset, skeletons bearing the marks of Roman artillery might have belonged to victims of one such battle – although this is still hotly disputed. Not far away at the hillfort of Hod Hill, however, unambiguous evidence remains of the outcome of the war in the west.

Behind the main rampart of the Iron Age defences, a line of small quarry ditches can still be made out which, perhaps early in the spring of AD 44, the area's inhabitants had dug to increase the height of the rampart. Maybe the advance scouting cavalry of the Roman army was already in the vicinity. Certainly, the people here would by now have known that the Romans were in Britain in force and were heading their way.

That they felt they could resist is perhaps not as extraordinary as it sounds. They must have seen Romans and known that, technologically, they were not much superior. Apart from some siege engines and artillery pieces, their equipment was not much different from that available in Iron Age Britain. The main weapons for both sides were swords, spears and arrows and the body armour of the period – a form of chainmail – had been 'borrowed' by the Romans from the northern tribes. What *was* different, which perhaps the leaders at Hod Hill had failed to notice, were the resources and organisation available to the Romans. While an Iron Age chieftain might have had a full set of weapons and armour, his men did not. In the Roman army everyone had the full equipment. The Roman army also had logistical backup: it thought ahead about how to move its troops, how to feed them, how to deal with the sick and injured, how to replace troops and supplies. For the Britons in Hod Hill there was no such backup and bravery alone proved no defence against the Roman army.

On the battle at Hod Hill the archaeology is silent, but the outcome is still writ large over the surface of the hillfort. Shortly after the defences had been improved, a section of the old ramparts was cordoned off with distinctively Roman ditches and banks, which turned a corner of the old Iron Age enclosure into a fort for the newly triumphant Roman army. The hillfort was taken and the inhabitants cleared out: the story of victor and vanquished written in turf.

The native people who fought here and elsewhere were not annihilated. Suitably subdued, the new authorities needed them to provide Rome with money, which she would get by making them pay tax. We can see into the lives of these new, probably reluctant, Roman Britons if we travel west, to where some of the less glamorous buildings of the Roman era survive. Just outside Penzance in Cornwall lies the ancient village of Chysauster, a long-abandoned huddle of stone houses on a gently sloping hillside overlooking Mount's Bay. Around the end of the first century AD, despite our modern obsession with 'what the Romans did for us', this was not a very Roman-looking world. If we could have accompanied a villager up the hill to the settlement we might have recognised a few character-istically Roman elements in their clothing – the typical bronze 'fibula' brooch, for example, like a type of early safety-pin, holding the two ends of their cloak together. We might have seen Roman pottery being washed in the stream – plates, cups and bottles, local wares, imports from other parts of England and perhaps some from overseas. But the houses were not square-cornered Roman villas: they were stone roundhouses, not dissimilar to those of a thousand years earlier. Ducking through the narrow winding passages between them we might have caught snatches of an old Celtic language, and inside we would have found beaten-earth floors instead of delicate mosaics. These people were the farmers of Roman Britain, and their lives had changed little with the invasion; they worked the land, paid taxes to local chieftains, perhaps enjoyed some of the material culture of Rome – brooches, pottery and wine – but did not live what Togidubnus might have considered a Roman life.

However, for those who could look beyond their village there were new possibilities in the Roman world. For the few with ambition, the arrival of the Romans offered the chance of something rare in the Iron Age world: social and financial betterment. From the little we know about class structure in the pre-Roman period it seems that social boundaries were rigid. Those born into one class or social group died in it, as had their ancestors and as would their children. After the invasion, however, something new appeared, which had appealed to Tancinus when he signed up for the Roman army in Spain all those years before. Opportunity.

To meet the new entrepreneurs of Roman Britain we must head for the new types of town springing up in the south of the country. In London large-scale trade was the order of the day in a town buzzing with Gaulish traders, money-lenders, spivs and conmen all eager to make a *denarius* or two out of the Roman military presence. In Colchester there was the *colonia*, the model settlement of retired soldiers from all over the Empire, living a thoroughly Roman retirement on the money with which they had been paid off. But if we followed Watling Street out of London, we would come to a third type of settlement: the native Roman town of Verulamium near modern St Albans in Hertfordshire. The Iron Age people living there, according to Roman sources, were from the tribe of the Cattuvelauni – whom Julius Caesar had fought a hundred years earlier. This time the Cattuvelauni knew which side their bread was buttered. They didn't just watch the Romans build the new town – they *were* the Romans.

The approach to the city shortly after the invasion, past the banks and ditches of the old abandoned Iron Age settlement of Prae Wood, would have marked the epitome of Roman Britain. Neat cemeteries lined the roads outside the city limits where the deceased were cremated in the Roman style. Beyond the gate a wide street lined with impressive private houses, all with square corners, some with under-floor heating, baths, gardens, even classical fountains. Behind the shuttered windows lived the same people who, only decades before, had ruled from Prae Wood, the aristocracy of the late Iron Age. Gone were the days when they impressed each other, and their people, with heavy gold jewellery or shows of communal hospitality in the roundhouse. Instead, neighbour competed with neighbour to acquire the luxuries of the Roman world and take their place in the official hierarchy of town life as prescribed in the Roman model. These leaders now aspired to the 'decurionate', the class of a hundred city fathers who made up the *ordo*, or council, which ran the town, organised its celebrations and festivals, controlled its trade, sat in judgement in its courts and commissioned its splendid classical buildings. To be a decurion was to be Roman and to be Roman was best. Tacitus described cynically how the Romanising process worked under his father-in-law, the Governor Agricola:

In order to encourage rough men who lived in scattered settlements (and were thus only too ready to fall to fighting) to live in a peaceful and inactive manner, Agricola urged them privately and helped them officially to build temples, public squares with public buildings, and private houses. He praised those who responded quickly, and severely criticised the laggards. In this way, competition for public recognition took the place of compulsion. Moreover, he had the children of the leading Britons educated in the civilised arts, and openly placed the natural ability of the Britons above that of the Gauls, however well trained. The result was that those who had once shunned the Latin language now sought fluency and eloquence in it. Roman dress, too, became popular, and the toga was frequently seen. Little by little there was a slide towards the allurements of degeneracy: assembly rooms, bathing establishments, and smart dinner parties.

But Agricola wasn't doing this out of the goodness of his heart:

In their naïvety the Britons called it civilisation, when it was really all part of their servitude.

Yet the Britons of Verulamium seemed to enjoy their new cells, and buying the luxuries they craved in the forum with the newly introduced Roman currency. In the shops you could find high-quality tableware from northern France, oil from Spain, Italian marble (for that inscription to commemorate your good works) and perhaps even Chinese silk. In return these same entrepreneurs exported their own exotic products to other parts of the insatiable Roman 'Euro zone', including a waterproof cloak known as the birrus Britannicus and a woollen rug called the tapete Britannicum – the Barbour jackets and tartan rugs of their day. So popular was British beer that the price-fixing Edict of Diocletian of 301 set its beer at twice that of its Egyptian equivalent.

Where a space had been left for a theatre (when the *ordo* could afford to raise one), a smaller building might have spoken to us more eloquently of how the lives of these people had changed. It was erected (or perhaps rented) by a man who, only a few years before, had probably lived beyond the city limits in a prehistoric community not unlike the one at Chysauster. Now he had a shop. It didn't sell duffel coats, silks or even beer. Instead it sold convenience: it was Britain's first public lavatory, and its owner charged the good citizens of Verulamium to use it. It was a little revolution in thinking.

Only a few years earlier the idea of paying to relieve yourself would have seemed risible anywhere in Britain – as would the idea of any room having a specific function. But a room set aside as a public convenience, which you must pay to use, was the Roman way, and the people of Verulamium clearly wanted to be as Roman as possible. If that meant spending money instead of ducking behind a bush, then so be it.

It also says a great deal about the owner. Here was a man who had quickly got the hang of town life, who understood how people behaved in towns, what made towns 'Roman' and what people were prepared to do to live like that. Gone were the days when he would have farmed for a living. He was now in the service industry, on the way up. If his business worked well he might die a Roman citizen – perhaps a decurion. That could never have happened in Iron Age society, but as a Roman he could become, in theory, anything he wanted to be.

But while some of the old aristocracy thrived in their new show-houses, lapping up the opportunity for outrageous consumption, and while others got a foothold on the ladder of success by servicing their ever-more elaborate needs, not everyone was benefiting. The Roman army had not arrived in Britain on a mission to civilise the barbarians, it had come to make a point and take a profit. If you wanted an easy life you could 'do as the Romans'; if you chose to cross them, you could die. When one tribe faced that choice, they turned their anger first not on the foreign legions, but on their own.

The revolt of Queen Boudicca of the Iceni has often been seen as the impotent but violent reaction of an old power to the arrival of a new one. But its causes and effects ran deeper into the lives of the people of Britain and affected more than just an old aristocracy and a new imperial power. The

Boudiccan revolt showed up the faultlines in British society as it descended into a short but bloody civil war.

The initial causes of the revolt centred on Boudicca herself. Her husband Prasutagus had been one of Rome's 'client kings' in much the same way as Togidubnus. On his death he had left the inheritance of his kingdom split between the Roman Emperor and his daughters – perhaps he hoped to help his people retain a degree of independence. If he did, he was wrong. Soon after, the Roman procurator – the chief financial officer of the province – the rapacious Decianus Catus, made an inventory of Prasutagus' goods, clearly as a precursor to taking full possession of his wealth and kingdom on behalf of Rome. According to Tacitus, who recorded the story some fifty years after it happened, when Boudicca objected she saw a side of Roman rule her husband had been spared: she was whipped. Further insults followed, including the rape of her daughters and the cynical calling-in of huge Roman loans, some lent by the illustrious Roman orator Seneca, which must have threatened the Iceni aristocracy with bankruptcy. But it was a general and deeper feeling of frustration that drove thousands of ordinary Britons to support Boudicca in her attempts to reassert self-determination. The clue to the real reasons behind the revolt lies in the targets of their fury: not the foreign civil servants who had so humiliated the Queen of the Iceni, but the inhabitants of the three towns that represented the three main aspects of Roman rule. First, Camulodunum (Colchester), the garrison town inhabited by retired Roman soldiers and built on the land of the Iceni's allies the Trinovantes, brought wealth into the area but also exploited its resources; its population lorded it over the locals and generally acted in a thoroughly imperialist way. Second, Londinium (London) was a commercial hotspot filled with the winners in Roman society, the foreign merchants feeding the army, the speculators, the officials and their cronies. But Boudicca's army saved their particular hatred for the residents of the third town, Verulamium, inhabited not by foreigners but by native Britons: these were the people who had become as Roman as the Romans and profited by it. In short, they were traitors.

For the inhabitants of Verulamium the arrival of Boudicca's army marked the end of their world. Today when archaeologists dig in the city they still come across a layer of black ash dating to AD 60 or 61 that covers the ground, and all that remains of the beautiful city. We only have Roman accounts of what happened here – they should never be entirely trusted – and they give a terrible flavour of this war between Britons with simply different beliefs. Tacitus said:

The inhabitants of Verulamium, a municipal town, were in like manner put to the sword ... The halter and the gibbet, slaughter and defoliation, fire and sword were the marks of savage valour. Aware that vengeance would overtake them, they were resolved to make sure of their revenge, and glut themselves with the blood of their enemies.

The slightly more excitable Dio, playing perhaps to a more tabloid audience, added:

The worst and most bestial atrocity committed by their captors was the following. They hung up naked the noblest and most distinguished women and then cut off their breasts and sewed them to their mouths, in order to make the victims appear to be eating them; afterwards they impaled the women on sharp skewers run lengthwise through the entire body.

It was probably more the destruction of the city than the murder of its inhabitants that marked out the revolt. The

Roman authorities had reasonable warning of Boudicca's approaching army and the city might have been evacuated long before it arrived. As such, save for any unfortunate stragglers her army met on the road, the death toll was probably lighter than lurid Roman accounts might suggest. There can be little doubt, however, that those Roman Britons who fell into Boudicca's hands received as little mercy as she and her family had, and when those evacuees who had escaped her wrath returned to their city they found she had left an unforgettable calling card: the total destruction of their Roman aspirations.

Boudicca's revolt did not succeed. The Roman bargain had always been backed up by force, and the survivors and the fallen of Verulamium were avenged by the legions. On Watling Street, at a still unidentified location, probably in Warwickshire, the Roman forces brought the Queen to battle. Tacitus, always prone to exaggeration, stated that eighty thousand of her followers died, compared to only four hundred Romans. But the numbers are really irrelevant, and however many died the result was clear: annihilation of Iceni resistance to Roman rule. The Roman experiment had been shaken but had not fallen. Londonium, Camulodunum and Verulamium would all be rebuilt. The people of Britain could adapt to it (or, perhaps among the poor, largely ignore it) but they could not oppose it.

Nor did the revolt delay town building elsewhere. At key sites all over the province towns were springing up, often at sites originally chosen for garrison forts but now no longer on the front lines. Some were full *coloniae*, others little more than small tribal centres, but with them came all the advantages, and many of the disadvantages, of modern urban life. One of the strangest of these sites is Silchester in Hampshire. While most Roman towns in Britain went on to become centres in medieval and later times, Silchester failed. On approaching it today you walk past a huge, empty amphitheatre before the great stone walls of the city rear up in front of you. Walk through one of the gateways and you find yourself in an empty field.

The towns of Roman Britain undoubtedly had their allure just as their modern counterparts do today. A family walking through the gates at that time was perhaps hoping to escape the strict social order of the countryside, or perhaps had a skill to sell. The town offered freedom for a select few (perhaps 1 per cent of the population) from the strain of agriculture and providing directly for their family. It also offered entertainment. No doubt newcomers looked excitedly at the amphitheatre as they passed, reminded of the free entertainments that the town's ruling élite would put on there on public holidays. Indeed, holidays themselves might have been a novelty for those used to the relentless daily rounds of the agricultural year. Perhaps the daughter of the family clutched an amulet like that found in Leicester which reads, 'Verecunda the actress loves Lucius the gladiator'. Gladiators were the superstars of their day, heroic, dashing, often tragic characters, the pin-up idols of every town girl. Then there were the baths, a cornerstone of Roman propaganda for the good life, where cleanliness, luxury and gossip came together and where every aspiring decurion took his first faltering steps up the slippery slope to political power. And education was on offer too, anything from basic literacy for children to the more ethereal delights of Greek philosophy or perhaps a more practical knowledge of such novel concepts as contraception, which might help the erstwhile country-dwellers to take more control of their future. Or perhaps they were simply looking forward to modern housing, with mains sewers and plumbing.

But there was another side to urban life. The bustling town of Silchester was a long way from an Iron Age village. Thousands of people lived there, but an incoming family knew so few, compared with the close-knit social group they had left behind in their village. Making friends is surprisingly difficult when you're surrounded by hordes of people. Then there was crime. Who was going to pay to remove the graffiti that had appeared on the outside of their house? It was a problem recorded in an inscription found in Bath. In a place where it was easy to be anonymous, it was an easy crime to commit. It was also noisy and tiring. For all the benefits of the public baths that Romans so frequently extolled, you wouldn't have wanted to live too close to them. If you had found lodgings, as the orator Seneca did, above a bath-house you might have complained as he did:

I live above a public bath. I can hear all sorts of irritating noises. There are groans when the muscle-men are exercising with their weights. Some unfit men just have a massage and I hear the slap of hands beating their bodies. Ball-players come along and shout out the score in their match. Drunks have arguments, thieves shout when they are caught, some men sing in the baths. People dive into the pool with a great splash. There are shouts from those selling drinks and snacks.

Nor, despite the mains sewerage, was Silchester a healthy place either. So many people living so close together encouraged disease, and life expectancy was lower in the Roman towns than it would be in the middle of the Dark Ages. It was not urban by the standards of a visitor from Rome – indeed, they might have viewed it as more of a 'garden city' – but it was a long way from the Iron Age village. Health problems were made worse by stress. A tile from Londinium bears the scratched inscription 'Austalis has been going off on his own now for 13 days'. Was the writer worried about him or checking up on why he was not pulling his weight in the tile factory?

But what of the small villages beyond the walls of the town? Undoubtedly for those living near Silchester there were benefits to be had. It would have attracted long-distance trade and the opportunity to buy the little luxuries that everyone was so fond of. The Roman roads marching across the landscape to the town gates were perhaps a visible sign of this connection with the wider Roman world. But it is doubtful how useful widely heralded innovations such as straight roads were to the people of the countryside. Contrary to popular myth, roads were not a Roman introduction: Iron Age Britain was covered with a network of roads and tracks, not perhaps as well built as the Roman ones but they had served a different purpose. The fine filigree structure of the Iron Age transport system was about encouraging local contact. The Romans had built trunk roads, long-distance highways connecting nodal towns. Their purpose was more to do with keeping those who lived in the 'Roman way' in touch with each other and the authorities than about encouraging the local economy. It is doubtful whether these were even great trading routes, the majority of long-distance trade probably being carried out using faster, more efficient waterborne transport. What the roads did bring to every country district were the two most visible signs of British subjugation: the army and the tax collector. So, a villager might have been less than impressed by the arrow-straight road passing over his farmland to the gates of the city, particularly as he might have been forced to help build it.

Nor perhaps was he much taken with the other great innovation that supposedly arrived with Roman rule: the monetary system. The single Roman currency – the euro of its day – was undoubtedly a powerful weapon in the spread of Roman culture and influence, but the idea that it changed British life can be overstated. The Roman introduction of coinage to Britain was not the setpiece of classical organisation the Romans would have had us believe, as we would have found out if we had tried to buy anything with it in the countryside around Silchester. The problem was that the system had only been half thought-out. When coinage was introduced, the only denominations available were huge – the equivalent of a day's wages or above. Now, if your coins were all worth what amounts to perhaps hundreds of pounds you had to be careful what you bought. Remember, no change could be given. It was fine if you wanted to buy a house or a couple of cows, but not so good if you were after a spot of lunch. The bemused Britons tried to alleviate the problem in some areas by introducing their own small change – a rather shoddy group of locally produced coins called 'barbarous radiates' that archaeologists believed for a long time were fakes. In fact, they were a desperate attempt by the people of Britain to make this new-fangled monetary system work, something they must have assumed the Roman authorities wanted them to do.

The reason behind the shambolic introduction of coinage to Britain might have had less to do with poor organisation than Roman motives. The coinage was not introduced by a benevolent empire to kick-start the British economy. It was essential that coinage reached all parts of British society because tax was paid in it. It was a simple three-part system. First, the state paid its soldiers and administrators in coin; second, they spent those coins in the local community, buying the goods and services they needed to survive; third, the coins that had been handed over to the locals in return for those goods and services were collected up again by the tax officials – and so the whole system went round. As the purpose of coinage was tax, the Romans had seen little need to introduce small change so they hadn't bothered. Outside that economic loop, the monetary economy, in the early days of the province, didn't exist.

So, if the Roman way of life couldn't be found in the coins in the pockets of local villagers, had it reached into their lives in any other way? To answer this, we might travel to Somerset, to a site that had been sacred to the people of that part of Britain since long before the Romans arrived. From deep pre-history this had been a magical place, a boggy, sulphurous landscape wreathed in clouds of steam that hung over the only natural hot spring in the country. By AD 200, however, while it retained its importance, the oozing bog had been replaced with a smart Roman settlement called Aquae Sulis: modern Bath. The hot spring had been contained in a Roman bath where wealthy locals could take the waters, just as the great and good of the city continued to do for the next eighteen hundred years. But this was not simply a health spa: it was a religious centre and a window on to the mysterious ritual life of Roman Britain.

In this elaborate complex we might have found lounging decurions enjoying the waters, fitness fanatics exercising with weights, friends sharing lunch and a game of dice, and orators writing speeches – all keeping at least one eye on the slaves guarding their clothes from the ubiquitous bath-house thieves. Relatives might drop in to pay their respects to ancestors com-memorated there – indeed, it housed the tomb of the auxiliary soldier Tancinus. But there was another side to the social life of this place – and a rather antisocial one at that. Among the stalls set up in the complex there was a particularly popular one where everyone, from wealthy city gents decked out in full

Roman garb to shabby villagers, might queue, not for food or drink but for something more intangible – justice – in the form of small sheets of beaten lead. Having purchased a lead sheet its new owner would scurry off to a darker corner where he or she began scratching on it with a bronze stylus, then folded it and threw it into the seething waters of the pool. The ordinary people of Roman Britain were doing what comes naturally: cursing each other. In the 1980s many of those lead packets were recovered by archaeologists, opened and read. For the first time in nearly two millennia, the people of Roman Britain spoke out:

May he who has stolen Vilbia from me become as liquid as water . . .

Docilianus . . . to the most holy Goddess Sulis. I curse him who has stolen my hooded cloak, whether man or woman, whether slave or free, that . . . the goddess Sulis inflict death upon [him] . . . and not allow him to sleep or [have] children now and in the future, until he has brought my hooded cloak to the temple of her divinity.

The Bath curses, and those from the Gloucestershire temple of Mercury at Uley, offer a unique insight into a world heavily Romanised in some respects but still deeply 'British' in others. The concerns of those who issued the curses are familiar – the day-to-day problems of life with awkward neighbours, adulterous spouses and petty thieves, no doubt exacerbated by the anonymity of town life and the absence of a police force. Each hoped that the god of the bath-house would intervene and either restore their loss, punish the transgressor or preferably both. But it is the people who wrote these curses who tell us most about this time. The fact that each appears in a different handwriting suggests that one aspect of Roman life, literacy, had penetrated deep into society. Even people with only one name – a sign of lower-class origins – had written their own curses in Latin. But Roman authority hadn't completely won them over: one woman referred to herself in her curse as the 'head of the household', which was possible in the Iron Age world but theoretically illegal in Roman society where women were considered minors all their lives. Clearly, however, she wasn't in fear of the magistrates and didn't believe that the god to whom she was appealing would mind much either. In fact, she seemed to have a distinctly Iron Age attitude. And there perhaps lies the key. The god to whom these people appealed was the god who gave the place its name, 'Sul'. But Sul was not a Roman deity: it was a more ancient Iron Age god who had probably been haunting this place for centuries, if not millennia, before the Roman invasion.

Of course, taking on local gods was not unusual for the Romans. One of the great strengths of the Roman system was its ability to accept foreign religions. Some foreign cults became fashionable with Roman citizens, such as the Indo-Iranian cult of Mithras, always popular among the professional soldiery, who approved of its all-male adherents, strict moral codes and seven degrees of tortuous initiation. Interestingly, it was particularly disapproved of by the growing band of Christians who considered its central ritual of a shared meal and Mithras' birthdate, 25 December, a devilish mockery of their own religion. For those with an even stronger stomach there was the eye-watering eastern cult of Cybele, which required its priests to castrate themselves with iron tongs, a pair of which have been found in London.

Even where local gods were not taken on wholesale, attempts were made to ally them with similar Roman gods. Thus the

Celtic god Taranis was equated with Jupiter as both had power over thunder and lightning – indeed, *taran* in modern Welsh still means 'a thunder clap'. Equally, when Roman influence arrived in Bath the authorities didn't inflame the locals by casting aside their gods: instead, they pointed out that Sul was similar to their goddess Minerva and combined the two as 'Sulis Minerva'. Provided the locals accepted the divinity of the Emperor – more a test of loyalty than of faith – they were free to worship whomever they wished. The dominance of the Iron Age Sul even received tacit recognition in the Roman name for the town. It was not Aquae Minervae or even Aquae Sulis Minervae, but Aquae Sulis. The Romans might have chosen the names, but it was clear who was still in charge.

Neither had the requirements of these old religions gone away. Roman authors claimed that one of the Emperor's main aims in 'civilising' the barbarian world was to ban human sacrifice. This injunction, instigated by the Emperor Augustus was often used as a reason for subjugating peoples and was a common criticism of British druids. But while the practice might have been outlawed in Roman Britannia, the fourteen baby skeletons discovered under the Roman temple at Springhead, Kent, and foundation human sacrifices (perhaps not unlike the girl buried under the Bronze Age house at Cladh Hallan) from Verulamium, Wroxeter in Shropshire and London suggest that old rites might have been tolerated, if not encouraged. More sinister still, the body recovered from Grewelthorpe Moor in North Yorkshire in 1850, described as wearing 'a green toga, dress of scarlet, stockings of yellow cloth and a nailed shoe' (now dated to the third century AD) hints at the survival well into the Roman period of the type of sacrifice that befell Lindow Man.

If in the south and west of Britain Roman ways remained

only a thin veneer on a more ancient culture, in the north it was more variable still. The great paradox of northern Britain in the Roman period is that while it remained to a large extent a militarised zone where the army 'enforced' a Roman way of life, it was here that some of the most Roman Britons in the country lived. And to meet them, we have to join the army.

The Roman army has gone down in history as a war machine, a fearsome, disciplined and highly organised professional body in which the needs of the individual were subordinated to the greater good of the Empire. But the real Roman army is far more interesting, and human, than that, and when we look into the soldiers' lives we get a glimpse into the world of some people for whom the Romans really did change everything. The army in Roman Britain consisted of two elements: the legions, made up of professional citizen soldiers, and the auxiliaries, soldiers from around the provinces of the Empire but not yet its citizens. While the legions were the storm troops of the day, it was the auxiliaries who provided the peacekeeping forces along much of the edge of the Empire, usually serving in a country other than the one where the regiment was raised (for obvious safety reasons). If the legions were the household cavalry of the day, the auxiliaries were perhaps the Gurkhas.

If we take the old military road from Carlisle east along Hadrian's Wall, that most famous of Roman frontiers, we reach the fort at Birdoswald, once the home of the 'I Cohors Aelia Dacorum Millaria', the first cohort of Dacians, Hadrian's Own. These were a detachment of Romanians, far from home on one of the bleakest frontiers of the Roman world. In the forts along the wall there were others like them – Spaniards, Belgians and North Africans. They were not Roman citizens and they were certainly not British; rather, they were a wildly cosmopolitan cross-section of the peoples of the ancient world, but they were unique in that they wanted to be Roman and they would in time become British. They were perhaps the real Roman Britons.

The forces that had drawn our Romanian cohort to the edge of the world were ambition and the hope of self-improvement. For the Dacians, a conquered people themselves, joining the auxiliaries offered some small compensation for their defeat at the hands of the Emperor Trajan. The army asked for twenty-five years of your life at locations it chose, but in return it offered education, training in a number of crafts, a pension, medical care in the only professional hospitals in the ancient world, and not too much danger of real fighting. At the end of service, you received some money or land and, most valuable of all, Roman citizenship for yourself and your descendants, with all the privileges and tax breaks that that brought with it. As a people the Dacians had failed to *beat* the Romans, so the Dacians of the 'I Cohors Aelia Dacorum Millaria' had *joined* them.

If army life would make these people Roman, their location would make them British. By the time the Emperor Hadrian visited Britain in AD 122 his predecessor Augustus's dream of an infinitely expanding empire had collapsed and Hadrian was happy to mark out the limit of the Roman world with the construction of the wall that still bears his name. This was to be a permanently manned frontier, and a posting here was more than just a short tour of duty – despite the obvious homesickness of men such as Caius Cornelius Peregrinus, who dedicated an altar to 'Fortune the Homebringer' at his posting at Maryport in Cumbria, far from his native Saldae (Bejaia) in Algeria. Of course, there were compensations for this lifestyle, and despite the army prohibition on marriage during active service, civil settlements quickly grew up around such static units as the Dacians' on Hadrian's Wall and many unofficial marriages must have taken place. The children who resulted were not only half British, but when their fathers retired they might inherit his Roman citizenship. As the generations passed and as, in the later Empire, soldiers' positions in the army became hereditary, these enclaves were not just more Roman but more British. For a sixth-generation Dacian with a whole line of British ancestors and perhaps only one Romanian, home was Cumbria. The idea of returning to Dacia after his army service would have seemed ludicrous. He and the descendants of his Spanish, Dutch, German and Belgian counterparts were the real Roman Britons. And with more troops stationed in Britain than in any other province of the Empire they were a growing band.

So, if we could walk along the precipitous cliff at Birdoswald towards the fort, some time in the third century AD what would we find? Following the road from the west, which runs in line with the wall, we come first to a civil settlement or *vicus*. This bustling village has grown up outside the gates to the fort and exists to serve the needs of the soldiers and in return to relieve them of their pay. It's a chaotic mass of shops, brothels and bars, a noisy world of locals selling what they have and soldiers buying whatever they can get. Here the monetary economy is in full swing. The pay chest arrived in the fort only days before and the men have silver to spend in the same ways that soldiers have for generations both before and since. But it is not simply a red-light district. Passing through the unplanned cacophony of the *vicus* we come to the west gate. Ahead lies the perfect 'playing-card'-shaped fort, a model of Roman military precision. Compared to the filth and din of the *vicus*, this is the epitome of Roman organisation. Everything is carefully laid out, just like it says in the Roman military manuals. This is the home of the famous 'Roman war machine'. All will be order. Or will it?

Our first surprise is that the gate is open, not locked to keep out the barbarous locals. As we push our way through the crowd, we come upon a surprising sight and an explosion of sound. Certainly, the interior of the fort is laid out just as the regulations suggest, with neat lines of barrack blocks, a perfect grid of roads, rows of granaries (holding the statutory one year's supply of grain that all forts were required to carry), and the commander's house, all in their correct places. But this is not the quiet well-ordered world we might have expected. There are people everywhere – men, women and children, soldiers and civilians, traders, prostitutes, beer-sellers, military contractors and beggars. Animals are wandering the streets, horses, poultry, pigs, sheep and dogs, creating a ripe smell that is not improved by the work of the nearby tannery. The military manual says that each barrack room is the home of four soldiers but inside it is actually the cramped quarters of four families. Wives are preparing food on the little hearth at the back of the room while their children play in the street outside, dashing from barrack to barrack. Traders and hawkers wander the streets, avoiding the careering children and looking in doorways for likely customers among the recently paid soldiers. Accents stranger than the Roman dialects of the locals can also be heard: people not just from the south but from the north of the wall are here, and they're not Scottish warriors infiltrating the enemy camp. These men and women are more interested in trading than raiding and stand arguing with the guard over the customs duty he is trying to levy on their goods.

As we approach the commander's house we might bump into another, more exotic trader. He is Barates – today we know about him from the information on two tombstones, his own and his wife's (if the Barates mentioned on each is the same man). Should we be able to stop him for a moment and ask him about his life, we'd be talking to one of the most cosmopolitan, yet not untypical characters of the wall. A Palmyran from Syria by birth, he came to Britain as flag-seller to the army. Since then he'd bought a slave girl, perhaps directly from her impoverished family, freed and married her. She was a young Englishwoman, a member of the Cattuvelauni tribe who had once fought Julius Caesar, and a startling cross between old and new worlds: a toga-wearing Roman wife who sported the thick gold neck torques worn by her warlike ancestors. But when we meet Barates, she has died, aged only thirty, although she might have been married to him from the age of fourteen or fifteen. All he has left to remind him of her is the memorial he commissioned at South Shields in County Durham. Beneath the traditional Latin text on the stone he has had a more heartfelt line inscribed in his native language, Aramaic. It reads simply: 'Regina, freedwoman of Barates. Alas!'

Leaving the flag-seller, we can look through a window of the headquarters building to see the commanding officer at his desk. He's due to take his prize dogs hunting – a favourite hobby among officers stationed on the wall – but new orders have changed his plans. Instead of hunting he's writing a persuasive (he hopes) speech to read later to the men. He must take a force north of the wall and he knows that orders are not enough to get his men to obey: he'll have to persuade them, just as the troops in France in AD 43 had to be persuaded to invade Britain in the first place. The men of the Roman army whom he knows are not selfless, obedient automata about whom Roman writers eulogise: they're a volatile, suspicious band of men interested primarily in what Rome can do for them, not what they can do for Rome.

Next to where the commander sits writing, and beside a package of dainty leather shoes he has recently imported for his wife, we might also see a pile of thin birch and alder sheets. These are the everyday correspondence of the fort, written in soot-black ink on wooden sheets with thick iron-nibbed pens. Normally such things were so fragile they would never survive the centuries – indeed, they were not designed to – but remarkably we can even read some of these notes, thanks to a discovery further east on the wall at the fort of Vindolanda. After use, the notes were thrown away just as we might bin an old Post-it. But at Vindolanda many were thrown into a boggy pit where they survived until modern excavators recovered them:

Claudia Severe to her Lepidina, greetings.
I send you a warm invitation to come to us on 11 September for my birthday celebrations, to make the day more enjoyable by your presence. Give my greetings to your Cerialis. My Aelius greets you and your sons. I will expect you, sister. Farewell, sister, my dearest soul, as I hope to prosper, and greetings.

Those are the authentic words of a woman of Roman Britain, showing the pleasures and concerns of everyday life 1900 years ago. The above letter would be valuable as Britain's first party invitation but it is doubly unique: while most of it was written by a scribe the final farewell is in Claudia Severa's own wobbly script. Dating from AD 100 it is the earliest known handwriting in Latin by a woman.

Another letter, this time an intelligence report from the first century AD offers further insights:

The Britons are unprotected by armour. There are very many cavalry. The cavalry do not use swords nor do the wretched Britons take up fixed positions in order to throw javelins.

Whether this refers to Britons outside the fort or perhaps even new recruits to the army we don't know but it tells us one thing – the nickname the Roman soldiers had for the British people: *Brittunculi*, 'wretched' or 'little' Britons.

Inside the fort the son of an officer is copying out a piece from Virgil's *Aeneid*, which has also survived, although the writer might have wished it hadn't. Like schoolchildren across the ages his mind had wandered from the painfully formed capital letters of his text and he'd left off the ending of the passage. In another hand someone – probably his teacher – has written '*seg*', short for *segnis* – sloppy!

Back at Birdoswald, the commandant is still writing his speech, hopefully to better effect. An expedition north of the wall was not unheard-of – indeed, the Roman frontier was at times further north along the line of the turf-built Antonine Wall, while before that Governor Agricola had taken the legions into Scotland. The line had settled now, however, on Hadrian's Wall, and beyond that, at least in the Roman mind, lay the barbarian world.

Of course, as we've seen in the fort, the wall is not an impenetrable barrier, and the people who lived north of it were not slavering barbarians clawing at its gates. While it might have suited some wealthy writers in Rome to characterise the boundaries of the Empire as barbaric and dangerous, stepping north across Hadrian's Wall did not mean falling off the edge of the civilised world, as the commander at Birdoswald would have known. Indeed, for many years Roman policy in the north seems to have been conducted as dialogue – an attempt to 'butter up' the inhabitants and seduce them into accepting Roman rule in return for the comforts of Roman life. At the Scottish hill site of Traprain Law near Edinburgh, well outside the Roman province, huge amounts of Roman pottery, wine jars and even a hoard of Roman silver suggest that not all Scottish chieftains turned away Roman overtures. Indeed, had we been able to interview the ruler of this ancient site we might have found that he considered himself a client king of the Roman Empire, much as Togidubnus had been in the south. But there remained a crucial difference in Scotland: although some rulers might have taken on the Roman mantle, ruled in the Emperor's name and perhaps even collected his taxes, most did not and, despite numerous costly campaigns, Scotland never fell into Roman hands. In fact, the campaigns had perhaps the opposite effect: the prehistoric peoples of Scotland remained even more elusive than their English counterparts, a disparate group of regional clans, but in fighting Rome they might have found a common cause. To the Romans these were the 'Picts', a people defined more by being 'not Roman' than being anything else. Their emergence as such in the face of the Roman menace might mark Scotland's first step on the road to nationhood.

However, if we leave the thriving cosmopolitan forts of Hadrian's Wall and head south again in the third century, we might find that the Roman way of life there was not perhaps as healthy as it was in the supposedly barbarian north. As we saw at Verulamium, town life was quickly adopted by some of those Britons with most to gain from the change. An old aristocracy had learned a new way of exerting their influence, and a new class of entrepreneur had emerged to service this new mode of urban life. But the great town experiment was not proving the unmitigated success that we modern city dwellers like to think it must have been. In the streets of Silchester by around 270 the changes would have been clear for all to see. Perhaps with the inducement of citizenship gone (the Edit of Caracalla in 212 had made all freeborn inhabitants citizens of the Empire) people no longer aspired to the decurionate; certainly there was little sign of any decurions left in residence. The impressive magisterial residences lining the roads would have been partly abandoned. Had we looked into their crumbling courtyards we might still have found people there, but not the old aristocracy.

It seems that the burdens of urban life for the rich had proved too onerous. It cost money to be a decurion and while the fame it brought was all well and good, money was more important. The people who would have stared back at us now from the old townhouses were from a different class of society: squatters and beggars from the margins, drifting through the long-abandoned halls of the nobility. At the centre of town the official buildings were still running but their function had changed. In the place of shops and courts, many units appear to have been given over to metalwork in what might have represented a state-controlled arms industry. They churned out weaponry for a nervous central government that had little time left for theatre, processions and the other traditional roles of their once grand civic centre. Above the sound of hammer on iron there was little of the hubbub of normal city life. It was a grey, lifeless place, an administrative centre but hardly a living city. It was not yet empty so it could hardly be called abandoned, but it was already a city of ghosts.

The rich and the rulers of late Roman Britain had not gone away altogether. No revolution had swept through the boulevards of southern towns while we were on Hadrian's Wall. We could still find these people, but we would need to look for them in the countryside from where they had come. They were the inhabitants of that most famous class of Roman building: the villa.

Our image of the villa is still one of classical sophistication. From the time when Togidubnus first looked proudly at his mosaics in Fishbourne in the first century to when the owners of the villa at Hinton St Mary in Dorset had the newly fashionable Christian monogram of the Greek letters 'chi' and 'rho' – the first two letters of the word Christ – set into their floor three hundred years later, villas seem perhaps the most Roman part of Britain. For some villa owners in late Roman Britain, this was an age of success unparalleled in the rest of the Empire and life was still sweet. The villa complex at Woodchester in Gloucestershire had sixty-five rooms, while it has been estimated that at Bignor in Sussex, the villa's eight-hundred-acre estate sustained two hundred sheep, twelve teams of ploughing oxen, fifty other cattle for meat and milk, and a staff of over fifty who brought in some ten thousand bushels of grain a year – a handsome profit for any farmer. The owner of Lullingstone in Kent, meanwhile, judging from the relatively small heating system there, probably only used this vast and beautifully decorated villa for the summer, retiring perhaps to the warmth of his London home in the autumn. The owners of these places were perhaps like eighteenth-century aristocrats: people who had made a fortune in the towns and retired to country life to avoid the inconveniences and costs of city dwelling. Exactly who they were, however, we will never know as, just at the time they began this renewed burst of building, the Roman habit of recording good works in inscriptions fell out of fashion. Perhaps as these were private rather than public monuments, their owners didn't feel the need to put their names to them.

But the luxurious complexes at Lullingstone and Hinton St Mary were not the average experience of life in the countryside any more than Chatsworth House or Windsor Castle are average country cottages. While some of the élite had built what were perhaps Britain's first 'stately homes', Roman life for most, even those rich enough to own their own land, was more prosaic. The sad truth is that while Roman rule might have opened up new markets, introduced new crops and possibly increased management efficiency, in four hundred years there had been virtually no technological innovations in Roman farming, which still relied on hand- (or slave-) operated Iron Age equipment.

For those who could not exploit the sorts of economies of scale present at Bignor, life was a little more rudimentary, even if their aspirations were just as high. At Rudstone in Yorkshire we might have found the type of Roman farmer who lived in this more realistic world. His villa was not of the highest quality, and was decorated in a style somewhere between slapdash and shoddy, which speaks volumes about its proud owner. The Roman Empire in the third and fourth centuries was a place of increasing tension. At times the imperial succession hung precariously in the balance: generals vied for the throne, using their own legions to press their case, and all the time pressure increased from the 'barbarian' peoples beyond the Empire's rim. This world was a long way from the high days of early Empire when Augustus rebuilt Rome in marble, and the central structure of Roman administration often faltered.

Yet here in the wilds of Yorkshire the owners of Rudstone were still impressing their friends and family with a pale, slightly confused native interpretation of the classical world. The Venus mosaic has, rather politely, been called 'rustic' where perhaps Togidubnus would have labelled it 'rubbish'. It is not so much an approximation of classical art as an aping of it – a mass-market DIY interpretation of a bespoke classical ideal that was already just a faint memory. The workmen who made it were certainly not the finest craftsmen imported from Italy – indeed, the style is 'naïve', but it is clear that the owner of Rudstone was just as keen as his wealthier counterpart at Bignor and Lullingstone to associate himself with the illustrious Roman past. While the great villa owners might have sneered at such pretension, it should also be remembered that the owner of Rudstone was still a step or two above the inhabitants of the small Iron Age-style farms that even now made up 90 per cent of rural settlements. On the continent, the really wealthy late Roman Empire villa owners were probably sneering at the classical pretensions of the owners of Lullingstone.

By the early fifth century both the social wannabes at Rudstone and their grander cousins in the major villas were in further trouble. Britain was now divided into five provinces with little overall cohesion. The vast panoply of Roman and Celtic gods had in theory been replaced with the official state religion of Christianity, although the 'pagan' treasure from Thetford in Norfolk, with its reliefs of the god Faunus, suggest that not everyone was toeing the party line. Recently it has even been suggested that the famous mosaic of a figure standing before the chi–rho monogram at the Hinton St Mary villa is more likely to be an image of the villa owner associating himself with a fashionable Christian logo rather than the earliest depiction in existence of Christ as was previously thought. Certainly the only way to get on in late Roman society was to be at least nominally Christian: it was as important for your career then as it was to hold a Communist Party card in 1930s Russia. However, a state religion had failed to bring about much sense of unity in the Empire. In fact, Christianity itself was riven with factions and heresies, one of which had originated in Britain in the beliefs of a man called Pelagius.

The Emperor Constantine might have believed that Christianity would hold together a fragmenting empire but by the fifty century that looked a vain hope. In the west it was on the point of collapse when, an early source says, the British wrote to the Emperor Honorius asking for protection from the barbarians. Honorius, too busy to worry about this distant province, is reported to have told the Britons to look to their own defences. But there was little with which to defend Britain, and perhaps little left to defend. The legions were long gone, to fight in other provinces and support other claimants to the imperial throne. The money supply had failed, and the stream of silver that kept the heart of Roman Britain pulsing had gone. The soldiers at Birdoswald might have waited a few months for the pay chest to arrive, but in the end they were forced to look to their own livelihoods. The idea of returning to Dacia can have meant nothing to those whose families had lived and died on the wall for centuries. Instead they melted into the countryside around them, where their descendants probably still live today. Despite their Romanian, French, Belgian or German ancestry, this was home. The gates of the fort fell down and the impressive granary was built over, but Rome's greatest legacy, her people, remained.

With the money gone, the administrations in towns began to fail too. The squatters and looters who had wandered the old mansions for over a century now took control of the basilicas and courtrooms. In the grand villas simple hearths were cut through once-beautiful mosaic floors, while in Aquae Sulis the steaming spring waters bubbled away through the cracked bath walls.

Yet if a sense of being Roman had left these shores, a sense of being British had not. Within little more than a generation Britain had returned to a pagan, rural society that was little different from the one that Tancinus had witnessed when he had disembarked with Claudius's legions nearly four hundred years before. Old hillforts, such as Cadbury Hill in Somerset, were again occupied – that one supposedly by the legendary King Arthur – and the old religion, only ever lightly covered by a veneer of Roman and then Christian ritual, re-emerged. In the gloom of sub-Roman Britain new battlelines were assembling and a new breed of hero was preparing to fend off another enemy. The Britons had returned to their old haunts to defend themselves against a new kind of barbarian.

It was almost as though the Roman invasion had never happened, except for the monumental ruins that littered the landscape. For a few hundred years Britain had bought into a European trading empire (albeit without having had much choice in it) and in that time had briefly become a single entity called Britannia. But the cost had been high in the perhaps irrecoverable loss of some of its prehistoric customs and sensibilities. Now the onerous requirement of the Roman world had gone and a new age was approaching. Free from the huge costs of Roman control, many must have hoped it would be a golden one.

4
Land of the Wolf

The Britons consulted how they might obtain help to repel
the frequent fierce attacks of their northern neighbours, and
all agreed with the advice of their king, Vortigern, to call on
the assistance of the Saxon peoples across the sea. This
decision, as its results were to show, seems to have been
ordained by God as a punishment for their wickedness.

Bede

Some time in the eighth century an Anglo-Saxon poet stumbled
into the decaying remains of an ancient city and began to record
the sad sights around him:

Wondrous is this stone-wall, wrecked by fate,
the city-buildings crumble, the work of the giants decay.
roofs have caved in, towers collapsed,
barred gates are broken, hoar frost clings to mortar,
houses are gaping, tottering and fallen,
undermined by age. The earth's embrace,
its fierce grip, holds the mighty craftsmen;
they are perished and gone. A hundred generations have
    passed away since then . . .

He came from a world where building in stone was unknown
and could only imagine that a race of giants had heaped up
the crumbling stone monuments all around him. It must have
happened centuries before, he thought, in a land of legend. In
fact, it had been only a few hundred years since the lost world
he was walking through had been the thriving Roman city of

Bath, so completely had the memory of that time been erased. But this was a story more connected with him than he might have believed. There is a good chance that his ancestors had once walked in these streets. There is also a chance that it was his ancestors who had brought them to ruin some time during one of the most obscure periods in British history: the fifth century.

The term 'Dark Ages', so often used about this period, has more to do with how brightly the Victorians imagined the classical world (and subsequently their own) shone, rather than how dimly remembered this time was or how ignorant its people were. No doubt the world of sub-Roman Britain, as this time ,is now generally known, was a far cry from the early days of the Roman province, but Rome had not suddenly abandoned Britain: it had rather mutated and faded away over a time frame measured in centuries, not weeks. For the large-scale villa owners, the good times might have been drawing to a close, but for the small farmer, for whom Rome might never have meant more than another tax burden, life was little different.

What has undoubtedly changed is our view of these people. In drifting back into many of their pre-Roman ways, the people of Britain largely slipped from written history and the brief glimpse of names and faces we gained during the Roman occupation is again clouded. Britain had re-entered an era of myth and legend, whose people can speak to us only through archaeology. Their voices are silent again so the physical remains of their life must speak for them.

Finding them is difficult. Without the centralised administration necessary to build roads and basilicas, and the trade to provide exotic goods, the mark that the people of sub-Roman

14. *The Bronze Age houses at Cladh Hallan in the Outer Hebrides contained a secret. Beneath their floors human remains had been deliberately interred. Stranger still, in the case above and one other, the bodies had previously been kept preserved above ground for 600 and 300 years respectively before their final burial. This makes them the only known mummies from the British Isles.*

15. *Iron Age offering. A perfectly preserved set of copper alloy shears, still with their original wooden case. The indentation in the centre of the case was for a whetstone which is now lost. These exquisitely crafted tools were carefully placed in the water at Flag Fen, along with thousands of other items, perhaps as gifts for the gods of this watery world.*

16. *Village life. The Iron Age settlement reconstructed by the late Peter Reynolds at Butser in Hampshire is as close as we can get to life in some of Britain's first true villages. A similar settlement was the scene of the Winnal Down party (see text).*

17. A defended land. The Iron Age hillfort at Danebury in Hampshire dominates the local landscape. The appearance of hillforts and other 'defended' sites in the Iron Age might suggest that life in this era was becoming more dangerous. This was not just a fortress but a settlement, meeting place, market and religious centre.

18. A defender's tale. Whilst hillforts were not purely military, Iron Age Britain was no garden of Eden. The diamond-shaped hole in the forehead of this human skull from Danebury was made by a spear point similar to the one shown above it. The owner of the skull did not survive this injury.

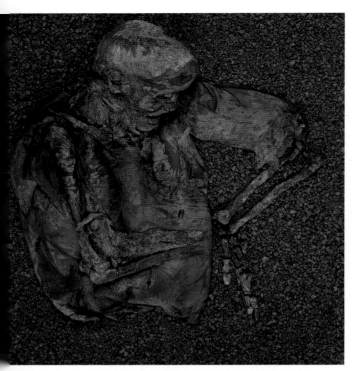

19. *The end of prehistory. The body of Lindow Man was preserved in a peat bog from his death in the first century AD to his rediscovery in 1985. He appears to have been a victim of human sacrifice – perhaps one of the last to suffer this prehistoric Iron Age ritual before the practice was, in theory at least, banned by the Romans.*

20. *Tribal branding. The White Horse at Uffington in Oxfordshire has survived as one of the most powerful images from prehistoric Britain. Standing at the junction between three tribal groupings in Iron Age England, it was perhaps the 'logo' of the people on whose land it lay and also appears on their coinage.*

21. *The height of fashion. The black and white geometric mosaics at Fishbourne Roman palace in Sussex were laid by continental Roman craftsmen for a member of the new pro-Roman elite in Britain. Sadly this Mediterranean style of flooring proved impractical in the colder British climate and braziers had to be brought in, which warped and scorched the tiles (top left).*

22. *Beyond the Villas. Life for most people in Roman Britain did not involve villas, hypocausts and mosaic floors. The ruins of the settlement at Chysauster in Cornwall give a less glamorous but altogether more typical view of life in Roman Britain.*

23. *Conspicuous consumption. For the Britons who wanted to buy into the new order the Roman world offered some material comforts. Aspiring Roman Britons in Verulamium could eat from imported Samian ware bowls, have their houses decorated with Roman wall paintings and tap into the sophisticated worlds of Roman art and culture.*

24. *The price of success. The Roman inhabitants of Colchester in Essex didn't get the chance to enjoy this particular imported luxury. These Mediterranean dates were carbonised in the fires that raged after the Iceni queen Boudicca sacked the city.*

25. *In the eye of the beholder. This late Roman mosaic known as the Rudston Venus has been politely described as 'rustic' and is a world away in style from the 'Venus' statuette from Verulamium. The villa owner who commissioned it clearly wanted to allude to the world of classical literature, but the interpretation is distinctly local and a little confused.*

26. *Not in polite society. The real voice of ordinary Roman Britons can be heard not in classical plays or orations but in documents such as this lead curse from Bath in Somerset, which begins:* 'May he who has stolen Vilbia from me become as liquid as water . . .' *and is followed by a list of names. Such inscriptions usually implored the gods to take revenge on a thief, known or unknown, a rival in love or even sometimes a charioteer and his horses (if a particularly large bet had been placed against them in the races).*

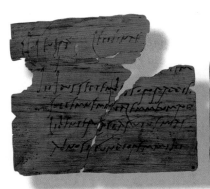

27. *Letters from the frontier. These Roman documents written on thin sheets of wood were discovered at the fort of Vindolanda on Hadrian's Wall, and represent the domestic correspondence of the fort. On the small fragment a piece of Virgil's Aenid has been copied out rather badly by a child. Next to it another hand (probably a teacher's) has written 'seg', short for segnis – sloppy! The larger pair of sheets contain a birthday invitation to Sulpicia Lepidina from Claudia Severa. The last line on the bottom right is in Claudia Severa's own hand and is the earliest known writing by a Roman woman. It reads:* 'I'm expecting you, sister. Keep well, dear heart, as I hope I will too; goodbye'.

Britain have left on the landscape is slight. The vast majority of the structures in this world must have been organic – made of wood, turf and thatch – and they have left little or no trace, except in some remote places, like Tintagel in Cornwall.

Tintagel is now, thanks to the romantics of the nineteenth century, for ever associated with King Arthur. This was the time in which the Arthur myth was born and, while an individual called Arthur has always proven elusive, people like him, if they ever existed, probably lived at this time and in places like this. For those in charge of the administration of the provinces of Britain, the collapse of central Roman authority did not mark an immediate descent into anarchy. Britain simply did as Honorius had suggested and looked inwards for governance and protection. Former administrators of the Empire now effectively became local overlords – the city councillors had become kings.

Had we approached the village of Tintagel from the landward side in the fifth century we would have walked into the world of such people. Now the high street is filled with gift shops and cafés, all named after Arthurian figures, but the great crag itself is substantially as it was all those centuries ago. The value of a place like this in the insecure days of the Roman withdrawal is still clear to see. Almost entirely cut off from the land, except for a narrow, treacherous isthmus, and protected from seaborne attack by precipitous cliffs, the promontory is almost a definition of the word 'impregnable'.

Overlooking the isthmus, instead of the Norman castle that now guards the site, there would have been a humbler group of stone buildings, not impressive by Roman standards but the home of rulers nevertheless. Inside, the population was not under siege: the withdrawal of the legions had not sent everyone scurrying for the hills to escape the predations of advancing barbarians. In the halls here, high-quality imported pottery was still in use, and luxuries such as spices and wine. Excavations have actually revealed more Byzantine (Eastern Roman) pottery at Tintagel than anywhere else outside the Mediterranean. If we want to know how it got here we need only look out of the window towards the little sandy cove far below us, with room for a huddle of trading ships to moor. Rome, in as much as it ever reached so far into Cornwall, had gone, but the Cornish dialogue with the classical world, ancient even at the time of the conquest, continued.

The people of fifth-century Tintagel were almost certainly not just average farmers. Indeed, they might have been the rulers of the area and they probably did not share their trade in the Mediterranean world with their underlings. In the first place they were Cornish, then perhaps British and, judging from their continuing interest in what the late-classical world could offer them, possibly even 'Roman'.

The great irony about the leaders of sub-Roman Britain was that they might have still considered themselves Roman, even though the trappings of the Roman world had fallen away from these shores and, perhaps, despite how superficially they had taken root there in the first place. Yet they were a group who, through centuries of myth-making and story-telling, were eventually reborn in the person of a single great British hero, King Arthur. That Arthur should be a folk memory of a tiny group of British people who considered themselves Roman is perhaps testimony to how varied and tangled British national roots are. If we could meet Arthur we would not be confronted by a 'knight in shining armour' but a defiant late-Roman government official, still clinging to the titles and modes of the Roman era, perhaps even dressed in Roman style and sporting a Latin name. Take this image, mix it with later European romances and a dash of earlier folklore, add aspects of the dimly remembered water rites of the Bronze Age at Flag Fen – now mutated into the story of the Lady of the Lake – and the medieval Arthur emerges on horseback, in plate armour, squinting into a mythological sun.

The history of this time can, in truth, barely be called history at all. Nearly everything we know of the events of the fifth century was written down by a monk called Gildas more than a century after they happened. The title of his book, *The Ruin of Britain*, should give us a clue that it is not an even-handed record of events. Gildas had a specific purpose in writing his book: to castigate the ruler of his own day for squandering the benefits their ancestors had bestowed on them and, more generally, to remind everyone that 'things ain't what they used to be' – which, of course, they never are. But in his hell-and-damnation tale we get as close as is historically possible to some of the leaders of sub-Roman Britain as they squared up to a new threat. It was people like these who ruled the rump of Roman Britain and had to face the coming storm.

Although the Roman influence in Britain had gone, along with the vexatious problems of tax and military control, that did not mean the country would now be left in peace. The native rulers of late-Roman Britain had applied to Rome for help because they were threatened, and when Rome turned its back on that plea, the threat grew stronger. The problem was perhaps rooted in earlier centuries when the Emperor Hadrian had first laid out the limits of Empire and, in the process, created a physical definition of barbarianism: the world beyond the Roman walls. Even since, the ambitious and disaffected of the non-Roman world has been pressing on those boundaries, exploring their defences, looking for cracks. The threat they posed was severe: on the south-east English coast, between

Brancaster in Norfolk and Porchester in Hampshire, a series of vast forts still stands as testament to the late Roman Briton fear of the barbarians from beyond the Empire.

One such stark witness to troubled times lies at Pevensey in East Sussex, where a complete circuit of walls twelve feet thick still encompasses an area of over eight acres, towering over the surrounding coastal landscape to a height of twenty-eight feet. When they were built in the fourth century, these huge fortifications were probably naval bases designed to suppress Scandinavian and Germanic piracy in the English Channel and North Sea. According to a fourth- or early fifth-century document called the 'Notitia Dignitatum', which appears to be a late-Roman list of military dispositions, these were the 'Saxon shore forts' and came under the control of a Roman official called the Count of the Saxon Shore. The occasional piracy these forts were designed to repel might have worried Roman authorities and perhaps the big villa owners with overseas orders to fulfil, yet it can hardly have bothered the average farmer. But with the abandonment of the Roman experiment that threat changed subtly and soon affected everyone.

If we survey the landscape of the fifth century on which this drama was about to be played out we might not be shocked at what we find. Life in the countryside was continuing much as it had before: the population were surviving, the old gods still received their dues and, in return, the sun rose each day, the seasons passed and the crops grew. There is even evidence that town life was continuing, although it would probably not have been what a first-century Roman would have considered civilised urban living. Perhaps the dream of an organised state, but one free from foreign control, was working; perhaps this *was* a golden age. If so, it was short-lived. With the western Roman empire in a state of collapse, the annoyance of barbarian raiding and piracy had grown into the full-scale threat of invasion. The Saxon Shore forts that had once pro-visioned the long-defunct British fleet now had to hold back a more fearsome tide than the one that lapped their walls twice a day.

The reason for the Saxon invasion of Britain, where these invaders came from, why and how many are still hotly debated issues. The meagre historical sources on the period, none of which were written by anyone who had lived through it, tell an apparently clear story, but religious authors like Gildas and, later, Nennius, were in the business of finding simple, deity-based answers to what were probably complex questions. These histories tell us that the sub-Roman King Vortigern invited some Germanic mercenaries to help him protect his lands from another troublesome group of barbarians who were threatening the coast, the Picts. Aid arrived in three ships led by Hengest and Horsa, brothers from what is now Jutland in Denmark.

Vortigern had invited the wolf into the fold. When Hengest and Horsa saw how rich the land was, and how poorly defended, they turned on their employer and seized Britain for the barbarians. Town and village were put to the sword, the rivers ran with blood, and the broken remnants of the people of Britain retired to the mountain fastness of the north and west, leaving a pristine land for the Germanic tribes to colonise. All very neat. As the Anglo-Saxon Chronicle for 449 puts it: '. . . they then sent to the Angles, and desired them to send more assistance. They described the worthlessness of the Britons, and the richness of the land. They then sent them greater support. Then came the men from the three powers of Germany; the Old Saxons, the Angles and the Jutes.'

The truth is almost certainly more complicated, but a lot

harder to find. In fact, there had probably been Germanic people in Britain from the late Empire onwards. Their love of fighting and undoubted military prowess had made them an excellent choice as mercenaries, and they were used regularly to prop up Roman forces. Even that was hardly a new idea, though: the Dacians on Hadrian's Wall in the second century AD had, only a generation before, been a dangerous barbarian nation, conquered by the Emperor Trajan.

But the dynamic had changed. There is some evidence that the coastal homelands of these people were suffering from the rising sea-levels in this period that were also affecting some parts of Britain – most noticeably turning the Isles of Scilly, twenty miles off the Cornish coast, from two large islands into the necklace of tiny islands and rocks they are today. Such flooding along the North Sea coast might have forced some families, perhaps whole peoples, to move. Elsewhere in Europe, better recorded barbarian nations were also on the move and in numbers. So, were the Angles, Saxon, Jutes and various other barbarians really mustering just over the horizon?

At Pevensey Castle in 491, the Anglo-Saxon Chronicle tells us, we would have witnessed the answer. The Saxon Shore fort, built in the twilight of empire was no longer a naval base, or home to a Roman legion: instead, it was filling with hundreds of people from the local area – men, women and children all hurrying through its gates while lookouts glanced nervously from the towers towards the line of black streaks gliding across the sea towards them. Within hours sleek Saxon ships had drawn up on the beach. Warriors emerged from them and quickly laid siege to the old fort and its poorly equipped defenders. In precious little time, both walls and men had crumbled under the onslaught and the Britons gathered inside were massacred. So says the Chronicle.

There was, of course, resistance, led, according to Gildas, by a shadowy 'Roman' figure called Ambrosius Aurelianus who defeated the Saxons at the still unidentified battle site of Mons Badonicus. This lone character, one of the last representatives of an even half-Roman authority in Britain, might have been the man that myth-makers later called Arthur. But Gildas goes on to say that his victories were squandered by his successors and that the Saxon triumph was soon complete.

But away from the minute quantity and dubious quality of the written history of the period, is there any evidence for this mass migration from Germany, the subsequent slaughter of the British population and its replacement by these ruthless invaders? We have already witnessed many events since the Mesolithic period that have, at one time or another, been interpreted as mass folk movements, from the farming 'revolution' to the arrival of Beaker People, and even the Roman invasion, only to find that in fact they probably didn't involve so much a movement of people as ideas and influence. Nor is it likely that the picture was the same across Britain. In Scotland the Picts were not defending themselves but joining in with the attacks, while the rulers of Tintagel were a comfortable distance from the front line of the Saxon shore.

However, a hundred years later changes had taken place that it would have been hard to ignore: in much of southern and eastern Britain Anglo-Saxon styles of dress and art, housing and lifestyle had been adopted and, more importantly, the Anglo-Saxon language was in use everywhere – the language which, though somewhat adapted, we use today. In modern Spain, France and Italy, Romance languages are spoken, derived from Latin as you might expect in the heartlands of the Empire, but English is different. It is not based on Latin, or on the old Iron Age 'Celtic' languages but instead on a barbarian Germanic language, despite our millennia of pre-history and four hundred years as a Roman province. That alone betrays that radical change must have taken place by this time in Britain. Even in the twenty-first century about a third of our words are Anglo-Saxon, as is our entire system of syntax. When Churchill promised to 'fight them on the beaches' he was basically speaking Anglo-Saxon.

Recently it has also been possible to look into another unique form of biography that we and our ancestors carry or carried with us: DNA. In rare instances it is possible to extract ancient DNA from bones and teeth, and some material has been re-covered from the people alive at this time. By looking at the Y chromosome – the male chromosome, which is only passed down the male line – it has been shown that anywhere between 50 and 90 per cent of the 'old' British male family lines appear to have been wiped out at this time and replaced with Anglo-Saxon genetic stock. While genetically the people of southern England and Friesland, a province of the Netherlands where some Anglo-Saxon invaders seem to have come from, are identical, those to either side of Offa's Dyke between Wales and England are not, which implies that the genetic heritage of the modern population of southern Britain lies on the conti-nent and not with the native Britons of the sub-Roman period. But DNA studies are not proof positive: however rigorous the science of DNA sequencing, these conclusions are drawn from data using the more subjective and arcane art of stat-istical analysis, and there are, of course, 'lies, damned lies and statistics'.

The real answer to the fate of the people of sub-Roman Britain lies probably in a combination of circumstances. In the west and north, life might have continued little changed, while on the Saxon shore it seems that the Anglo-Saxon Chronicle's tale of blood and savagery might hold the frightening ring of truth. Whether the people of, say, Suffolk were literally rounded up and killed to a man or driven from the area, or whether many simply kept their heads down and adapted, as they had many times before, to a new way of life under new masters, will probably never be fully known. But if we had stumbled upon a village of this date in that area, we would soon have been aware that we were in a new world.

At West Stow in Suffolk there once stood one of the earliest Anglo-Saxon settlements in England. Today much of the site has been reconstructed on its original foundations. In AD 500 it would have contained a small huddle of rectangular buildings, not particularly neatly arranged; the homes of four or five families. The most solid-looking buildings were wooden halls where these families lived, their doorposts carved with the twining, snaking decorations they loved and their thatched roofs steaming from the fires within. Clustered around them were the working buildings, a group of huts, known as *grubenhaüser*, where perhaps looms and craft-working tools were kept, and beyond them,the pens and paddocks of a few animals: ducks, hens, sheep and a pig or two.

If we could have watched the owners of these buildings return from their work in the fields, we would have seen that the men looked more like the weary farmers they were than the fearsome Germanic warriors of the Chronicles, and wielded nothing more offensive than an iron scythe. Inside the grubenhaüs the fading light may have caused one woman to rub her eyes, set aside her hand loom and call across her children in Anglo-Saxon to gather up the hens and return them to the safety of their coop for the night. Across the way in a central, larger hall, perhaps a slave dragged benches around a central fire in preparation for the evening's entertainment. A stranger had perhaps arrived in the village, a 'scop' or travelling poet, the living memory-bank of these people: come to tell tales in return for food, shelter and perhaps some small gift.

The stories told in this period are only known to us from later written accounts. The scops learned stories by heart and passed them down the generations by word of mouth. But written poems from the seventh and eighth centuries, themselves perhaps survivors from this time or before, tell us much about the loves and fears of this still pagan world.

After the scop had issued the traditional call to attention – '*Hwaet!*' – the hall would fall silent to listen. His alien, but curiously familiar language contained words we might recognise. The intimate language of these supposedly 'barbarian' people survives, in particular: 'Ich love fay' – I love you; 'daoling' – darling; 'mood' – mood.

His poems and stories would deal with the everyday concerns of these people. This was a highly structured, kin-based society, where immediate family groups held allegiance to larger extended families and even larger kin groups beyond that, from the head of the household to the head of the village, right up to the King. Blood and belonging was important and expulsion from the bosom of this family group was their greatest fear: 'I am choked with longings. Gloomy are the valleys, too high the hills, harsh strongholds overgrown with briars: a joyless abode. The journey of my lord so often cruelly seizes me. There are lovers on earth, lovers alive who lie in beds, when I pass through this earth-cave alone and out under the oak tree at dawn.'

So speaks the female writer of 'The Wife's Lament'. Perhaps due to her husband's banishment, she has been thrown out of her kin group and forced to live in an earth cave at the base of a tree. Yet it is not so much the hardship of living in a cave that tears at her heart-strings, but the thought of being out of the love and protection of her lord. Her lost and lonely voice rising into the cold night air above the little settlement of West Stow is a far cry from the fire and brimstone that the Chronicles associate with Hengest and Horsa.

Other than the echoes of the hopes and fears of these people that linger in later Anglo-Saxon poetry the main way in which we can grasp something about their beliefs is through their death rites. Just outside West Stow we would have found a small burial field where the ancestors of these people lay. The preferred rite here was cremation: the dead person's body was burned with some of their possessions, the residue gathered up, placed in a handmade pot and buried in the field. There were also a few inhumations – whole burials – perhaps of the more important leaders of the community, although bones are not always a good guide to 'who's who'. What is important is that these pagan people were buried with many of the objects they had known in life, presumably in the belief that they would be able to take them to the next world. So, in the pots and graves of such huge pagan burial grounds as Spong Hill in Norfolk, where over two thousand individuals were excavated, many objects have been found that must have mattered to the 'ordinary' people of early Anglo-Saxon Britain: brooches carved with swirling geometric patterns, silver finger rings, amber and glass beads and bone combs; useful everyday items such as spindle whorls – pierced clay discs attached to a stick for use in spinning wool; miniature tweezers and razors that perhaps had religious or magical significance. The bones tell a story of lives that rarely reached what we might call middle age and of hard-worked joints, riddled with arthritis.

At the other end of the scale, of course, the leaders at the top of this society were buried in considerable state. Most famous among them must be the man uncovered beneath a barrow at Sutton Hoo in Suffolk, still resplendent in his longship, and surrounded by the most famous treasure ever uncovered in these islands. The man at Sutton Hoo, possibly the pagan king Raedwald of East Anglia, or one of his successors, was very different from the people buried at Spong Hill. While the site is rightly famous for its beautiful gold jewellery, hoards of foreign coins, enamelled hanging bowls and magnificent decorated helmet, other finds hold clues to a great change about to sweep this cosy rural world, from the illustrious court of Raedwald to the farmers at West Stow. Among the finds at Sutton Hoo there were a number of items of the type archaeologists refer to as 'ritual'. We might perhaps have expected to find the peculiar stone mace with bronze stag finial in the grave of a pagan king, but perhaps not the two silver spoons marked 'Paulos' and 'Saulos'. The names reflect a new influence growing in this society: Christianity.

Why the man at Sutton Hoo was buried with these spoons – which have been tentatively identified as christening spoons – is a matter of debate. Later sources suggest that Raedwald trod a difficult line between allowing Christian worship but not banning his old pagan religion. Perhaps he had the spoons buried with him to hedge his bets. We might imagine a nervous Raedwald standing at the Pearly Gates waving his spoons furiously at St Peter in the hope that it might distract him from looking at the huge pagan longship and treasure behind him. Equally he might have seen them simply as spoons, and cared little for what was written on them.

According to the history books, Christianity was re-introduced to Britain by St Augustine, sent on the orders of Pope Gregory in 596 to convert this pagan people to the 'true faith'. Of course, Britain had been at least nominally Christian under the later Roman Empire when Christianity was the official state religion. A group of impressive treasure hoards from the period suggest that some parts of Britain, or of British society, were indeed devoutly Christian. Possibly the world's oldest communion silver was found at Water Newton near Peterborough, and, of course, the Hinton St Mary mosaic is claimed by some to be the earliest surviving depiction of Christ. This does not, of course, mean that everywhere and everyone was Christian, or that Christianity meant to them what it does to us. Certainly, in many areas, this Roman state religion seems to have faded quickly with the collapse of the province. There is a chance, however, that it might have survived in the north and west, where a distinctive Celtic form of monasticism grew up, well away from the predations of the Germanic pagan tribes. However, in the areas now ruled by Anglo-Saxon kings (which stretched from Wessex to Northumbria) and away from the Christian enclaves of Scotland and Wales, paganism was the rule.

The true nature of that religion is difficult to understand as these were an illiterate people, but the Germanic gods who held sway seem to have been the same as those in the German homelands. This pantheon is, in turn, not very different from that of the Celtic gods who had inhabited the hillforts of Iron Age Britain and dwelt just beneath the surface of Roman religious life. As such, we might expect that any Britons still living in Anglo-Saxon areas (if we assume they were not all murdered or expelled) could easily adapt to the new names as they had done during the Roman occupation, but retain their own beliefs fundamentally intact. But with the arrival of Christianity, that was no longer possible. Christianity was not a religion forgiving of other faiths. It did not allow for more than one God; nor was it keen to equate its God with anyone else's. Paganism was wrong and Britain would now form the battleground of a propaganda war to prove it. In the end, all that would be left of the old religion were the names of the days of the week: Monday, after Monan the Moon, Thursday, after Thunor, god of thunder, Tuesday, after Tiw, god of justice. The last surviving vestiges of a long dead religion.

The new evangelists brought the whole weight of the educated Christian world to bear on the problem of converting Britain. Its priests were literate men, skilled in story-telling, diplomacy and rhetoric. Their first targets were often the wives of kings who, once converted, could use their feminine wiles to persuade their husband to follow them, or at least to allow priests to preach on their land. At the other end of the scale, stories of the daily presence of the Christian God in people's lives and the dire consequences of His wrath were preached to the masses. They appealed to a storytelling culture, offered peace of mind in an uncertain world and promised damnation to those who transgressed.

Bede, often called the father of English history, used such stories himself in his *Ecclesiastical History of the English Church and People*, which documents this extraordinary conversion process. He tells a simple tale, of fear, faith and miracles, which would have spoken directly to many a Saxon farmer:

... no rain had fallen in that province in three years before his arrival, whereupon a dreadful famine ensued, which cruelly destroyed the people. In short, it is reported, that very often, forty or fifty men, being spent with want, would go together to some precipice, or to the sea shore, and there, hand in hand, perish by the fall, or be swallowed up by the waves. But on the very day on which the nation received the baptism of faith, there fell a soft but plentiful rain; the earth revived again, and the verdure being restored to the fields, the season was pleasant and fruitful.

These events occurred, according to Bede, in the Sussex village of Bosham near Chichester, which he had never visited and of which he can have had little idea, living, as he did, in Jarrow, Northumbria. Had he been to Bosham he would have known that it is a very flat area: no precipices or cliffs to throw yourself off. But that wasn't the point: neither had most of his audience. Bosham might have been anywhere where the people worried about the vagaries of the weather, their crops or the health of their families – and that was everywhere. It was a simple message for people with simple concerns. Ignore the Christian God and you will be punished; accept him and you will be blessed.

The new religion required more, however, than a basic outward show of conformity. Christianity was a personal religion with an interest in every aspect of everyone's life. While the great and good argued about points of philosophy and doctrine, the priests were changing the social fabric of society at its most basic level: the family. In a society based around kinship, this was perhaps a harder task than changing any outward show of religion. To begin with, the acceptance of polygamy in pagan society was rejected by the Church, which opposed it in sermons and went as far as legislating against it. Casual relationships became a thing of the past. The Church required marriages to be '*au fast*' – legally binding between two people 'till death us do part'.

Not that death provided an escape from the influence of the early Church. The Christian burial rite was generally inhumation, and, perhaps more importantly, Christianity introduced the concept of 'you can't take it with you', to which many pagan Anglo-Saxons would undoubtedly have replied,

'Why not?' Persuading the people of Britain to stop burying their loved ones with their possessions would be an uphill struggle. Old habits – and these were very old habits – die hard and for a long time into the Christian period people were being buried with the odd item such as the seventh century infant from Barton-on-Humber in Lincolnshire buried with its breast-shaped feeding pot. Perhaps the mother had been unable to breastfeed the child and the pot substitute had failed. Perhaps the pot was to help the baby feed on its lonely journey to the next life without its mother. Either way, by Christian standards it shouldn't have been there. But it was.

One boy standing on the cusp of this revolution was a young aristocrat's son called Guthlac. His life spanned these old and new worlds: he was brought up in the pagan household of his wealthy family but died a Christian saint. His biographer, Felix, in trying to explain the promise of the boy's youth, had terrible trouble reconciling the wild days of pagan childhood he recorded with the saintly unworldliness of Guthlac's later life, but in doing so he caught for ever a snapshot of a family at the end of the pagan heroic age:

. . . the child was initiated into the noble arts of his forefathers in his parental palace . . . Then when the powers of adolescence came upon him . . . recalling the mighty deeds of primitive demigods, as if startled from slumber with awakening intellect, he assembled his troop of minions and turned to arms.

The young saint had formed his first warband and set out on the old pagan path designed to bring him booty and fame. It appears he was successful:

And though he laid waste the cities and hamlets and castles of his enemies with fire and sword, gathering immense booty for his confederates assembled from different races, yet as if guided by divine counsel he sent back a third part of the accumulated plunder to its owners.

The returning of a third of the plunder shows that Guthlac's biographer was having difficulty reconciling his hero's actions with Christian doctrine although it is perhaps doubtful if his victims were all that grateful, preferring him not to have taken any of it in the first place. Of course, Guthlac repented of this way of life and retired from pillaging to adopt Christianity. The new religion must have offered people like him something more than the old pagan ways.

If Christianity had one advantage over the religion it was slowly displacing, it was literacy. The central theme of Christian teaching was the power of the Word, and the faith was spread by literacy and education. There had been some formal education in Britain before, as the unfortunate Roman boy copying Virgil knew only too well, but this had largely been available only to the select few sons of the select few. Now the newly flourishing monasteries offered opportunities to a wider public, who would join the faith.

Bede himself had been a beneficiary of this system. If you travel to Jarrow today you will find that the chapel in which he worshipped is still there, at least in part. On walking through the west door towards the chancel if you look up to the left you will see the foundation stone of the monastery. Bede would have been about twelve when it was put in place on 23 April 685, and had already been in the care of this monastery's sister house at Wearmouth for five years. Shortly afterwards he moved to Jarrow to begin his adult monastic life, which he describes simply in the few words of autobiography he has left us:

I Bede was born on the lands of this monastery at Jarrow and on reaching seven years of age, I was entrusted by my family to the Abbot Benedict for my education. I have spent all my life in this monastery and while I have observed the regular discipline and sung the choir offices, my chief delight has always been in writing.

This is just about all Bede tells us of himself – the story of a no-doubt scared little boy leaving home for mysterious world of the monastery. It must have been a daunting prospect; one which would withdraw him from his family and kin but which offered the prize of opening his mind up to a world of knowledge that stretched far beyond their horizons.

The ability to write would change British history forever and the simple writing tools of the period excavated at Jarrow – the metal styli, oyster-shell ink-pots, hide scrapers and stone rubbers that the young Bede might himself have used – are the instruments of a revolution more important than all the gold and silver in the Sutton Hoo treasure. Literacy brought with it the opportunity to codify laws, create land deeds, transfer property, record history, and speak to people distant in place and time. Bede's joy in writing was not that of a man who has found his medium, but the exhilaration of someone seeing a world of knowledge for the first time and knowing that, through his books, he could transmit that wonder across both time and space.

It would be wrong, of course, to imagine that everyone was as lucky as Bede. There were others – Cuthbert, prior of the famous monastery of Lindisfarne and one of the greatest Anglo-Saxon saints, had begun life as a simple shepherd boy in Scotland – but the monasteries of the seventh century didn't offer a universal comprehensive education. Indeed, their benefits might still have been reserved largely for the children of the privileged, or those fortunate to have been born on monastery land, as Bede was. But the monastic education of boys like Bede and Cuthbert marked the beginning of a system of formal education in Britain, those franchise has been expanding ever since.

The success of the Christian Church in Britain did not go unchallenged. While kings could be persuaded by political debate and the people won over with miracles, the growing wealth of the Church attracted the attentions of an unwelcome group of visitors:

This year came dreadful fore-warnings over the land of the North-umbrians, terrifying the people most woefully: these were immense sheets of light rushing through the air, and whirlwinds, and fiery dragons flying across the firmament. These tremendous tokens were soon followed by a great famine: and not long after, on the sixth day before the ides of January in the same year, the harrowing inroads of heathen men made lamentable havoc in the church of God in Holy-island, by rapine and slaughter.

Britain was proving once again that being an island does not guarantee being left alone. The 'heathen men' of this excitable account in the Anglo-Saxon Chronicle were Vikings, and the year was 793. From their point of view the raiding made perfect sense. Monasteries were vast treasure vaults in convenient out-of-the-way places, with good access for longships, and guarded by unarmed pacifists. For any pagan warrior worth his salt, they must have been hard to resist. For the Church, however, these brutal raids represented an approaching Armageddon. Of course, the recently converted farmers in the fields of Britain probably knew nothing of the raids on these distant and ex-clusive monasteries but in attracting the Vikings the Church had introduced them to a land of opportunity. Soon they would return, and change the shape of everyone's lives from northern Scotland to the south coast of England.

For the Norse peoples of Scandinavia, the gateway to Britain was not the Channel or the Thames but the Scottish islands, and it is on those islands that evidence of their presence can still be found today. On the Brough of Birsay, a tidal island just off the north-eastern tip of the main island of Orkney, one of these Viking settlements still stands. Excavations here have rather given the lie to the simple view of Vikings as bloodthirsty lads in boats on a violent away-day. Certainly, when the first Viking boats arrived in the late eighth century, the local population must have either collaborated or run away. Across the western world these were violent times, and few peoples, Christian or pagan, would simply go home if politely asked. But the Vikings were not just in Britain for a season of monastery plundering. They were farmers and builders, and they had brought with them a rich and varied culture that they would mingle with Scotland's own.

Had we found ourselves washed up on the beaches of the Viking settlement on the Brough of Birsay around 810 we might not have been in for as hard a time as we might have expected. As we walked around their cliff-top settlement in the winter sun we would have found a complicated group of buildings, including byres, barns and a smithy, and further up the hill a Pictish symbol stone, carved with an eagle and three warriors, evidence of the earlier inhabitants of this place. Whether those people had left the island to their new Norse owners, been driven off or killed by them, or simply integrated into the Norse population we cannot tell. If the new Norsemen were fearsome warriors, however, they also had a taste for luxury. A heated building with stone-lined drains running under the benches around its walls might have been an early form of sauna where these Vikings relaxed after a hard day's work.

At the centre of the community was a hall, over twenty metres long, which was clearly no temporary structure. Inside, benches surrounded an oblong hearth in a single windowless room, lit only by the flicker of whale-blubber oil lamps. Here many of the people of the Brough sat, slept, ate and perhaps listened to sagas of their great adventures across the North Sea. This building was made of wood, brought to the western Orkneys by longship. Huge squared timbers of Norwegian pine were pre-cut back in Norway and sent across 'ready for assembly': the first Ikea delivery in history – a flatpack house for the island's stylish new Scandinavian inhabitants.

And there, perhaps, lies the difference between the hysterical reports of the Christian chroniclers (who had always played up the dangers of paganism, like Bede with his suicidal Bosham villagers) and the truth. Vikings were certainly keen on plundering churches, but they were not only day-raiders. Some built permanent settlements, which meant that they intended to stay. So everyone had to get used to them.

While the Norwegians in Scotland were settling down relatively peacefully, the Danes were causing more of a stir further south. The Anglo-Saxon Chronicle speaks of great 'heathen armies' arriving in the spring to rape and pillage over the summer, then returning home to Scandinavia in the autumn leaving the people of England to lick their wounds. In the autumn of 851, however, the Chronicle records an ominous change in their plans: instead of returning to their boats and sailing back across the North Sea, they stayed. By 1 November 866 they were at the gates of the Anglian city of York, and everyday life there was about to take on a decidedly Scandinavian flavour.

There can be no doubt that the initial flavour they tasted was blood. Much has been done in recent years to rehabilitate the image of the Vikings, but in violent times, it would be foolish to assume that these invaders were averse to a little rape and pillage. The Anglo-Saxon chronicler puts it bluntly: '. . . having collected a vast force they fought the army at York; and breaking open the town, some of them entered it. Then there was an immense slaughter of the Northumbrians, some within and some without.'

The king of Northumbria, Aelle, suffered possibly the worst fate: he was sacrificed by the Viking leader Ivarr the Boneless. According to the Viking *Saga of Ragnar's Sons*, Aelle's ribs were cut from his back, his lungs removed and draped over his shoulders in a ceremony known as the 'blood eagle'. If the leaders of Anglo-Saxon England could expect no mercy, then for the people of York the invasion must have seemed like the end of the world, and for many it probably was. But what happened next was even more extraordinary. The Vikings were now in charge of a well-placed major settlement and a cowed, if resentful population both inside York and beyond its walls. Yet their presence did not turn this place into an Anglian concentration camp but a commercial success. Walk down the streets of what is now Jorvik a hundred years after the Viking conquest and you will see a whole different side to the Viking way of life.

The moderately successful Anglian settlement of perhaps some two thousand people is now a thriving city of over twenty thousand, its river banks lined with longships returning from Scandinavia, the French coast, the rivers of northern Russia and beyond. The streets have been divided into neat, equally spaced plots for single- and two-storey houses with a yard behind, and between the various crafts. On Coppergate the cup-makers, from whom the street gets its name, are producing piles of wooden food bowls, ready to be filled by the butchers selling favourite Viking foods such as beef or the fishmongers with their barrels of oysters. Elsewhere tanners, weavers, leather workers and dyers are at work. Tradesmen from the ships sell exotica such as silk caps from China, cowrie shells from the Red Sea and amber from the Baltic in return for hard silver currency, which they jealously guard in padlocked boxes. In a doorway two old men are playing a favourite Viking board game, *hnefatafl*, while their wives haggle over the cost of cheap, mass-produced brooches. Noticeable for their absence are the hordes of snarling Viking warriors.

Passing a cup-maker turning a block of ash on a lathe we might not think he represents much of a revolution but he does: for a start he might be either Christian or pagan, and speaks perhaps a dialect somewhere between Old Norse and Anglo-Saxon. This is a tolerant society, as a glance at the coins on his table shows: they bear images of both a Christian cross and a pagan Thor hammer. Furthermore he is a specialist. Since the decline of Roman cities, perhaps as early as the third century AD, there has been little room in Britain for professional craftsmen outside a few specialised commercial centres, such as Southampton and Ipswich. At West Stow the blacksmiths, furniture-makers and weavers were not tradespeople working full time in return for money, but farmers and their families doing these jobs in their time away from the fields. This man is a professional. Jorvik is a city again, just as it was when it was Roman Eboracum, when Constantine the Great was declared Emperor here. The Vikings might have arrived in Britain in a welter of blood and violence, but they had brought a gift with them. Large-scale urban living had returned.

Although we have no contemporary accounts of Jorvik, we

do have a description of the Viking town of Hedeby, now in modern Germany on the border with Denmark. When the Arab writer Ibrahim al-Tartushi visited around 950 he described a strange scene perhaps not too different from what we might have met in Jorvik:

Schleswig [as al-Tartushi calls Hedeby] is a very large town at the extreme end of the world ocean. In its interior one finds fresh water sources. The inhabitants worship Sirius, except for a minority of Christians who have a church of their own there. They celebrate a feast at which all get together to honour their god and to eat and drink. He who slaughters a sacrificial animal puts up poles at the door to his courtyard and impales the animal on them . . . so that his neighbours will be aware that he is making a sacrifice in honour of his god . . . Babies are thrown into the sea for reasons of economy. The right to divorce belongs to the women. They let themselves be divorced when they are so inclined. Artificial eye make-up is another peculiarity; when they wear it their beauty never disappears, indeed it is enhanced in both men and women. Further: never did I hear singing fouler than that of the Schleswegians, it is a rumbling emanating from their throats, similar to that of a dog but even more bestial.

While the people of Northumbria were getting used to the rites and voices of their new neighbours, far to the south the Viking presence was having similar effects, although this time not just on Viking areas. Since Alfred the Great's victory over the Danish army of Guthrum in 878, England had theoretically been divided in two along the line of the old Roman road of Watling Street, which ran from London to Chester. To the east of this line lay the 'Danelaw', an area at least in principle under Danish control; to the west lay Alfred's kingdom of Wessex, the last and most powerful of the Anglo-Saxon kingdoms. This division had come about as a practical solution to the years of raiding by Viking warbands and the long-term presence of Danish armies in the south, although it should probably not be thought of as some kind of 'Maginot line'. Crossing Watling Street (still a major road today) in 900 in either direction was probably no more dangerous than it is now. It is hard to know if the inhabitants on either side were aware of the difference between them. There may have been administrative differences in some areas and taxes were paid to different overlords, but it was never a line on which one side people spoke Danish and the other English.

What the Danelaw did prove to be was a spur for development. The Danish presence in England was always seen by her Anglo-Saxon rulers as a threat, and Alfred and his successors combated this by creating their own English social solution. The key to the defence of Wessex against Viking attack was not a large standing army, extended lines or defence or massive investment in military technology, it was shopkeepers. The small towns that sprang up across Wessex at this time were not simply the bright idea of local people out to make a silver penny or two, they were part of a concerted and planned development of settlements called 'burghs'. Some were built on Roman sites, some in Iron Age hillforts and some were new. Should you find yourself flying over Wallingford in Berkshire today, you would look down on a thriving modern town, but hidden just beneath the surface is an ancient story. The rectangular shape of the settlement, the even grid of roads, the neatly demarcated housing plots are all ghosts from the ninth and tenth centuries. The layout you look at is the one devised and ordered by Alfred as part of his bold plan to protect Wessex from Viking attack. Instead of defending one central royal stronghold, which he knew the Vikings would eventually besiege and probably take, or building a string of forts that could be starved out one by one, Alfred built burghs, planned and defended civil settlements a day's march apart, which were self-supporting and distributed power across the country. Knock out one, and others filled the void – exactly the reasoning that lay behind the US military's development of the Internet.

The burgh created a new class of Anglo-Saxon, the counterpart to his Anglo-Scandinavian cousins in Jorvik: the local traders who thrived in their planned city and exploited the transport links being built between them and who, from Alfred's point of view, could hence afford to defend their town and would fight to preserve their way of life. And it was a successful way of life, the rebirth of localised urban culture in the south and the origins of many of the hundreds of little market towns that still lie scattered across the country.

So successful was the policy that by around 955 the kings of Wessex could consider attacking the Danelaw and bring it back slowly into the Anglo-Saxon sphere of influence. As a result the rulers of Wessex could call themselves Kings of England for the first time without any sense of irony. Indeed, when Edgar, Alfred the Great's grandson, was crowned in Bath in 973 he accepted the homage of not only the magnates of Anglo-Saxon England but also the rulers of Scotland and Wales. The nations of Britain were being born, and with them came the earliest dawnings of the structures of government and law that we live with today.

Today the power of the state and judiciary reach into every life, no matter how remove from the centre of power, but this had not always been the case in Anglo-Saxon England. It had been a land of many kings and kingdoms, each distant from the everyday concerns of the people on their land. With the birth of England came the need to rule it – a vast undertaking – and new laws soon made their way into even the smallest communities.

To walk into Pewsey Vale in Wiltshire today is to enter a landscape that would have been familiar to the people of this new world. Standing on the hills that rise to either side of the flat, green valley we might let the years slip away, and find ourselves back in 900. We could then have looked down, much as we can today, on a series of small settlements strung out along its length, connected by a road from which droveways led off up the valley sides to the sheep pastures above. We might even have been able to pick out some individual houses, a little larger and more sophisticated than those at West Stow some four centuries before, but still basically rectangular buildings made almost exclusively from wood, leather and plant fibres. There was a newer type of structure in each village now, though, always aligned east–west, perhaps with a semicircular eastern end: the village church. In some areas this might have been rebuilt in stone: a wonder of the age.

Standing close to the valley's edge lies a peculiar little hill, known as Swanborough Tump and it is towards this that we might have seen the villagers of Pewsey slowly heading. Swanborough Tump was the parish council chamber of its day, where the government of this small piece of England was carried out. England was ruled by division: the nation as a whole had been divided by the King between his most loyal and favoured subjects, who in turn subdivided it between theirs. This whole valley might hence have belonged to the King but each part was controlled by one of his lords, who might have parcelled it out to his retainers. In return for the land from the king the lords provided military service, including raising troops for the King's conscript army, the *fyrd*, guaranteed to keep communication routes open, and repaired defences. Hence, through the chain of command, one man could rule a nation. It was the start of a system of aristocratic land tenure that endured for centuries.

But the high politics of national government were not what interested the people who ran their affairs on Swanborough Tump. They stood at the other end of the scale, at the basic level of government and law enforcement, the 'Hundred', which, theoretically, was a division of a hundred families. The Hundred Court meeting at the Tump once each lunar month heard all judicial cases relating to the area from petty theft to capital murder. To keep in touch with the wider kingdom, a royal official might have arrived to announce a new decree, or promulgate new laws. Not everyone from the Hundred would attend, just the adult free men of the area (that is, free men over the age of twelve, at which tender age a Saxon boy officially became an adult). It was a first step towards local government as we know it. In silent recognition of this, the hill still carries the memory of such gatherings: 'Swanborough Tump' means 'the Hill of the Common Man'.

The immediate effects of such a meeting might have been evident on the highest point of the valley's edge. Against the evening sky, silhouetted for all in the valley to see, stood a gallows upon which from time to time the body of a condemned man swung, like the pendulum of some macabre village clock. Executions occurred on the very edge of the Hundred as a warning to those passing through. This was the dawn of a great age of lawmaking in which kings repeatedly drew up codified lists of crimes and their appropriate punishments. Murder, theft or some sexual offences might have brought a victim to his death, or crimes more indicative of the period, such as witchcraft or army desertion.

Witchcraft was seen as a genuine problem. And one which might have very real effects on everyday life. A property deed of 975 explains how a piece of land came into its owner's hands via such a case:

Then the bishop gave the land at Yaxley to Thorney and that at Ailsworth to Peterborough. And a widow and her son had previously forfeited the land at Ailsworth because they drove iron pins into Wulfstan's father, Ælfsige. And it was detected and the murderous instrument dragged from her bedchamber; and the woman was seized and drowned at London Bridge, and her son escaped and became an outlaw.

The 'murderous instrument' mentioned in the deed was a wax model of Ælfsige – a voodoo doll – into which the widow and her son were accused of sticking pins in the hope of bringing about his death. The 'murderous instrument' was clearly considered proof positive of guilt, although one wonders if acquisitive landowners were tempted to invent such charges in a bid to seize a vulnerable widow's land.

But if the crimes were becoming clearer and more codified, the process of confirming guilt could still be very strange. In small communities where privacy was almost non-existent, many cases at the Hundred Court probably relied on evidence such as the effigy above or the testimony of villagers who had witnessed the act. The innocent or guilty party would appear before the Hundred Court with 'oath helpers', who would swear to the accused's innocence or guilt, assuming they could find some people to swear that.

The more contentious cases were played out in the village church. In the tenth-century mind, be it that of a great philosopher or a local farmer, the worlds of God and man were intimately linked. God did not wait in silence for the 'last blast of the trumpet when he would judge the quick and the dead', but was believed to be actively engaged in the world, ordering events, letting His will be known and guiding His people. This was an age when saints still performed miracles, rivers might run red with blood, and natural disasters were seen as divine punishments. As such it seemed to fall naturally that in legal cases where proof was difficult, the all-seeing eye of God was invoked to provide the solution. Take the accused to the church and let God sit in judgement.

The handful of stone churches that survive from this era give little clue now of what happened inside them at such times. Our image of the village church is of a peaceful, contemplative place, with light streaming through stained-glass windows on to ancient stone floors. It is a world where flower arrangers silently go about their task, where congregations gather once a week, and where, in between, a perfect silence descends over the tombs of long-forgotten ancestors. If you enter the Anglo-Saxon church at Brixworth in Northamptonshire today that view would undoubtedly be reinforced. Walk into it eleven hundred years ago, and you might be forgiven for thinking you had stepped not into a little piece of heaven, but into a circle of hell.

Your first, overwhelming, impression would be the smell – not of damp or flowers but of burning flesh – then the sound, the sharp intakes of breath from the crowd gathered in the nave, the screams of the man they are standing around, and the pious mumbling of the priest in the chancel. And there's the unusual heat. Perhaps now you might dare to open an eye and witness the scene beyond: the scene of God judging man, Anglo-Saxon style, in a trial by ordeal.

Its logic was simple, if gruesome. The accused was summoned to church where a great fire would have been lit. When the brazier was blazing, an iron bar was placed in it and heated until it was red hot. At a nod from the priest the bar would be removed and placed on a wooden post. The job of the accused was then to pick up the burning hot bar with his naked hand and carry it a prescribed distance, often nine paces. The law prescribed in great detail who should witness this and how:

And an equal number of men from either side [of the case] are to go in and stand down the church on both sides of the ordeal; and all those are to be fasting and abstaining from their wives at night; and the priest is to sprinkle holy water over them all – and each of them is to taste the holy water – and to give them all the book to kiss, and the sign of Christ's cross. And no one is to continue making up the fire after they begin the consecration; but the iron is to lie upon the embers until the last collect; then they are to lay it upon the post, and no other words are to be spoken inside, except that they are earnestly to pray Almighty God that he makes the whole truth plain.

Having walked the length of this grisly assault course, the accused would drop the bar and his burnt and blistered hand would be bound with a clean dressing.

Three days later the accused, and no doubt the crowd, would return to church, where the bandages would be removed. If the wounds were healing, God was protecting the innocent and the man was free. But should they have festered the message was clear: the inner corruption of the guilty heart had prevented them healing and God had turned His face from the man, who was guilty. Justice could then be done.

The victim of an ordeal did not have to rely solely on the will of God however. By the late Anglo-Saxon period a sophisticated knowledge of medicine had grown up, and was practised among the wealthy at least by professional physicians. It would, no doubt, have been useful to a post-ordeal suspect. But health and medicine was also within the realm of the Church. After all, the God who healed the hands of the innocent could clearly heal anyone else He chose, or perhaps who asked. The peculiar mix of herbalism, prayers and charms that make up such medical works of the period as the wonderfully named *Bald's Leechbook* draw heavily on the involvement of God in effecting cures in intractable conditions. In the case of 'Fiend Sickness', the book recommends making up an ale of twelve herbs in a church bell, then having a priest say certain chants over it after mass. It is then drunk for nine days – a magical number in the Saxon world – accompanied by more prayers and chants. The cure might be herbal in origin, but God made it effective. Other remedies required no physical medicine: caught up in tenth and eleventh century medical manuscripts these 'charms' were probably survivors from pagan times but clearly had a place among the herbal cures and prayers that made up the later Anglo-Saxons' medical arsenal. One of the strangest is the 'Charm Against a Wen' – a form of tumour. It is a charm that may have been in use since the days when West Stow was inhabited:

> Wen, wen, little wen,
> here you must not build, here have no abode,
> but you must go north to the nearby hill
> where, poor wretch, you have a brother.
> He will lay a leaf at your head.
> Under the paw of the wolf, under the eagle's wing,
> under the claw of the eagle, may you ever decline!
> Shrink like coal on the hearth!
> Wizen like filth on the wall!
> Waste away like water in the pail!

Become as small as a grain of linseed,
  and far smaller than a hand-worm's hip-bone and so very
    small
  that you are at last nothing at all.

However odd the mix of Church and state, dimly remembered pagan ritual and Christian liturgy might seem to us, it
worked. Britain in the tenth century was becoming a stable,
relatively peaceful island. But life for its villagers was still hard.
The Julian Work Calendar, drawn up in 1020 in Canterbury
and designed to teach monks the saints' days, is illustrated with
the toils of working people over the seasons of the year. The
sketches of men and women going about the labours of each
season could almost have been drawn from life: a vivid collection of pock-marked, balding, smiling, grumbling and
bemused-looking Anglo-Saxons. The life depicted here would
have been familiar to nearly every family in Britain: the
men drinking beer, the shepherds chatting idly, always with
one eye on their sheep, the blacksmith shoeing a horse, and
the labourers in the field, their backs bent, scythes in hand,
gathering in the harvest.

The calendar certainly shows a world of unremitting toil
and the skeletons of Anglo-Saxons from this period have the
worn, arthritic joints of men and women who had worked
hard for their living. But it was a successful world, far distant
from the sub-Roman Britain from which it had emerged only
six hundred years before. Gone were the days of hiding from
Germanic invaders or Viking warbands, and the towns and
cities that the Romans had left crumbling were thriving again.
Much of the basis of the structure of rural life was already in
place, the lords in their manors, the villagers tending the fields,
the priests in their parishes, the lawyers writing laws. English

was emerging as a universal language, preferred since the days of Alfred the Great to the more formal but fossilised Latin: the language of the people was also the language of the state and the law. Life was hard but the people in at least some of Britain could get on with living it in a stable, structured society.

Far from the concerns of villagers, life at the top of society could still be turbulent. The Vikings would finally achieve their goal with the installation of the Norse Cnut as King of England, but he had little effect on the life of those caught up in the unending cycles of the life described in the Julian Work Calendar. There were other Vikings on the horizon, however, who would. As a prosperous and relatively stable island, Britain was again attracting the attention of foreign would-be kings, and these Northmen would not be sailing from Scandinavia but France and they would leave their mark on nearly every city, town and village in the country. Britain would suffer one final wave of invasion, its most famous: the Norman Conquest.

5
Free and Unfree

The first and shortest classification of persons is this, that all men are either free or unfree.

attr. Henry of Bracton, *c*.1210–68

A visitor passing through the prosperous Anglo-Scandinavian market town of Norwich in the late eleventh century would have been struck by a disturbing sight. Until recently the town had been one of the success stories of late Saxon England, and one of its most densely inhabited boroughs. Now it was a building site.

It was not simply a case of urban renewal. Standing by the work site any traveller might have noticed something rather stomach-turning. Beside the huge mortar pits and stone-dressing camps that had sprung up all over the town loomed piles of earth dug out and heaped up to form a great mound – but this was not just ordinary earth. From among the rubble, stones and soil the occasional broken human skull stared out. In fact the ground was littered with human remains, pieces of stone monuments, grave slabs, coffins, scraps of shroud and the decaying remnants of their one-time inhabitants. No doubt a shocked and resentful huddle of locals stood around the site, bearing witness to the destruction of their church and the desecration of their graveyard. Beyond them the workmen, themselves press-ganged townsfolk, continued to dig up the bodies.

And this was not all: nearby a bustling line of ninety-eight shops and houses, not unlike those of Jorvik in earlier centuries,

145

had been demolished, and the former owners of the plots had received precious little in the way of compensation. Perhaps they had salvaged a few possessions before the work gangs moved in but that was all.

But it was not just their homes that the locals had lost. Their livelihoods were also in peril. The old market-place at Tombland (from the Norse, meaning 'open space'), where the town's trade had been carried out since the days of the Dane-law, had a new rival. Just over a mile away a new market had been built and new traders, with new privileges, had moved in. It looked as if they were going to make a killing. Norwich wasn't what it used to be, and it never would be again.

The Norman Conquest had come to East Anglia, not in the form of a vast foreign army but in an insidious game of mind control. At Battle, in Sussex, the Conquest had been about military might, as King Harold had discovered to his cost, but the conquest of Britain as a whole would not involve the large-scale dispossession of the Anglo-Saxon population, simply the superimposition of a new system of control upon them.

The Normans did not arrive in their hundreds of thousands eager to displace the local English. Instead an old and successful society was decapitated by a new élite. Out of a population of around two million people in 1066 only about ten thousand were foreign invaders, but they were set to replace the ten thousand most important people in Anglo-Saxon Britain. From this group would come nearly ever new baron, lord, bishop and priest, while the old rulers of this society would find themselves completely dispossessed. By the time the Domesday Book had been compiled in 1086, three-quarters of the assessed value of the country would be in the hands of just two hundred laymen and a hundred churches. After 1070 the Normans appointed no Englishman to any senior religious position and it would be three hundred years before English names reappeared in the ranks of priests and sheriffs. That was the basis for the real Norman Conquest, and that was what had happened to the people of Norwich.

The Norman plan in Norwich was as simple as it was brutal. The new élite in East Anglia took a successful market town and imprinted on it the unmistakable marks of Norman control. The old Saxon church of St Michael's was demolished and a new Norman cathedral was built – far grander than the old building. It was an awe-inspiring demonstration of the Conquest, built in stone and encased in dazzling white limewash. Not only was this a larger, more sophisticated building, it was also the new centre of the bishopric of East Anglia – recently moved from Thetford (and shortly before that Elmham) in Norfolk – with a new Norman bishop, Herbert de Losinga. In a rather half-hearted gesture towards the old ways of worship, a replacement for St Michael's was built, a mile out of town on a steep hill on the wrong side of the river, where those who refused to worship at the Norman church could suffer for their intransigence. All that remains today to hint at the splendour of the original Anglo-Saxon church is a beautiful walrus-ivory cross, uncovered during excavations on the site in the nineteenth century, prior to the building of a public lavatory.

Before the new cathedral foundations had even been started, that other classic piece of Norman architecture, the castle, had arrived in Norwich. It was the 'signature piece' of the Conquest, and shortly after the battle of Hastings, a wooden castle, probably of the motte-and-bailey type, was built here. In some ways it was little more than a fort, a palisaded wooden building on a man-made hill, surrounded by an enclosed area at its foot, but it made a profound point. The people of Norwich had probably seen fortified houses before – Anglo-Saxon England had not been an Eden and at Goltho in Lincolnshire there is archaeological evidence that the manor there was fortified before 1066. Nor was the castle necessarily a Norman idea: one of the earliest had been built in Anjou by the notorious Fulk the Black, a man who, some claimed, was a direct descendant of the devil.

What was undoubtedly different were the sheer numbers, their scale and, of course, the nationality of their owners. Within a short period a sizeable part of the middle of Saxon Norwich had been cleared and the first timber castle built. This was replaced later with a more imposing and ominous stone keep, placed conspicuously in a position where anyone anywhere in Norwich might be reminded of who was in control. As late as 1137 the Anglo-Saxon Chronicle was still complaining: 'And they filled the whole land with these castles. They burdened the unhappy people of the country with forced labour on the castles. And when the castles were made they filled them with wicked men.'

The cathedral and the castle were the reason behind all the building work in Norwich and the desecration of the graveyard. But the new Norman overlords did not think the town was without value. In fact, they were keen to ensure its economic success – they just wanted it to be done in a Norman way. That was why they had built the new market-place away from Tombland, to bring the market under Norman control, and why they were encouraging merchants from France to move to the city and set up a French quarter. The new bishop was one of these entrepreneurs: he had purchased the bishopric of Norwich (along with the abbacy of Winchester in Hampshire for his father) from the King for the huge sum of a thousand pounds. Herbert clearly believed that the incomes from the bishopric would more than compensate for his initial out-lay. The only hitch in his plan was the Church's official dis-approval of the buying of clerical positions – the sin of simony – and he later found it necessary to have a picture of himself painted on the ceiling of his new cathedral buying his office, then repenting of his sin. Indeed, the building of the new cathedral was an act of atonement on his part. Needless to say, his repentance did not lead him to give up his lucrative new office.

The conquest of Norwich was remarkably complete, con-sidering how few Normans were involved in it. The cathedral brought power and influence – to a new Norman clergy; the castle provided security – but not for the Anglo-Saxon locals; the market brought new prosperity – to a new class of Norman and French merchant. And this type of conquest was not unique to Norwich: between 1070 and 1130 every major church in the country was rebuilt and perhaps a thousand castles sprang up. In previously virgin territories new markets were laid out in planned new towns, over five hundred of which were built between the Conquest and 1350, always in the shadow of a Norman church and castle.

But if the conquest seemed complete, it was not unopposed. History is generally written by the winners, as the Bayeux Tapestry shows so eloquently, and the voice of Anglo-Saxon resistance in the years after the Conquest was faint and quickly faded. Nor was it the voice of the ordinary people of Britain, the farmers and labourers who had, in many senses, merely swapped one master for another. But in the years just after the conquest, and close to the building site of Norwich, it can be heard in the words of a monk from Ely in Cambridgeshire, who was composing a book called the *Gesta Herewardi* – the Deeds of Hereward.

The writer of the *Gesta* was one of the last of his kind. His book was not a strictly historical account of a life but a 'ripping yarn' of Anglo-Saxon derring-do, a last cheer for a group of people whom the Normans were erasing from history. Although it was possibly based on first-hand information from some people who had fought with Hereward – and Hereward seems to have been a real man – it included many fictional elements in the heroic and often bloody Anglo-Saxon style. The tale of Hereward, as told in the *Gesta* and greatly elaborated in later medieval documents, is the story of one man's violent fight against the Norman Conquest. It is not the story of an 'ordinary' man: Hereward seems to have been a landowner, so those working his land perhaps had little more sympathy for him than they had for the Norman who replaced him. But in the violent, often unpleasant and resentful character of Hereward lies at least some memory of the struggles of that class of Saxon landowner who lost everything in the Conquest. Hereward the Wake stands for every dispossessed and angry Anglo-Saxon, and his story is, perhaps, their swansong.

You wouldn't have liked Hereward if you had met him in the years leading up to the Conquest. The son of a local landowner, he was a teenage tearaway in the mould of the young Guthlac, but clearly not destined for sainthood. Dispossessed by his father, he had become a mercenary, working both in England and on the continent. On hearing of the Conquest, so the tale goes, he returned home to find that his father's estate, now in his brother's hands, had been confiscated by new Norman lords and his brother's head was displayed on a stake outside the house. Hereward, who was not renowned for his self-control, flew into a rage, killed all those indoors and set his face against the new masters of Britain. In the process he had changed from mercenary to avenging angel, or perhaps Angle. In Norman parlance he became one of the *silvatici*, a member of the Anglo-Saxon resistance who melted away into the forests and swamps as the Normans approached.

The young rebel headed for the centre of resistance to Norman rule in eastern Britain, the Isle of Ely, a superbly defended position surrounded by open water, bog and impenetrable fen. Here he took control of a group of renegades, including the rump of the army that had escaped from the battle of Hastings and began to cause trouble for the Normans. Aided by Danish raiders, still a common sight in what had once been the Danelaw, Hereward despoiled Peterborough in Cambridgeshire, taking the treasure from the abbey before the new Norman Abbot Thurold had arrived. Incensed by this and the growing band of refuseniks gathering round the Saxon Abbot of Ely, William the Conqueror sent nearly two-thirds of his army to surround Ely and smoke out the rebels. A classic game of cat-and-mouse ensued, using all the latest military tricks. William's army began to build a causeway across the fen and Hereward responded by setting fire to oil poured on the waters around the workmen. The Normans replied by protecting their army with the latest development in psychological warfare, a witch, who, the *Gesta* records: '. . . harangued the Isle and its inhabitants for a long time, denouncing saboteurs and suchlike, and casting spells for their overthrow; and at the end of her chattering and incantations she bared her arse at them'.

In fact Ely was never taken by force but, tellingly, by guile. Eventually the abbot, whose monks had been fighting alongside Hereward, tired of the siege and agreed to show the Normans a route to the island – no doubt in return for some unidentified favour. Ely was taken, but Hereward slipped away into the fen and out of history. He was perhaps furious with the abbot for siding with William, but according to the *Gesta*, he himself ended his days no differently:

And so Hereward, the famous knight, tried and known in many places, was received into favour by the king. And with his father's land and possessions he lived on for many years faithfully serving king William and devotedly reconciled to his compatriots and friends. And thus in the end rested in peace, upon whose soul may God have mercy.

The story of Hereward takes us into a world where the Conquest is not a foregone conclusion, where local rebels or Danish allies could still undo what had been achieved at Hastings. But it is not the story of the majority of people who experienced the Conquest. Hereward's world was full of earls and bishops and he was only interested in who sat at the head of the table, not those below the salt. He was, perhaps, the last vestige of that group of wealthy young men who had been forming warbands in the old heroic pagan tradition since the Anglo-Saxons themselves had been the invaders.

Elsewhere in the fen, however, others were resisting, if passively. Our knowledge of this group comes from one remarkable autobiography, dictated to a monk at the abbey of St Albans in Hertfordshire by one of the rebels, Christina of Markyate. Her account of the life of an Anglo-Saxon hermit is unique, the only surviving report of an ordinary Anglo-Saxon's experience of the Conquest and the only female voice to come down to us from this time. Like Hereward, Christina was not just a Saxon peasant. Her family were wealthy landowners in Huntingdon who had every hope of finding an advantageous marriage for their daughter among the new Norman élite.

Indeed, her family seems to have taken a realistic view of the situation: her aunt became the mistress of the soon-to-be Bishop of Durham, Ranulph Flambard, one of the architects of the Domesday Book and, later, the first man successfully to escape from the Tower of London. Christina, however, seems to have experienced the other side of the Conquest when Ranulph, staying in her parents' house, tried to rape her when she was just fourteen.

For Christina's parents, a good marriage was of paramount importance for their daughter, themselves and their family. But if they had hoped it might ally them to the new regime they were to be disappointed. Christina had visited St Albans Abbey as a child and vowed to become a nun, which would, of course, preclude her from marriage. This was not in her family's interests and, possibly through the intervention of her aunt, Ranulph Flambard was asked to arrange her betrothal and marriage to a man called Burthred. In stubborn defiance of the 'new order', Christina refused to consummate the marriage. Her horrified parents, desperate to retain their position in the new scheme of things, tried every trick available to change this, using magic potions, hiring groups of youths to kidnap her, as well as trying to get her drunk. It was even reported that her mother 'in the end swore that she would not care who deflowered her daughter, provided that some way of deflowering her could be found'.

However, Christina's one-woman fight was not over, and she escaped the clutches of both husband and family by disguising herself as a man, leaping from a window and riding off on horseback. Now effectively on the run, she joined an underground religious resistance and became one of a band of mystical hermits who travelled eastern Britain. They provided a focus for passive resistance to the new Norman Church. Passed from safe-house to safe-house by local clergy, they were the recusant priests of their day, secretly keeping alive the old Saxon ways in the face of the overwhelming might of the Norman religious machine.

It was clearly a dangerous life, particularly with an angry husband on her trail, and Christina only found safety in Markyate with a kindly hermit called Roger. He hid her in a small cupboard behind a door wedged shut with a tree-trunk. Inside, she would apparently sit all day in silence on a stone, unable to move or even to wear thick enough clothing to stay warm. Such was her initiation into the religious life. On Roger's death Christina emerged, no doubt somewhat bewildered and, according to her own account, rather constipated. From there she found shelter with another mentor, before finally finding herself under the care of Geoffrey, Abbot of St Albans. She seems to have become something of a guru to him, advising him on the business of the abbey and on the spiritual Anglo-Saxon world that was fast fading. To celebrate their relationship – apparently platonic, despite the monkish gossip of the day – he presented her with a psalter that depicts them together. In return she provided him with hand-stitched underwear. She ended her days in Markyate, having inherited Roger's cell, and turned it into a small priory for women, which survived until the dissolution of the monasteries under Henry VIII.

The extraordinary events in Christina's life are a unique insight into the last days of the Anglo-Saxon aristocracy and Church. But the desire of her family to integrate into the new Norman order proved little more than wishful thinking: within twenty years only two of around four thousand Saxon thegns (barons) still held their lands and title. The intimate experience of Saxon Christianity would not survive much longer. In villages and towns across Britain, Anglo-Saxon saints were repudiated, their shrines and churches razed to the ground. In their place came the vast, expansive, reformed Christianity of the Normans, expressed in the huge stone vaults of cathedrals and bishops' palaces, and the economic might of the new all-male, financially savvy, monastic orders. It was still Christianity, but on a corporate scale.

While the lives of the Herewards and Christinas of the age were turned on their heads, it is harder to see the effects of the Conquest in the fields and villages of Britain, beyond the relentless replacement of the old wooden churches. Finding the 99 per cent of the population who were still living a rural subsistence life in the countryside is complicated. Few, if any, documents written by them survive and the homes and fields where they lived and worked have been built on and ploughed over many times since by later generations of farmers and labourers.

What we do have, courtesy of Ranulph Flambard and others, is the Domesday Survey, a huge reckoning of the ownership and value of large tracts of Britain at two dates: just before the Conquest and at compilation, around 1086. The information it contains often seems a little bald, but it gives us a snapshot of parts of rural Britain. In Pinbury in Gloucestershire the Domesday details are supplemented by a survey undertaken by the manor's owner, the nuns of Caen in Normandy, in about 1120, which gives us a clearer glimpse of this world.

Domesday for Pinbury states: 'There are three hides. In demesne are three ploughs. Eight villeins and a smith with three ploughs. There are nine slaves. A mill at forty pence. It was and is worth four pounds.' By combining this with the later survey it is possible to decode this cryptic entry and look at a Domesday village. Each of the three ploughs mentioned 'in demesne' would have been pulled by a team of eight oxen and were used to work the lord's land, using the labour of his tied tenants and slaves. Another three ploughs were owned by those tied tenants, who each owned perhaps two or three oxen, which they teamed up to work their own holdings. This could only be done when they were not working for the lord, who, the late survey claimed, demanded five days' work from each of them every week. The smith – a blacksmith – might have had some land to work but his main job was repairing agricultural equipment, such as plough shares, iron cartwheel tyres and scythes. The nine slaves worked solely for the lord, six operating the three demesne ploughs and the other three caring for the manor's animals, which in 1120 included seventeen cattle, a horse, 122 sheep and ten pigs. The mill made its profit from charging the estate peasants to grind their corn.

Pinbury was a small settlement, but a reasonably typical one. For its owners in Caen it was just a source of money – the four pounds mentioned in Domesday, which was presumably partly raised from selling the produce of the demesne. For the eighteen or nineteen families living there, including the slaves, villeins (peasant-farmers), smith and priest, it was their world – a village of perhaps ninety people surrounded by seven hundred acres of cornfields, some pasture for the sheep and cattle and perhaps a small wood for fuel and building materials. Each villein here tended around forty acres of land on the two days of the week when they were not tending their lord's, and from this they fed their family and sold any surplus to help pay the lord's rent, which formed the rest of the four-pound value of the manor.

But neither Domesday nor later surveys gives us an intimate view into the people's lives. To see how they lived we must find a village that hasn't changed and for that we need to find a village that hasn't survived to the present day. Among the humps and bumps in fields that mark the sites of these deserted villages we can still conjure the ghosts of twelfth-century villagers.

Nearly forty years of excavation at Wharram Percy in Yorkshire have made it possible to imagine this world, the people who inhabited it and the sights and sounds of their everyday lives. Now, as we stand outside the roofless church that today lies at the centre of an open field, we might imagine, as the setting sun casts long shadows over the grassy mounds around us, that those humps are houses. Wharram is a living village, whose central street is lined with wooden cottages. At one end stands the manor house, which rules this little world, the home of the landowners or, in this case, their agent, the bailiff, to whom all the villagers owe their living. He controls nearly every aspect of secular life: he runs the local courts, collects fines, rents and taxes, demands labour and services from the people and musters the men when the call to battle comes. Most of the people he controls are 'tied' to his employer, the landlord; indeed, in theory they belong to him. In some documents their children are even referred to as a 'litter', using the terminology of animal rearing to describe them. They must work on the lord's land for most of the time, as at Pinbury, and they must pay rents on their own land, either in cash received from selling their surplus, or 'in kind', as at Strathearn in Scotland where the rent around 1200 was paid in grain, malt, cheese, fowls and game. More exotically, the medieval rent for the Isles of Scilly was paid during some periods in puffins. In return for their service and rents the villagers receive the right to work a small parcel of land from which they feed their families, and perhaps some protection from the predations of other landlords. It is a world of Norman haves and Anglo-Saxon have-nots, and it is no coincidence that modern words for animals, such as 'pig' and 'cow', are Anglo-Saxon while the names of the luxury foods they produce, 'pork' and 'beef', are Norman French. The villagers did the work, and the lords enjoyed the results.

Walking into one of the villagers houses we are entering an alien world. This village is not the chocolate-box image of rural England, with its thatched cottages and smoke curling from a hundred little chimneys: these people live in longhouses, rectangular buildings about thirty feet long by fifteen wide, divided with wattle partitions into a communal 'hall' for cooking and eating and a more private 'chamber' for sleeping. This is the home of a single family, two parents, their children and, perhaps, a servant or two. In a little place like Wharram, nearly all young adults would have spent some time in service in other villagers' houses, particularly if the head of the household was a widow who needed help in the fields. Nor does this place live up to the cosy modern image of the rural farm.

There are no cowsheds and byres, no farmyard, no separate pigsties and sheep pens: the animals live in the longhouse too, protected from the winter cold by the same fire that warms the family. They are corralled at one end of the building in winter, when the Yorkshire weather makes keeping them outside impossible. To improve sanitation, the floor at that end slopes to allow the animals' urine to run away from the living area. All the same, the smell must be quite potent as it mingles with the thick smoke from the chimneyless, dung-burning fire.

But we would be wrong to think that these people live like animals. They may define their social space differently from us but they have many of the same cares. The floors of the main part of the house are dished, due to the incessant sweeping that keeps the place meticulously clean. Nor are the occupants unconcerned about their appearance: in the wooden chest in the chamber we might find a brave collection of metal brooches and dress fastenings, perhaps a pair of scissors and a decorated belt. There is some concern for security too: the door has strong iron hinges and a lock from which hangs a bunch of keys. There is little in the way of furniture or valuables in the house but there is a small pile of money – silver pennies: this is a sophisticated monetary economy where the traditional bartering has given way to paying with coins. If we look closely we might even see that some coins have been clipped to remove small amounts of silver in an attempt to make the money go a little further.

Nearby a bow and a quiver of arrows with worn tips is a reminder that men were expected to practise archery regularly. Their lord was obliged to provide a number of fighting men for war, should the King demand it, and it was his duty to make sure that his men were ready. The tools of a more peaceful but no less arduous everyday life also lie around: the iron firedogs on the hearth for cooking, the wooden bowls, and cups made from moulded cow horn. Against the hall wall are propped the benches, trestles and table-top used for the two daily meals, served at about ten in the morning and four in the afternoon. In the corner the iron share of a recently repaired plough and an iron scythe speak of a life spent in the fields.

To meet the villagers of Wharram we must return to the ruined church where, as part of the large-scale investigation of the village, the graveyard was excavated by archaeologists. Analysis of the bones from seven hundred people buried here gives us our best view of a medieval rural population anywhere in Britain. Life for the villagers in Wharram was hard, and began with the lottery of surviving birth and infancy. Babies were breastfed for around the first eighteen months, which helped to develop their immune systems in a pathogen-rich world and acted as a form of contraception for their mothers. Only about half lived to adulthood, but of those half again might reach over fifty. Strangely, twice as many people here were left-handed as commonly occurs today, perhaps representing a natural rate of left-handedness in an era before children were forced to use their right hands. Among the adults there were more men than women, perhaps because women were more socially mobile and were attracted to the nearby city of York by the prospect of paid work. Excavations in York seem to confirm this, with more female remains there than male. Of the women who stayed, osteoporosis was a main cause of health problems in the over fifties, but a healthy diet, including plenty of fish – this was a time when the Church forbade meat on Wednesday, Friday and Saturday – might have alleviated it. The freshness of the fish, when it arrived so far inland, was another matter.

The lives of the villagers of Wharram were highly structured and centred round the institutions of their village – the manorial court and the church. An inflexible class system marked out the rights and duties of all, from the lord of the manor at the top to the slaves at the bottom. Below the lord, 'sokemen' could, with some justification, call themselves free as they owned rights in land and benefited from certain legal privileges. Next came the 'villeins' – peasant farmers often making a reasonable living and holding between them 40 per cent of all the land mentioned in Domesday – then the 'bordars' and 'cottars', who made up nearly as high a percentage of the population as the villeins but held only 5 per cent of the land. The poorest cottars could take pride in possessing *some* land, unlike the slaves, who owned nothing. But even the slaves had something to look forward to: by 1200 slavery had been all but abolished in Britain – indeed, the nine slaves recorded in Domesday at Pinbury were no longer referred to as such by 1120.

The rights and privileges of these groups, and most import-antly the rights of the lord, were maintained in the regular courts, where the community gathered to regulate its world. As the population increased, Lords took more direct interest in their manors – higher prices and lower wages made them more profitable – and a burgeoning legal system, operating through these courts, developed to support this. The end result would be to wipe away the subtle distinctions between the people of the village and legally class all the people of Britain into just two main categories, free and unfree, the latter being defined by the thirteenth-century legal writer Bracton as: 'Some-one who wakes up in the morning not knowing what the lord will expect of him that day.'

The courts that once upheld these definitions, the 'Courts Baron' for the free and the 'Courts Leet' for everyone else, used to exist in every manor in Britain, dealing with the day-to-day problems of village life and ensuring that the lord of the manor, and ultimately the King, received his dues. Even today a few 'Courts Leet' survive, stripped of much of their power, but still acting out the legal rituals of a lost medieval world. High on the North Yorkshire Moors the castle of Danby was never an impressive fortification, even in its heyday, and today it lies partly in ruins, but once a year it gives a glimpse of how every manor in the country must once have been run. A Court Leet is still held in the hall annually, presided over by the lord of Danby, as it has been for the last seven hundred years. Today much of the court's power has gone and the lord has few rights other than to fine villagers who misuse the local common grazing land.

Cases brought to the manorial court were investigated by a

jury appointed by the lord (old Saxon trials by ordeal had been largely abolished by the early thirteenth century), and covered everything from infringements of common land and border disputes to the more serious crimes that plagued an often violent society. Without a standing police force, individuals often took the law into their own hands. The results could be bloody, as an entry in the Chronicle of a St Albans monk, Matthew Paris, for 1248 shows:

For a certain Norfolk Knight ... Named Geoffrey de Millers, wretchedly lead astray, one night secretly entered the house of a knight called John Brito to sleep with his daughter. But he was prevented by some people placed in ambush ... He was seized, savagely thrown to the ground and badly wounded. Then he was suspended from a beam by his feet with his legs stretched apart, so that he was completely at the mercy of his enemies, who disgracefully mutilated him by cutting off his genital organs, though he would have preferred to be beheaded. Thus wounded and castrated, he was thrown out half dead.

On a more mundane level the courts saw to the maintenance of the roads, fences and ditches, conveyed land, and appointed a variety of local officers, including constables, ale-tasters, dog-muzzlers and 'pinders' to round up stray animals on common land. On the judicial side they dealt with trespass, libel, assault and breach of contract. In court the accused might be asked to explain their actions or provide friends to vouch for them. The guilty party (also decided by the jury) would then be judged, and a punishment decided upon – often a fine.

In fact, the villagers at places like Danby and Wharram were plagued by fines. There were fines for not turning up in court, fines for not providing service to your lord, fines for grubbingup hedges, fines for digging illegal ditches, and fines for not paying fines. For those classified as 'unfree' their lord's reach went further still: into their social lives and moral values. They had to pay for a licence to marry, to move, to educate their sons, to have children out of wedlock; for women who were sexually active but not married, there was a 'leirwite', a fine for 'lying down'. Even death didn't provide an escape: the heriot – a fine of the family's 'best beast' – was payable to the lord of the manor on the death of the head of the household. It was a considerable loss for any poor family. Some tried to evade the fines by appealing to the King's Court in an attempt to escape the control of their lord. In 1224 William, the son of Henry of Pilton in Rutland, cheekily petitioned the King's Court to restore his free land to him, which he claimed had been taken by Bartholomew, son of Eustace. Bartholomew countered that William was not free but one of his villeins, for which he provided evidence of William's onerous services. The case was dismissed and sent back to the manor court. That court, of course, was overseen by Bartholomew himself, who probably didn't look kindly on William's petition.

Most common in the local courts were fines for petty fraud. The mill in every settlement was a common cause of litigation. Lords usually retained the right to grind in their mill all the corn in their village – a convenience to the villagers for which the lords charged a premium. Poor villagers were naturally unwilling to pay and a thriving trade took place across the country in small, illegal handmills in which a family could grind their own corn. Almost certainly, had we looked into one of the darker corners of any house in Wharram, we would have seen such a mill, and its owner would tread a delicate line between grinding enough corn in the lord's mill not to be noticed and the rest in her own mill to save money. When she got the balance wrong, she was liable to find herself in court and fined.

Similar problems arose for the lord with the assizes – laws that regulated the size, weight and strength of staple foods. Each year he would appoint ale-tasters to ensure that locally brewed beer was sold in the correct units of the correct strength. Brewing was a popular way of making money, particularly for women, and even a little village like Brigstock in Northamptonshire had thirty-eight brewers. The job of ale-taster was thus highly desirable, and at the end of the taster's year in office it was usual to fine him too – allegedly for failing in his duty but in reality for having been lucky enough to drink free ale all year.

The increasing legal complexity of local courts and the growing obsession among landowners with recording laws and cases in writing has often been seen as a sign of how oppressed the people of rural Britain were, but, in fact, the increasingly legal world in which they were forced to live was also providing benefits not seen in other European countries. The lords recorded events to increase their own power but that recording also had the effect of permanently memorializing the customs and rights of the people. The men and women who arrived at the manor court were not ignorant fools, there to be bamboozled by clever London lawyers, they were becoming astute participants in a legal system that worked both ways (if weighted in favour of the lords). Even in villages where few could read and write, everyone was aware of the value of charters for transferring land and they were accustomed to even more sophisticated documents. By the mid-thirteenth century even vagrants were required to carry certificates of good character. In Essex, in 1248, five men were acquitted of theft, then forbidden to return to the county without 'their testimonial of trustworthiness'. Receipts for goods were also coming into use, something the gullible John le Keche and friends must have wished they had got when they were accused of theft in 1291. In the end they were acquitted by the jury but reprimanded for buying animals 'without the warrant that they could have had'. Legal documents were becoming ubiquitous. In every longhouse on Wharram's street we might have found a box that held six or seven written deeds setting out the rights of the tenant to their land or property.

Groups of villagers were even beginning to club together to take on their lord in court. The tenants of South Petherton in Somerset hired a lawyer in the late thirteenth century for the considerable fee (even for a lawyer) of five pounds. They claimed in court that their lord had seized goods worth a hundred pounds from them after they complained about his attempts to confiscate the property of widows who had committed adultery. Clearly they resented the interference of the lord in their lives and, rather than being disobedient or running away, they used the law as a new, if often unsuccessful, way to fight.

Nor were villeins content with legally challenging their lord: in an increasingly literate world they were taking on each other. At Hinderclay in Suffolk the court rolls show two villeins, Nicholas and Robert, continually hiring lawyers to press their claims in a sophisticated dispute over property rights and debt. From the surviving documents it is also clear that they were using the law to air more personal grievances: the claim and counter-claim had as much to do with the discovery by one of the litigants that his wife was having an affair with the other as they did with property and debt. In one extraordinary incident, Nicholas claimed he invited Robert to his house but Robert used the opportunity to sleep with his wife. When

Nicholas walked in and found them in a compromising position, he attacked Robert, tied him up and tried to turn the situation to his advantage by renegotiating a debt he owed him in front of several witnesses. It conjures a scene that might have come from the pages of the *Canterbury Tales* were it not, in fact, true.

If the local court record gives us an insight into the daily concerns of the people of rural Britain, the village church allows us to glimpse their deeper hopes and fears. The church had been central to rural life since long before the Conquest, but the replacement of all those wooden Saxon churches with stone Norman ones was perhaps the greatest single indication to the people of Britain of how their world had changed. A medieval church was not simply a place where you spent Sunday morning but the social centre of the village. The priest organised the religious festivals and services that marked out the agricultural year, it provided a billboard on which individuals might display their piety through gifts, it celebrated the stages of every village life, from christening to burial, and it provided moral guidance with a greater final sanction than that imposed in the local court.

Even the tiniest local church provided an extraordinary link between the ethereal, cultured world of European Christianity, centred on the great universities such as Paris, and the people working the fields. Following debates at the gathering of Catholic cardinals know as the Fourth Lateran Council in 1215 (an event that must have seemed distant to the villagers), the Church was changing, and that change would be communicated to ordinary people, wherever they were, through the little stone building in their village. A religion that had once preached that only the very righteous – monks – would get into heaven was now offering universal salvation. The Church would look after you from cradle to grave – a form of medieval welfare state – and offered the chance of eternal life at the end. Through devotion and moral rectitude, anyone could enter the new democratic heaven, and the route map to get there was painted on nearly every church wall in the country.

The Reformation, and perhaps more importantly the Civil War, have scrubbed the evidence of this world from the walls of all our churches. When Norman churches sprang up in every village, they were decorated with gaudy depictions of Biblical stories – the comic strips of their day – which provided colourful graphic descriptions of the lives of saints and the subjects of sermons. They were not 'high art' – but they represented the hopes and fears of the ordinary people of the village. A common theme in these pictures was the road to salvation (and the slippery path to hell) in the form of 'Doom paintings' – so called because they portrayed the final judgement on Doomsday: a magnificent, if stern, Christ stands in judgement, often above the chancel arch, with the righteous proceeding to heaven up one side of the wall and the damned falling into hell on the other. Look carefully at the individuals painted on each side: they are not simply 'standard' figures. Each is an individual, some may represent people in the village (perhaps those who paid most to commission the painting on their triumphant way up to heaven), whose beliefs are clearly displayed in the good and bad things they have done that they consider will interest God. At Trotton in Suffolk a more peculiar painting shows two naked men, one pious with all good things flowing from his body, and one damned, showing in lurid detail the parts of the body from which his sins emanated. At Chaldon in Surrey the whole process is shown on a 'ladder of salvation', which connects a group of devils at the base, demonstrating the wages and causes of sin, and angels above in heaven. Clinging

167

precariously to this ladder, the righteous are climbing to heaven, and the sinful tumbling past them to hell.

The people who commissioned the paintings were not lords of the manor or priests but the middling sort of villagers – the millers and freemen with a little money and a lot to prove. The few records that survive in churchwardens' accounts and bishops' visitation records from before the Black Death show that they arranged fundraising events to pay for them, no different in their way from today's church fetes or car boot sales. These included fancy-dress processions and the occasionally rowdy 'church ales' where the young men brewed a beer to be sold on behalf of the church. Decorations in the church were also often paid for by these fundraisers and their wives. One woman left her second-best dress to be made into a cushion for her local Lady Chapel, no doubt to replace a threadbare example she had seen there every week for years gone by. She also bequeathed her rosary to be kept at the back of the church for anyone who had forgotten theirs – an embarrassment which had perhaps happened to her on occasion but which she could now prevent happening to others.

While the church in villages like Wharram might have drawn communities closer together, in the burgeoning towns of the period it could just as easily drive them apart. In Norwich in 1150, many of the former complaints of the inhabitants had died away. Normans, Frenchmen and Anglo-Saxons were becoming harder to distinguish from each other and the insult of the partial demolition of their town after the Conquest had been forgotten in the light of its new financial success. Norwich was now a cosmopolitan place, with English, French, Flemish and Jewish communities. The Jewish inhabitants of Britain's rapidly growing towns provided an essential service enabling that growth: credit. In a Christian world that banned moneylending, only non-Christians could theoretically extend the lines of credit necessary to expand businesses and trade, and the Jewish community was at the heart of this industry. But success brought with it suspicion and this was growing to ugly proportions.

In Norwich the event that brought the tensions to boiling-point had occurred at Easter in 1144: the body of a boy called William was found just outside Norwich at Thorpe Wood. How this twelve year old apprentice tanner came by his death is uncertain but it was claimed that he was found hanging naked from a tree, stabbed and bleeding. His uncle, a married priest (still possible at this date), had blamed the Jewish community, who had only recently arrived in Norwich (in the 1130s), but no one had been prosecuted. Around 1150 all that changed, however, when a monk called Thomas arrived in the town from Monmouth, in Wales. He seems to have believed there had been a cover-up and went about interviewing witnesses and putting together what he claimed was a true account of William's death. In writing up the story he determined to turn the boy into a saint and a martyr, and for that he had to have been murdered. For a culprit, he saw no reason to look further than the Jewish community of the city who had initially taken the blame. His 'imaginative' account of how a young Christian boy was kidnapped by the Jews of Norwich, ritually crucified and his blood drained to make unleavened bread, spread like wildfire among the various communities in the city and the sinister fiction of the 'predatory Jew', desperate for the blood of Christian children, had been born. It was an image that would haunt the Christian imagination for centuries.

The birth of the 'blood libel' in Norwich in 1150 speaks volumes about the stresses and concerns of city life in this period of precocious urban expansion. A cult, with associated miracles, quickly developed around William and brought pilgrims and their money flooding to the city although his sainthood was never recognised by the papacy. Thomas was employed to run the shrine of St William, and the boy saint became credited with such wonders as drawing a valuable ring from the finger of a pilgrim – a rather self-serving miracle. Of course, many cities relied on local saints to help them prosper: saints brought money and religious orders, who provided some of the social fabric of the city. Monasteries and churches distributed charity to poor newcomers while they looked for work; they furnished hospitals for the sick and gave food to the destitute. Every city needed these services, and a saint could only help it to get them. Norwich had been in particular need of such a saint as the local candidate – St Edmund, a former Anglo-Saxon king of East Anglia who was allegedly 'blood-eagled' by Ivarr the Boneless, like poor Aelle of Northumbria – had been taken up by the nearby town of Bury. Since then there had been such competition between Bury and Norwich that the Abbot of Bury had extended his church by a few feet when he heard the new Norman cathedral of Norwich was to be larger than his own. Having a saint was good for business and Norwich now had its own, even if that had meant vilifying an innocent community.

It was not long before vilification went beyond a war of words and physical retribution was visited on the Jewish community. Those Christians in debt to Jewish money-lenders finally had a reason to default on their payments and perhaps take more violent action against those they blamed for their financial situation. What had been a useful line of credit could easily become a burdensome debt, and the opportunity to evade paying was not lost on the 'indignant' burghers of Norwich. And with interest rates sometimes as high as 43 per cent, it must have seemed a good time to stop paying. The Jewish communities in Britain would survive this first attack, but from now on, at times of social stress, they would frequently find themselves accused of ritual murder. On 16 March 1190 nearly the whole Jewish community of York was either massacred or committed suicide when their sanctuary in Clifford's Tower was attacked, after just such an accusation.

The Church also shamefully exploited xenophobic attitudes towards Jews, insisting they fast during Lent like Christians and wear distinctive badges – two strips of yellow cloth, six inches long and three wide – to identify them. While they were under the King's protection – all British Jews were theoretically his chattels – many Jews thrived, as long as he could claw back large taxes from their profits. However, in 1250, when Edward I secured credit from the Italian banking-houses of the Frescobaldi and Riccardi, who had somehow avoided the Christian ban on usury, he expelled the Jewish community from Britain and their role in helping to forge urban Britain was conveniently forgotten.

The spread of urbanism, particularly in the south-east, in the years between the Conquest and the Black Death of 1348, was extraordinary. Towns offered opportunities that village life could not, away from the daily grind of growing enough to eat while lining the coffers of your lord. In towns you could take paid employment, and this lured the young women of Wharram to York. On a much larger scale, it was the returns from such businesses that attracted a whole new group of entrepreneurs to Britain: monks.

The Norman Conquest had brought with it a wholesale reformation of the Anglo-Saxon Church. The personal, mystical, monastic experience offered by Christina of Markyate was replaced with a large-scale, reformed monastic tradition based around new religious orders. The reformation of monasteries was supposedly encouraged by the laxity of Anglo-Saxon houses, which were accused of luxurious excess and moral turpitude –indeed, the papacy had sanctioned the Norman Conquest for this very reason. Not all of the new orders lived up to their promise, though, and the wealthier ones, who lived largely off huge land endowments, seem quickly to have slipped back into easier ways. In St Albans, Matthew Paris wrote with some disgust at the excesses of the Abbot of Thetford, a member of the hugely wealthy Cluniac order, accusing him of '. . . indulging in immoderate feasting and drinking. He seldom went to mass, was seldom present at the canonical houses, and in the morning, drunk, he vomited forth his nocturnal potations.'

It seems also that the Abbot liked to invite his non-clerical friends to enjoy the luxurious monastic life with him, and Paris singled out one in particular: '. . . Guisgard, whose belly was like a bladder in frosty weather and whose body was a cartload, stayed longer; and all the monks' provisions were engulfed in the Charybdis of his belly. Afterwards, thoroughly gorged, he despised and insulted them.'

Perhaps he simply couldn't get enough 'Principal Pudding' for which a recipe survives. It was eaten at Westminster Abbey, and calls for six pounds of currants, 300 eggs and at least 181 pounds of suet.

However, one new order was renowned for its strict order and purity: the White Monks, or Cistercians. Yet, despite their strict regime, the experience of religion they brought with them had as much to do with profit as piety. The effect of the Cistercians' arrival in any area of Britain was immense. They were supposedly a withdrawn and contemplative order, divorced from the real world, but in fact they were the masters of Britain's first agribusiness. Their foundation at Meaux in Yorkshire was bequeathed to them by the Earl of Albemarle in lieu of a vow to go on pilgrimage to Jerusalem, which he was now apparently too old and fat to honour. The monastery was an offshoot of the great Yorkshire Fountains Abbey and, like all Cistercian houses, was supposedly a place of silent contemplation and fasting. The Cistercians devoted themselves to prayer and manual labour, unlike those who lived off land grants and rents. Cistercian monks were segregated from the outside world and even from their lay-brothers, who provided for them. They were not, however, divorced from economic sensibilities and they managed the Cistercian 'corporation' while the lay-brothers worked the estates that would change this part of Yorkshire for ever.

For the White Monks the attraction of Meaux was wool. It was one of Britain's main exports and a trade they intended to dominate. To do this they needed to build a port for their mother-house, the wool-producing Fountains Abbey, so they used the land at Meaux to build a new abbey that would, in turn, build a port to run Fountains's export business. That port would become the city of Hull. It was the industrious monks of Meaux who dredged the little settlement of Wyke, where Hull would grow up, who drained nearly the entire valley in which it stood, and widened and canalised the river to allow the container-ships of their day – cogs capable of transporting up to 300 tons of wool – into the port. They also expanded the transport infrastructure to bring the wool from Fountains to the port. Where villages or villagers got in the way, the Cistercians were ruthless. They took over Thorpe Underwood in North Yorkshire and dispossessed the peasants. In its place a sort of collective farm was set up where former tenants might work if they became lay-brothers – provided they were men. Those who did not want to join, along with the abandoned wives and children of those who had, could leave, although it is difficult to imagine where they might have gone.

Perhaps some went to Hull where there were opportunities for employment in the burgeoning import/export trade that the Cistercians were stimulating. As well as exporting wool, the city became a major customs centre for imports: it was the main route for wine into the north-east of the country and a primary entry-point for cloth dye. Free from the strict controls of a country lord, groups of townsfolk, both men and women, formed co-operatives to buy trading ships and cargoes. The villagers at Wharram Percy, some fifty miles distant, might even have bought some of their thrice-weekly fish ration from them: dried fish was regularly imported here from Iceland. Other innovations and ideas arrived through the port, including bricks for building (they were often carried on ships as ballast) and Britain's first frying-pans. By 1203 Hull was the sixth largest town in England and by 1290 it ranked third.

For the Cistercians, the twelfth and thirteenth centuries were a boom time. By 1300 there were over 1.5 million sheep in Yorkshire alone. Along with the sheep, the human population soared: labour grew cheaper, prices rose and some landlords made huge profits. In particular cities benefited. By 1300 London had a population of around eighty thousand, making it larger than the cities of Flanders or the Rhine valley, and not much smaller than Paris. Rents in the most expensive shopping street, Cheapside, had doubled in just fifty years. It was a thriving, cosmopolitan trading centre attracting all the problems that modern cities do. Richard of Devizes, in his *Chronicle of the Deeds of Richard I* of the late twelfth century, warns:

Free and Unfree

Behold! I warn you whatever of evil or perversity there is in any, whatever in all parts of the world, you will find in that city alone. Go not to the dances of panders, nor mix yourself up with the herds of houses of ill-repute; avoid the dice, the theatre and the tavern. You will find more braggadocios there than in all France, while the number of flatterers is infinite. Stage players, buffoons, evildoers ... druggists ... fortune-tellers, extortioners, nightly-strollers, magicians, mimics, common-beggars ... So if you do not wish to live with the shameful, you will not dwell in London.

London might have been a den of vice and iniquity, but it was becoming a very wealthy one. For the rich, times had never been better but the gap between rich and poor had never been wider. As the population boomed the manual workforce – the engine of the medieval economy – received less money for their labour and paid higher prices for the increasingly scarce staple commodities. By the dawning of the year 1300, they needed a white knight to charge over the horizon if their lives were to improve. What they got was a Horseman of the Apocalypse.

For the Cistercians and other large landowners, the spiralling population offered an endless supply of cheap labour with little or no bargaining power. But even these poor workers had one requirement that could not be bargained away: food. A rising population might have driven down wages, but it required feeding. While the weather remained good and diseases stayed away, all was well, but with each year as the population grew it would have taken a little less to push it over the edge into famine. After 1300 the scales were tipping.

We often think of the Black Death as coming out of the blue, suddenly hitting a merry Chaucerian world that had been unchanged for centuries. In fact, the fifty years leading up to it provided a grotesque overture to the coming carnage. After

175

poor harvests at the end of the thirteenth century, the misery set in for the rural population in the autumn of 1314 when heavy rains knocked down crops and caused widespread food shortages. The following winter was hard, as people eked out their supplies from the previous year and grain prices on the open market quadrupled. The next year, when the harvest failed again, there was nowhere left to turn. In a world where small-holders could rarely produce enough to store for over a year, the cupboards were now bare, and the Great Famine was about to begin. The Bishop of Winchester grimly noted a 60 per cent fall in the yield from his manors in southern England.

The people back in Hinderclay in Suffolk had more immediate concerns. They had long since given up suing each other and were now turning their legal minds to an increasingly desperate land market: the poor sold their livelihoods to the few remaining rich tenants in a last-ditch attempt to buy food. As the situation worsened, court rolls show prosecutions for increasingly petty offences, mainly the theft of food. In April 1316 John Bray of Wakefield was accused by his father of stealing a bushel of oats from him. While there might never have been much love lost between the pair, the shortage must have been acute for a father not to overlook the 'borrowing' of food by his starving son.

Food shortages continued into 1316 and 1317, accompanied by further crop failures and other horrors. The warm, wet weather encouraged disease in the one food source to survive the famine: the livestock. Diseases known as 'murrains', perhaps foot-and-mouth disease or similar, struck livestock in 1319, 1320 and 1321. Heavy rain also reduced salt production, making it harder for villagers to preserve the meat they could find.

Nor were they just falling prey to natural disasters: King

Edward I had spent the latter part of the thirteenth century and the first part of the fourteenth actively engaged in the conquest of Wales, then Scotland, imposing heavy taxes to pay for it. Reverses like the natural disasters of the early years of the century offered his enemies the chance to fight back. Scottish raids into northern England increased, and the ordinary farmers of the region bore the brunt of their wrath. In 1319 a Scottish army was raiding as far south as the valley where the Wharram Percy villagers lived.

Retaliatory English missions wrought similar havoc on the starving Scottish farmers north of the border. Money had to be spent on arms and fortifications, rebuilding pillaged communities and paying off bands of brigands. Between 1338 and 1340 the towns of southern Britain had to endure attacks from Edward's other enemy, France. All this against a background of crop failure and disease.

The immediate effect of these troubles was that the population of Britain, which had perhaps topped five million in 1300, was falling: perhaps half a million had died as a result of the famine and other disasters. Even the survivors were becoming what is euphemistically known as 'harvest sensitive' – always just a bad harvest away from starvation. In London people were trampled to death in queues for bread and there were even reports of cannibalism. It was in this weakened and bewildered state that the people of Britain faced up to the most cataclysmic natural disaster ever to hit our shores.

Black Death had been recorded in China since 1000 BC and since then had spread across Asia and Europe in several pandemics. The disease is caused by a bacterium, *Yersinia pestis*, and is today relatively simple to treat with antibiotics. In 1348 it was a very different proposition. Of the three forms of the disease, septicaemic plague, passed on by direct transmission into the blood, is the swiftest: the victim turns purple, due to haemorrhaging under the skin and often dies within hours of onset. The pneumonic form of the disease is passed on by inhaling infected droplets from a victim's breath and causes, among other things, bleeding in the lungs, which also leads to death.

Plague probably arrived in Britain in the summer of 1348 in its third, most infamous form: on the back of an apparently innocuous black rat that jumped ship somewhere on the south coast, possibly at Melcombe Regis near Weymouth in Dorset. That rat, like all rats, carried fleas, but these fleas carried plague. A bite from such a flea can lead to the infamous 'bubonic' form of plague. For the first two to six days after being bitten the victim might not even feel ill, but then the disease develops rapidly. Contemporary sources claim that the early symptoms included a rising temperature, sleeplessness, vomiting and sometimes convulsions. A splitting headache followed, accompanied by giddiness, intolerance to light, pain in the lower abdomen, arms and legs, and sometimes delirium. On the second or third day the temperature would fall, but the eyes became bloodshot and the tongue swelled, revealing a coating of white fur. Later it dried and the fur turned yellow or brown. Then pus-filled swellings developed under the arms, on the neck and in the groin – the buboes that gave the disease its name. From them, bacteria invaded the bloodstream and death followed swiftly on.

On the day that the black rat clambered ashore the people at Melcombe Regis were probably aware that a devastating disease was sweeping Europe, but they had no means of knowing how it was spreading or what they could do to stop it. In Weymouth docks, that rat found many others to carry its fleas and from that small 'beachhead' plague swept across the country at a devastating rate. Britain at this time is often thought of as a small world in which villagers rarely travelled further than a few miles to their local market. In fact, it was a vibrant, cohesive land, where monks, officials and traders regularly travelled long distances and where intensive trade between local towns and villages tied even the smallest community into a nationwide trading network. Pilgrimage was also becoming increasingly popular: to Canterbury after the assassination of Thomas Becket in 1170, and even further afield to Santiago de Compostela in northern Spain, Rome and Jerusalem. This network helped plague to spread with devastating speed: in some respects Britain had become a victim of its own success.

In the major towns and cities, the spread of plague from the south coast was closely monitored as travellers brought news of the latest place to fall victim. Of course, there is a good chance that the messengers brought it with them too, although a nervous Bishop Eddington of Winchester could have had little idea of that when he recorded, 'We report with anguish the serious news, which has come to our ears: that this cruel plague has now begun a savage attack on the coastal areas of England. We are struck by terror lest (may God avert it!) this brutal disease should rage in any part of our city or diocese.'

His prayers were to be in vain. Plague was already raging in his diocese only thirty kilometres away, and Winchester would become one of the worst hit places in Britain. The people of the town, however, expected Eddington to do something about it. In the autumn of 1348 life in Winchester still centred on its church, which provided an explanation of the origin of the world, the purpose of life and the celestial rewards and punishments that encouraged people to live a good life. Much that happened in the natural world was interpreted in terms of the will of God, and everyday events were viewed as evidence of His direct intervention in the minutiae of daily life. The Church acted as intermediary between this active God and the population who hoped to curry His favour and avoid His wrath. With the arrival of a disease that looked very much like a Biblical plague, they expected the Church to intervene with practical advice on how they could avert the catastrophe. If it was to retain its position in their minds it had to produce results quickly. Of course it couldn't.

Bishop Eddington might have believed in the power of the Church to prevent disaster as wholeheartedly as his flock did. In November 1348 he issued advice on how to avoid the Black Death: 'the approved teaching of the Holy Fathers that sickness and premature death often come from sin and that by the healing of souls this kind of sickness is known to cease'. The inhabitants of Winchester were instructed to say twenty-two penitential psalms of Wednesday and Saturdays and to join the brethren of the abbey in processing round the town each Friday. But this proved woefully inadequate. At his manor of Bishop's Waltham in Hampshire, where the ruined walls of his magnificent palace still stand, the plague had torn the heart out of the community. Of the 404 tenants who held land from him there, 164 were dead. At Quob, a hamlet in Hampshire, the manorial court roll records the death knell of an entire community, stating grimly that: 'All and each of the tithing died in the present pestilence.' The village was never inhabited again.

In Winchester itself, tensions between Church and town were growing. The abbey and cathedral of St Swithun's was continuing to bury the dead in its graveyard within the town walls, causing consternation among a population who were convinced that this might spread the plague further. Events came to a head on 21 January 1349 when a monk of the monastery, Ralph de Staunton, was attacked by an angry mob while performing the burial rite in the churchyard. One account says that the bodies he was burying were seized and thrown on to a rubbish tip outside the town. The respect in which the Church had been held for centuries was breaking down. Hoping to offer the people of Europe more than prayer, the Pope wrote to the medical faculty of the University of Paris for advice. We don't know if the response ever got as far as Bishop Eddington's palace, but it would have made little difference:

No poultry should be eaten, no waterfowl, no pig, no old beef, altogether no fat meat . . . It is injurious to sleep during the daytime . . . Fish should not be eaten, too much exercise may be injurious . . . and nothing should be cooked in rainwater. Olive oil with food is deadly . . . Bathing is dangerous . . .

By June 1349 the disposal of the heaps of putrefying bodies stacking up in Winchester's graveyards was causing serious problems. Royal records show that in that month the towns-folk, led by the mayor, 'assaulted in warlike array and with din of arms, the bishop's servants and the monks of the cathedral church and men bearing bodies to the graveyard, and when these fled, followed them with noisy threats of burning the cathedral church'. Only a handful of years before, such an attack on one of the most powerful bishoprics in the country would have been unthinkable. Now anything was possible. Eddington did not even have enough clergy left to try to calm his flock: nearly half of all his priests were dead, and some of those still living had abandoned their flocks and run away. The situation became so grave that Eddington's successor, William of Wickham, had to found a whole school to replace his missing priests: it survives as Winchester College.

With the Church patently failing in its attempts to prevent

the spread of the disease, people turned to more unusual preventive measures. For the wealthy a plethora of advice was available, including an Italian treatment that suggested:

In the first instance, no man should think of death . . . Nothing should distress him, but all his thoughts should be directed to pleasing, agreeable and delicious things . . . Beautiful landscapes, fine gardens should be visited, particularly when aromatic plants are flowering . . . Listening to beautiful, melodious songs is wholesome . . . The contemplating of gold and silver and other precious stones is comforting to the heart.

Such remedies did not come cheap, however. Chaucer, who was a boy of about ten at the time of the Black Death, comments in *The Canterbury Tales* that the physician liked gold in particular and had made plenty of it during the plague. For the poor, there was little more than superstition, although ironically this was as effective as the pronouncements of the academic establishment. Charms were widely worn and incense burnt to clear the unclean air, which was believed to harbour the disease. Even loud noises were considered effective and church bells were rung until there was no one left to ring them. In wealthier towns that could afford the latest technology cannons were fired in the hope that the sound would scare away the disease.

In most minds, however, the Black Death was a scourge from God that only prayer could prevent, and the failure of the clergy to help people achieve this changed the relationship between ordinary people and the Church for ever. Ironically, the one person who did not rely entirely on prayer was Pope Clement VI, who took to sitting between two large fires at his palace in Avignon in France. As the plague bacterium is killed by heat, this might have been of some benefit to him.

Back in Britain the plague had swept on past Winchester. In

Norwich (that great Norman success story), the guild hall records show that 57,374 people died out of an estimated population of around seventy thousand. The Jewish community, who had left in 1290, might have been lucky not to be there any longer for the suspicions and hatreds that had flared up in the St William case were now raising their ugly heads across Europe: in Strasbourg, on one day in 1349, two hundred Jews were burned alive, accused of having caused the plague. So bad did the situation become that the Pope was forced to issue a bull forbidding the plunder of Jewish houses and the murder of Jews, pointing out that they were suffering as much from the epidemic as the Christian population.

Closer to home the disease raced north. In Ely, where Hereward had made his last stand against the Norman Conquest, fifteen of the forty-three monks succumbed. At their monastery in Meaux, the industrious Cistercians were worse hit: only ten of their fifty monks survived the pandemic. As the disease dashed on, the Scots took the opportunity to prepare an invasion of England in what must have seemed the ideal opportunity for payback after half a century of English interference in Scottish affairs. According to Henry of Knighton, however, their initial glee at English suffering was short-lived and even before they had finished mustering near Stirling the army met an enemy far more deadly than any English bowman. Henry describes how this 'monstrous death' proceeded to 'winnow' the Scots, leaving five thousand dead. The remainder, fearful and weakened, returned home, taking the plague with them into the Scottish heartlands. After a brief respite in the winter of 1349, plague erupted there again, possibly in its most deadly pneumonic form, in the spring of 1350, leaving John of Fordun in his *Scotichronicon* to record: 'It generated such horror that children did not dare to visit their dying parents, nor parents their children, but fled for fear of contagion as if from leprosy or a serpent.'

Wales had also been severely hit. At Whitchurch one sad sequence of events tells a tale that must have been repeated across the countryside. In an attempt to keep up normal mechanisms of life, an inquest was called into the death of John le Strange, who had died on 20 August 1349. Inquests were normal part of village life by which the estate of the deceased could be ascertained and valued to prevent disputes. But these were not ordinary times. By the time the inquest met ten days later to decide on the fate of John's estate, his eldest son and heir, Fulk, was already dead too. By the time an inquest had been arranged for Fulk, his brother Humphrey was also dead. Only the youngest, John, was left alive, but with a wrecked inheritance. His three water-mills stood empty as there were no tenants left to grind their corn and his land was deemed worthless as all his villagers were dead.

To walk across Britain in 1350 would have been to walk across a dislocated and devastated world. The old system of manor and tenants was close to collapse as simply too few people remained to work the land. Henry of Knighton recorded the sight in his Leicester Chronicle: 'Sheep and cattle went wandering over fields and through crops, and there was no one to go and drive or gather them for there was such a lack of servants that no one knew what he ought to do. Wherefore many crops perished in the fields for want of someone to gather them.'

In many places the dead lay in the fields where they had fallen, there being too few living to collect and bury them. At St Mary's Church, in Ashwell, Hertfordshire, the graffito that one anonymous survivor scratched on the wall still bears witness to the bewildering shock of those who had to pick up the pieces: '1350. The people who remain are driven wild and miserable. They are wretched witnesses to the end. A strong wind is thundering over the whole earth. Written on St Maurice's Day.'

But when Britain awoke from the nightmare of plague in 1351, the news was not all bad for that 'remnant of the people'. In 1300 the country had been under-developed and over-populated. Now, with between a third and half of the population dead, that pressure was gone. As labour grew scarcer, the wages that surviving workers could charge rose. The King was so alarmed that he issued the 'Ordinance of Labourers and Beggars' to cap wages at 1346 levels, but among the labourers in the fields (and the lords with manors to run) it proved ineffective. Peasants suddenly had bargaining power, and a law made in London was not going to stop a tenant in Yorkshire looking elsewhere for better terms if his employer refused to pay more. Neither could those surviving lords afford to watch their few remaining labourers drift away to manors where the wages were better. Henry of Knighton noted the almost immediate rise in the value of labour in the shattered countryside:

After the pestilence, many buildings, great and small, fell into ruins in every city for lack of inhabitants, likewise many villages and hamlets became desolate, not a house being left in them, all having died who dwelt there; and it was probable that many such villages would never be inhabited. In the winter following there was such a want of servants in work of all kinds, that one would scarcely believe that in times past there had been such a lack. And so all necessities became so much dearer.

For the 'servants' who did remain, the cloud of plague would have a silver lining. The last fifty years had been a disaster for the hundreds of thousands who fell victim to famine and disease, but for the survivors, the Black Death would prove in many ways to be the White Knight they had been praying for. An age of opportunity was dawning.

6
Opportunity

Sceptre and crown must tumble down
And in the dust be equal made
With the poor crooked scythe and spade.
James Shirley

On 22 November 1357, Sir Roger de Cotesford received some good news at last. The preceding fifty years had been disastrous, with crop failure and famine followed by a three-year outbreak of plague, which may have killed up to half the population of Britain. Even now, new outbreaks of the disease were being reported around the country most years. But Roger had something to be pleased about. A messenger had arrived on his manor: the king had seen fit to grant him a writ allowing him to create a park on the site of his village of '. . . Tusmore which belongs to the said Roger and was, before the pestilence, entirely inhabited by Roger's serfs. Because of the death of those serfs, it has been, from time to time, empty of inhabitants, and so remains, and intends to remain so in the future.'

The daily medieval cycle of life at Tusmore in Oxfordshire had gone for good. No more church services, no more feast days and festivals, no Leet Courts, no levies, no target practice for the men and boys on Sunday. The open fields were empty and no tenants answered Roger's customary call to work on his land. Tusmore was dead, and in his hands, Roger held its death certificate.

*   *   *

The image of a post-Black Death Britain inhabited by a wraith-like population, stunned and bewildered by the cataclysm that had befallen them, staggering from one ghost town to the next abandoned village has proved pervasive. But life after the Black Death was not as simple or as bad as many had feared. Certainly there had to be changes in both the countryside and the towns to cope with the lower population but for those who had survived the disease there was opportunity.

Tusmore was not in fact a typical village. While Roger had taken the chance offered by the removal of his tenants to change the way he ran the place, the tragic tale he told the King was not quite true. Tusmore was finally depopulated by the plague but Roger failed to add that the village had been in terminal decline long before that. Even had his tenants survived, it was likely that they wouldn't have stayed. If the final nail in this village's coffin was the Black Death it was only the *final* nail. Other forces were at work in the countryside to change the relationship between lord and tenant, between the free and the unfree.

The immediate after-effect of the Black Death in the countryside was a shortage of labour, and for the field worker that could only be good news. Suddenly the man who had been worth a penny a day before the plague was worth twice that, sometimes more during the harvest season. Of course, some landlords were reluctant to pay the new, realistic rates, but the workforce now knew its value and could vote with its feet. Theoretically many farm labourers and tenants were still tied to their land and still owed service to their lord. Again theoretically, the price of hired-in labour was fixed. But these were desperate times for landlords. In the past a neighbourly landowner might have returned a runaway tenant to the next-door manor, but now that runaway was another much-needed pair of hands whom he might offer to protect. Emboldened peasants who thought they were getting a bad deal from their lord could move, and new, better landlords would protect them. Even in Scotland, where serfdom had persisted rather longer than in England, the concept of being 'tied' to the land was losing its grip, despite the best efforts of conservative lords like the Bishop of Moray who turned the pursuit of fugitive serfs into something of a hobby. Whether the lords liked it or not, the labour market was becoming mobile.

The idea of peasants setting their own rates of pay and moving to estates of their choosing caused uproar among the governing classes. The feudal system had been designed to tell the workforce what to do, not to offer them options. The government's immediate response was to try to legislate the old world back into existence. The opening of the 1351 Statute of Labourers put it bluntly:

Whereas late against the malice of servants, which were idle, and not willing to serve after the pestilence, without taking excessive wages, it was ordained by our lord the king, and by the assent of the prelates, nobles, and other of his council, that such manner of servants, as well men as women, should be bound to serve, receiving salary and wages, accustomed in places where they ought to serve in the twentieth year of the reign of the king that now is, or five or six years before.

This attempt to turn back the clock was doomed to failure. Not only had the heady concept of 'improvement' already firmly rooted itself among the more ambitious tenants but landlords themselves were eager to breach the regulations to gain the labour they needed to get their harvests in.

Neither was the population as happy to take their masters' word as gospel any more. The loss of so many had sent a seismic shock through the medieval mind. The Church – one of the largest landowners in the country, as well as the people's supposed spiritual guardian – had proved impotent in the face of plague. Bishop Eddington in Winchester had lost nearly 50 per cent of his clergy, Meaux had lost 80 per cent of its monks and even the Archbishop of Canterbury had succumbed. It seemed that God had no special favour for these people, and they had not proved a successful conduit to Him when the people needed it. Outside the religious world, the aristocracy hadn't fared much better: the King himself had lost a daughter. People of all classes had been mown down by plague, not just the poor, which again cast doubt on the 'divine order' of things and the right of a few to rule.

In this new world of doubt, attempts by landlords and special justices to enforce the Statute of Labourers caused growing resentment. Those accused of breaking it, such as Nicholas Thressher of Halsted – who, so the court heard, 'takes 2d per day, both in winter and summer, and 4d in harvest', were fined and such prosecutions were pursued so vigorously that the money raised in this fashion became an important part of many manors' incomes. As, under the statute, these proceeds could be deducted from the main form of taxation, the lay subsidy, the rich, who usually paid the subsidy, were encouraged to prosecute the poor, who were most likely to be caught out by the fines. Furthermore, villagers were urged to inform on each other, while officials, such as the constables, who were drawn from their ranks were expected to turn in friends and neighbours who broke the law. Tensions could only rise.

Clearly the attempts to cap incomes amongst the workforce were not working by 1363 when parliament introduced another law, which shows their disquiet at the continuing rise of the labouring classes. The Sumptuary Law of that year attempted

28. *Dark Age fortress. The peninsular at Tintagel in Cornwall has been associated with King Arthur since the nineteenth century, but excavations have shown that this was the home to real Dark Age Cornish leaders. From here they managed to maintain their connections with the Roman world even as the South East of England was falling under Anglo-Saxon control.*

29. *Saxon England. The reconstructed Anglo-Saxon village at West Stow in Suffolk gives us a taste of everyday life in pagan Anglo-Saxon England. Far from being a world filled with bloodthirsty warriors, this was an overwhelmingly agrarian society where the concerns of everyday life took precedence over warfare.*

30. Corporate raiders. The Viking ships such as this one carved on a picture stone in Gotland brought more than just an army to Britain. Vikings were world class traders: the skills that enabled them to navigate their way up rivers for surprise attacks also enabled them to trade across the known world, from Muslim North Africa to Russia and beyond.

31. Viking exotica. The 'Horn of Ulf' now in the treasury of York Minster amply illustrates the trading contacts of the Jorvik Vikings. The horn is made from African elephant ivory imported to Italy for carving and then brought to York where a local lord gave it to the church.

32. Raiders or traders? The Vikings' real success came not simply in raiding Britain but in setting up thriving trading colonies. In York professional craftsmen and women produced everyday items from woolly socks to coloured beads to provide for the burgeoning city population. Before this most Britons had made their own everyday necessities – now, in York, they could buy them.

33. *The circling years. The Julian Work Calendar is illustrated with domestic and agricultural scenes from the late Anglo-Saxon world. It depicts a rural way of life already firmly established by the early 11th century which would survive in a recognisable form until the Industrial revolution.*

34. *Saxon science. The late Anglo-Saxon medical compendium known as Bald's Leechbook uses herbs, prayers and pagan spells to effect a vast array of cures for everything from cancer to a woman's gossip. On this page is a handy cure for lunacy.*

35. *In every town. The most visible sign of the Norman conquest in many towns and villages was the construction of an earth mound with a wooden palisade on the top. Many of these 'mottes' would later be developed into full-scale castles from which the new Norman elite ruled. This well-preserved example tucked away in the corner of a later castle is at Berkhamsted in Hertfordshire.*

36. *David and Goliath. This late 12th century illumination from Winchester depicts a very overbearing Goliath in the guise of a Norman soldier being attacked by a plucky, and rather Anglo-Saxon looking David. Perhaps this was the illuminator's way of making a sly comment on his Norman masters?*

37. *Fusion. The Normans replaced nearly every wooden Saxon church in England. Their new stone churches in the Romanesque style were as much a symbol of conquest as their castles, but away from the centres of Norman power this building programme could be interpreted in a more native style. At Kilpeck in Herefordshire a typically Roman-esque Norman plan has been decorated in a uniquely Anglo-Saxon style; the Norman 'nook-shaft' pillars swarming with intertwining animal decoration are more typical of the Lindisfarne gospels.*

38. *Fallen idols. This peculiar walrus ivory crucifix shows Christ between Longinus and Stephaton; above are personifications of the sun and moon and, in the middle, the hand of God. Although it dates back to just after the conquest its layout is still very much Anglo-Saxon. It was found in Norwich in the nineteenth century amongst Norman building rubble, and was perhaps one of the last treasures of the Saxon church there.*

39. *The Ship of the Fen. The mediaeval cathedral at Ely in Cambridgeshire occupies the highest ground for miles around. Shortly after the Norman conquest Hereward the Wake chose this location for his final stand against the new Norman overlords. According to the Gesta Herewardi he made a good choice and the stronghold was only taken after the Abbot of Ely betrayed the defenders.*

40. The 'Ladder of Salvation'. This twelfth century wall painting in Chaldon church in Surrey opens a window into the minds of the mediaeval villagers who lived here. The 'ladder' shows the righteous ascending in triumph to heaven whilst the damned fall down to hell. In the lower right section cheating trades-people are forced to carry the symbols of their trade across a razor sharp bridge supported by enormous demons.

41. *A parcel of ground. For the average mediaeval villager before the Black Death, home was usually a single storey, chimneyless cottage similar to the one reconstructed here at the Weald and Downland Museum, and based on a thirteenth century excavated example from the deserted mediaeval village of Hangleton in Sussex.*

42. *Cathedrals to grain. At the other end of the scale to the Hangleton cottage, large landlords such as the church could invest in huge barns to hold the food tithes they took from their peasant farmers. The great tithe barn at Harmondsworth in Middlesex was built in 1426 and is the second largest surviving mediaeval barn in Britain.*

to restrict what clothing people of different social orders could wear to curb the 'extravagant apparel' of the working classes. Certain social groups were restricted to buying cloth of so-many-pence per yard and no more. Even the height of boots was dictated by rank. The law's main purpose was to slow the rapidly rising cost of manufactured goods, which Parliament evidently blamed on the lower orders having too much disposable income. But it also hints at the jealousies and concerns of a ruling class who were seeing their social inferiors dressing above their station and acquiring the wealth that was once their preserve. Just what would have happened if bailiffs had been sent to take the clothes from their back is another matter but perhaps fortunately (unlike in Florence where there really were fashion police who could break into your wardrobe), the law was never enforced. A trend had begun that could not be legislated away. A hundred and fifty years later, Sir Thomas More, the great Tudor author and statesman, could only see it ending in chaos and disaster:

For not only gentle mennes servauntes, but also handicrafte men: yea and almooste the ploughmen of the countrey, with al other sortes of people, use muche straunge and proude newefanglenes in their apparell, and to muche prodigall riotte and sumptuous fare at their table. Nowe bawdes, queines, whoores, harlottes, strumpettes, brothelhouses, stewes, and yet another stewes, wynetavernes, ale houses and tiplinge houses, with so manye noughtie, lewde and unlawfull games, as dyce, cardes, tables, tennis, boules, coytes, do not all these sende the haunters of them streyghte a stealynge when theyr money is gone?

Against the background of rising concern among the governing classes and rising resentment in the villages, the wider political world was also impinging on the people of Britain.

England was fighting France in a prolonged and expensive adventure that would become known as the Hundred Years War. While its immediate effects were seen only in areas that attracted French raiding and among those sent to fight, its influence would eventually be felt everywhere through tax. In Scotland, taxation was levied to pay the huge ransom of ten thousand merks required by the English for returning the Scottish king, David II: he had been captured after ill-advisedly invading England in support of his French allies, following their defeat at the battle of Crécy in 1346.

But the English were not to have it all their own way. To pay for the increasingly expensive and futile campaigns that followed the success at Crécy, the government decided upon a relatively novel concept, which has remained hugely unpopular from that time to this: direct taxation. In 1377, 1379 and 1380 poll taxes were ordered, which required a substantial majority of the population to pay direct tax for the first time. The first tax required everyone over fourteen to pay fourpence regardless of income, the second increased the age limit to sixteen and made some attempt at matching payment to income, whilst the third demanded the huge figure of twelve pence from everyone over fifteen, although with some provision for the rich to subsidise the poor. By the time the last poll tax was voted in, Parliament knew it was pushing its luck and, fearing the response of the London mob, met in the relative safety of Nottingham.

The immediate result of this last poll tax was evasion on a spectacular scale. In 1377 over 1.25 million people had paid up, but by 1381, when the 1380 tax was collected, this figure had dropped by a third: four hundred and fifty thousand people had apparently disappeared. It was almost as though another plague had struck. This time, though, the missing men and women weren't dead, they were hiding. Civil disobedience was not new – indeed, villagers probably concealed many things from their local courts and tax collectors before the Black Death – but the scale now was different. There was huge resentment that some of the poorest sections of the community, such as female servants, were required to pay in the same way as rich landlords. It is not surprising that stories of Robin Hood, the free-living rebel who hid in a forest and stole from the rich to give to the poor became popular at this time. In this world of doubt, the demands of the government were clearly no longer seen as divine law but simply as a request, and one that could be refused.

Of course, the government was hardly going to sit back while the population opted out of paying tax, and official inquiries were instituted to look into the mass evasion. When they reached Kent and Essex resentment boiled over.

At Fobbing in Essex the sergeant-at-arms of the Royal Commission into Tax Evasion rode into the village on 31 May 1381. Two days earlier John Bampton, its head, had summoned the people here to Brentwood, some five miles away and ordered them to pay the poll tax. They had refused so John was now sending in his enforcer. It seems that the people of Fobbing had been forewarned, however, for on the high street the sergeant met an angry mob who drove him out of the village. Enraged by these heavy-handed tactics, the people marched back to Brentwood and John Bampton's house, only to find that he had fled to London. If he had thought he would be safe there, he was wrong.

Soon the bailiff was riding between the nearby villages calling on locals to arm themselves and join him. Within a couple of days people from all over Essex had gathered under the command of one Thomas Baker of Fobbing and were marching on

London. The people of rural England were about to step out of the obscurity of local life and on to the stage of national politics. The fuse had been lit for the Peasants' Revolt.

If you walk along the Strand in London today you will come to one of the world's most famous and luxurious hotels: the Savoy. In fact, had you walked here in the spring of 1381 you would have come across a similarly spectacular building. Stretching from what is now Somerset House all the way to Charing Cross Station, stood the finest, richest palace in Europe and it too was called the Savoy.

This Savoy was not a hotel however, but a private home belonging to probably the most powerful man in Britain, John of Gaunt, son of the late Edward III and uncle to the present king, Richard II. On reaching the gates of the Savoy Palace in 1381 it is unlikely that you would have received a particularly warm welcome. Inside his palace John of Gaunt guarded the vast treasure he had accumulated, valued at over ten thousand pounds even before 1381 (in excess of 10 million pounds today) and that excluded the value of the palace itself. It was a fortune he was not renowned for sharing and the extreme extravagance of his lifestyle evoked widespread hostility. The people who paid for this lifestyle, certainly weren't welcome here.

The evening of 13 June 1381 would be different however. That night the whole of the Strand was bathed in a warm orange light. The smoke from the hundreds of chimneys that lined the street perhaps seemed thicker and more acrid. Everywhere there were people running down the street, some in panic, some laughing, and ahead a huge knot of people blocked the road. Pushing through we might have caught a glimpse of the reason for their gathering. The extraordinary Savoy palace was ablaze. The gates were broken down, their guards long fled, and in the courtyard there was a scene of pandemonium.

There were people here not just from London but from all over the south-east, hurling the property of Britain's greatest magnate out into the street and burning it. The people of Fobbing and a thousand similar villages had arrived in town.

In a corner you could have seen some men from Hertfordshire talking about their journey. This was not the first of John of Gaunt's properties they had attacked. After mustering in their home town of Ware they went first to his castle at nearby Hertford and burned that, before turning south down the Lea valley to London. Elsewhere Londoners were encouraging each other to throw valuable tapestries and silks on to the fires, rather than loot them. Many would have told you that this was about destroying Gaunt's ostentatious wealth, not stealing it. Even chests of money were consigned to the flames. One rioter reported that a man who tried to pilfer a valuable piece of silver was thrown on to the flames with his prize. Only the brave dared to remove items from this 'bonfire of the vanities' including one Joanna Ferrers, braver than most, who escaped across the river to Southwark with a chest of Gaunt's jewels.

Despite the apparently puritanical motives, some people were enjoying Gaunt's 'hospitality', although he, far away in Berwick, was quite unaware of it. Thirty-two men found their way into the extensive wine cellars and helped themselves to a better quality of drink than they were used to. They paid a heavy price for their revelry. The next morning their charred bodies were found among the collapsed timbers of the cellar roof.

An explosion heralded the sudden end of another rioter's evening. On finding what appeared to be a barrel of coins, an overzealous insurgent hurled it on to the fires, only to find it was filled with gunpowder. It was the last mistake he ever made.

The motivations behind the rioters at the Savoy that night were almost as diverse as the people themselves, yet an extraordinary degree of organisation and communication had managed to bring them all together at the same place and time. For some Londoners there was perhaps little more driving them than the desire for a good riot – indeed, some took the opportunity to massacre the Flemish merchants of the City probably for financial reasons. Others, like the men from Ware, were paying back John of Gaunt for having reduced wages on their estate while at the same time raising taxes for the war. Across on Blackheath, where large numbers of rebels gathered, there were more specific demands. Lead by Wat Tyler and a charismatic preacher called John Ball, they put their demands directly to the young Richard II at Mile End the following day. Interestingly this was not a rabid ultimatum to 'smash the state' but showed a careful appreciation of the problems of working people and a good knowledge of the laws that bound them. The inequalities felt by many were summed up by John Ball in his reported phrase: 'When Adam delved and Eve span, who was then the Gentleman?'

Their anger against their overlords was not directed at the King himself. Indeed, they went to great lengths to show their loyalty to him while counselling that his advisers, most notably John of Gaunt, had led him astray. They asked the King simply that 'no man should be a serf, nor do homage or any type of service to any lord, but should give four pence for an acre of land'.

Richard listened patiently to these requests and agreed to them, at least in the short-term.

The real anger of the mob was directed at the Church, the high officers of State and particularly at Archbishop Sudbury, who also happened to be the Chancellor as well as Archbishop of Canterbury, and Treasurer Hales. While the King was busy at Mile End with Wat Tyler, other rebels were breaking into the Tower of London where Sudbury and Hales were holed up. On entering the royal apartments, the mob showed little concern for the strict protocols of court life. One chronicler, Thomas Walsingham, declared: 'Who would ever have believed that such rustics and most inferior ones at that would dare to enter the chamber of the King and of his mother with their filthy sticks. They arrogantly lay and sat on the King's bed while joking and several asked the King's mother to kiss them.'

But the mob were not only there to joke, as Sudbury knew. In a desperate bid to escape he made a dash for the watergate that led on to the Thames but was seen by a woman and stopped. He and five other 'traitors', including Hales, were dragged unceremoniously to Tower Hill and beheaded. His head was then placed, like those of all traitors, on London Bridge before it was smuggled back to his home town of Sudbury in Suffolk. The skull rather surprisingly still resides in a vestry cupboard to this day.

Elsewhere in England other, more local targets were identified, including St Albans Abbey, whose charters were burned by a mob who believed that the abbot was suppressing a more ancient charter granting the town independent market rights. It was perhaps naïve of them to think that the abbey hadn't kept copies of the documents they were destroying, but it showed they knew that the bonds tying them to their land and lord were made of parchment and ink, not iron.

Just when things seemed to be going well for the rebels, their luck ran out. The day after the Mile End meeting, the King met the leaders again, this time at Smithfield, where the Lord Mayor of London, on the pretext of an attempt on the King's life, took the opportunity to assassinate Wat Tyler in broad daylight. The charters of freedom that the King's clerks were even then drawing up for the rebels were destroyed. The deal was off, the surviving leaders were rounded up and executed, and the vast majority of the rebels melted away into the countryside.

That there was no full-scale witch hunt for them says something about the new-found power of the working people and the origins of the rebels. After the revolt it was popular among chroniclers, who were generally horrified that the natural order of things had been disrupted, to claim that the rebels were simple peasants, thugs and bandits. But this was not so. The group who had come from Ware were led by a chaplain, an educated man, and the degree of organisation of the revolt, and the legal understanding shown by its leaders' demands, suggests that it was far from the 'dregs of society' who had rebelled.

We can meet one of the more troublesome rebels at his home in Ingatestone, Essex. William Smith might have been at John Bampton's house when the people of Fobbing arrived. He was just a serf, with a little land and a few animals, and held a position of respect in his community. He might have been one of those at the time who were rebuilding their homes with the proceeds of their increased wages. New ideas were coming into fashion in home design, with second storeys being added to the ends of some houses, allowing for a private upper bedroom for the owner. More was being spent on possessions as well, with better clothing (often in breach of the Sumptuary Law), more furnishings and household equipment, including even a small garnish of pewter on the cupboard alongside the wooden bowls. The food on the table was improving too: the largely bread-based diet was now supplemented with more meat, in particular fresh beef. A fortunate guest might be presented with bread made from wheat instead of the usual barley flour, perhaps even sieved or 'boulted' to make it white. Which of these new luxuries William could afford we will never know, but we do know that as a middle-aged married man he had been ale-taster – a position of some respect in the community and one he undoubtedly enjoyed. What he clearly did not enjoy was his servile status. He had seen opportunity appear in the wake of Black Death, seen the chance for cheaper land and higher wages, and he was damned if he was going to let the ruling classes take it away. Indeed, he seems to have taken quite a physical approach to settling his grievance: he was accused of attacking John Bampton during the revolt – no doubt to the delight of the villagers of Fobbing – and even of being an accomplice in the murder of a senior Essex official. He did not however hang for either crime. The village of Ingatestone needed its William Smiths, and this one was allowed to return to his home, becoming ale-taster once again in 1386. But the fire had not left his blood, and he continued to cause trouble for his lord, refusing to pay fines for having to be bound over to keep the peace in his dealings with the bailiff.

The reintegration of the rebels into local society after the revolt shows that they were valued members of the community. Their complaint had been justified and, while the revolt had failed in its major aims, it shook government policy and notably no further poll tax was levied. It had also left a lingering fear in the hearts of the ruling classes, as the contemporary poet John Gower vividly describes in his *Vox Clamantis*, an allegory of the Revolt. Despite his pleasure at the suppression of the rebels, he clearly fears that their time may come again:

So when the peasantry had been bound in chains and lay patiently under our foot, the ox returned to its yoke, and the seed flourished beneath the plowed fields, and the villein ceased his warring. Similarly, Satan's power lay prostrate, overwhelmed by divine might; but nevertheless it lurked in hiding among the ungovernable peasantry. For the peasant always lay in wait to see whether he by chance could bring the noble class to destruction. For his rough, boorish nature was not tempered by any affection, but he always had bitterness in his hateful heart.

In Wales he was proved right. There, the problems between lord and tenant continued to fester, in part because the lords were English and their tenants Welsh, and also because of the additional freedoms and tax-raising privileges the Crown awarded the 'Marcher lords'. Events finally climaxed when a member of the Welsh gentry, Owain Glyn Dŵr, brought Wales into full revolt in September 1399, demanding not just better treatment but freedom from English dominion. His open war against the English lasted for nine years and attracted a huge amount of support among rural peasants and urban craftspeople who resented the privileges of the English colonial towns founded in Wales after Edward I's conquest. They no doubt felt that laws that prevented them trading on equal terms with their English neighbours were grossly unfair – just as the Anglo-Saxons had complained of the privileges of Norman merchants in Norwich over three hundred years before. In fact, Glyn Dŵr's demands for a free Wales were not met and his rebellion ended in defeat before overwhelming English military pressure. However, the English towns of Wales were forced to change, and after Glyn Dŵr had disappeared into the hills, Welsh voices were heard at last inside the city walls.

In fact, across Britain many of the peasants' demands were

met to a small degree, but this came about through gradual change rather than public riot or legislation from the King. The great monastic houses on which the rebels had turned so savagely were themselves suffering problems. In the wake of the Black Death their incomes had not only reduced in line with other landowners' but were further diminished by a sudden drop in bequests. In this new age the great medieval orders were seen by many as failures for having done nothing to prevent Black Death. Instead, people looked to a more intimate religion, expressed in the work of the orders of friars, whose vow of poverty exempted them from accusations of religious excess, and the contemplative monastic orders who, through their isolation, had largely survived the Black Death and were viewed as 'favoured by God'.

At Mount Grace Priory in Yorkshire it is still possible to walk through the ruins of one of these 'new' houses. Founded in 1398 by the Carthusians, this was the last monastery established in England before Henry VIII's dissolution, and is a world away from the vast agribusiness in which the Cistercians were involved at Meaux. At the turn of the fourteenth century Mount Grace was a place of prayer, not business. The monks lived as hermits, each occupying small 'two-up-two-down' stone cells spaced around a large central cloister. Within each cell, the Carthusian monk spent his day in silent prayer, study and manual work, only leaving his enclosed world to tend his own small garden and join his brethren for three daily services in their church: Prime at six in the morning, Vespers at a quarter to three in the afternoon, and Matins at a quarter to midnight.

Lay-brothers serviced the needs of this extremely reclusive order. They ran the secular business of the monastery and prepared the meals, leaving them in hatches beside each cell door so they did not disturb the occupant's contemplation. It was a life with virtually no outside contact and, as such, came through the Black Death relatively unscathed. That proved to the local populace that God favoured the meek rather than the magnificent orders.

While many may have taken comfort from the thought that the reclusive and ascetic Carthusians were praying for them, others wanted more immediate contact with their religion and with those they believed to be closer to God. Against this background an extraordinary group of women came to the fore: the anchoresses. There had been a long tradition of female mystics in Britain but since the Norman conquest their role had diminished, as the followers of Christina of Markyate might have told you. The Norman Church was a large-scale administrative organisation, not a personal church, and it had had little time for hermits, mystics and prophets. In a world post-1350, however, things had changed: terrified of what they saw as the wrath of God, which had so recently and terribly been visited on them, and acutely aware of the Church's failure to prevent it or even to save itself, new forms of intercession were needed, and the hour of the female Christian mystics had come again.

To modern eyes the role of the anchoress would seem extra-ordinary. These women dedicated their life to solitary prayer and contemplation, confined in a small cell usually attached to the side of a parish church from where they could view mass through a tiny window in the church wall. This life of hermetic purity appealed to the traumatised minds of post-plague Britain, and to have an anchoress attached to your church became a considerable status symbol for a community. The parish offered her a place to live, food, drink and the respect of the community, and in return she prayed for the parish and might provide spiritual guidance for its people. To many it seemed a good deal – after all, the reclusive and isolated anchoresses in existence between 1348 had survived the Black Death – something we might put down to their isolation, but which to the medieval mind was clearly a sign from God.

We might have met an anchoress in many parish churches around the country, but to meet the most famous – and many became very famous even in their own lifetime – we need to return to Norwich in around AD 1400. Approaching the church of St Julian there we would immediately notice the small stone building attached to the side of the church, the home of the most famous of all the anchoresses – Julian of Norwich. Should we find the small door to her cell ajar we might see beyond a simply laid-out room, with a bed, trestle table and bench. In the wall there is a small hatch, not unlike those in the Carthusian monastery at Mount Grace Priory, through which parishioners pass food. Over in the wall of the church, a thin slanting window, known as a squint, gives her a view of the altar during Mass – her only other view of the outside world.

We know little about Julian's life, not even her real name: 'Julian' being taken from the patron saint of the church where she lived. But we do know something of her beliefs and what inspired her to live like this, thanks to two surviving books she wrote – the first books written in English by a woman. Julian tells us that in May 1373, 'when I was thirty years old and a half, God sent me a bodily sickness, in which I lay three days and three nights; and on the fourth night I took all my rites of Holy Church, and weened not to have lived till day ... And being in youth as yet, I thought it great sorrow to die'. During the illness she received a series of visions, which she described as sixteen 'showings', sixteen revelations of Divine Love, which brought her back from the edge of death:

. . . the upper part of my body began to die, so far forth that scarcely I had any feeling . . . And in this [moment] suddenly all my pain was taken from me, and I was as whole . . . as ever I was afore. I marvelled at this sudden change; for methought it was a privy working of God, and not of nature.

It seems that these revelations told her the path she should now take in life and, after she had undertaken a probationary period, the local bishop agreed that she might attach herself to the church of St Julian in Norwich. Here she was confined to her cell for the rest of her life.

But the Julian who lived here was by no means an unhappy or ill-treated woman. The role of anchoress was highly desirable and brought with it not only respect but kudos for her family. Anchoresses were literate and often came from the wealthier families in the village or town. The parish took pride in supporting her, and many probably saw her as more important in the salvation of their souls than their priest. Nor was it an entirely solitary life. Any number of people came up to the cell to talk to Julian through the grille in the wall, asking for advice or for prayers to be said.

Some anchoresses seem to have enjoyed considerable luxury as their parishioners vied to provide for them. But at the end of the day, one final ritual brought home to them the meaning of their unusual life. Before the squint in Julian's cell lay a freshly dug hole in the floor – her own grave. In the dwindling light of dusk, she would kneel here, as she did every day, to remind herself of her mortality and the purpose of her existence. Christina of Markyate, some three hundred years earlier, would no doubt have understood.

Julian's cell no longer exists: it was bombed in the Second World War, so we do not know if she was buried in it. But

550 years after her death, when another anchoress's cell was excavated at the church of St Anne in Lewes, the body of its occupant was indeed found in a grave by the squint where she had knelt every day, fulfilling the requirement of the *Ancrene Wisse*, the medieval manual for anchoresses: 'She should scrape up earth every day out of the grave in which she shall rot. The sight of her grave near her does many an anchoress much good. She who keeps her death as it were before her eyes, her open grave reminding her of it, will not lightly pursue the delight of the flesh.'

The increasing concern with what might happen to the soul after death did not only benefit the reclusive, mystical religious orders. In the towns, the need for individual salvation after death was being combined with the need for support and fellowship during life in the creation of a new group of institutions, the guilds and fraternities. The Black Death had affected towns severely: the overcrowded streets had proved the perfect breeding-ground for the disease. As a result there was now a desperate need for craftsmen and -women to fill the void – attracting an increasingly footloose rural population keen to escape the bonds of their manors. But towns were dangerous and anonymous places compared to the intimacies of village life. To go from a rural world of a hundred or so people where you knew everyone to a town of thousands of people where you knew no one would have been traumatic. These new organisations provided the help townspeople needed both for the protection of their livelihood and their souls.

The fundamental role of many of these organisations was religious. The fraternities offered a personal approach to salvation that involved individuals rather than large church organisations. After the terrible mortality of the previous fifty years, it is hardly surprising that people were concerned about death, their souls and, in particular, Purgatory. The view of what happened immediately after death had changed since the Norman Conquest and the idea that the dead just simply rested in their graves until the Day of Judgement had been replaced by the concept of Purgatory: there, souls were purged of their venial (excusable) sins before judgement. The living prayed for the dead to make this process as swift and painless as possible and to ensure their entry afterwards into heaven.

While this concept had existed before the Black Death it now began to exert an unhealthy grip on the minds of a people who had lost so much. The religious fraternities offered a form of religious insurance, guaranteeing that, after death, a member would receive a proper funeral and that masses would be sung regularly for their soul in the fraternity's chantry. Such a personal service seemed to offer a much better chance of salvation than the high masses of what was viewed as an over-mighty, over-wealthy and corrupt Church.

What was good for the soul was also good for business. Guilds and fraternities could do more than arrange for prayers. This was the age of the great merchant and craft guilds.

The guild system offered a structured career path for those prepared to bow to its rules (and had powerful means of excluding those who wouldn't). For the newly arrived teenager in town the guild offered apprenticeship in a trade. While he was now free of the control of his manorial lord, he was under the strict control of his master and the guild. As an apprentice he would be employed in the workshop of a master, learning the trade and abiding by the often strict moral codes of the guild. Members were required to avoid drunkenness – particularly in the face of the introduction of strong 'beer' (as opposed to ale) from the Low Countries around 1400. They should also avoid lewdness and any talk about guild business with anyone other than members and anywhere except in the guild hall. In return for his work, and perhaps a fee from his parents, the apprentice would be fed, sheltered and learn a craft. After a number of years, he might become a 'journeyman', a freelancer working for other masters but under considerably better conditions and for considerably more reward than an apprentice. Only when the journeyman married and proved to the guild that he had both the capital and the skill would he be fully admitted as a master, able to run his own workshop and employ his own apprentices.

The guilds of late medieval towns were more than just a cross between a professional body and a union however. They were central to the operation of town life, and their competitiveness and love of show provided much pageantry and splendour for both their members and those who aspired to their ranks. In the major towns each trade had its own guild, from blacksmiths and goldsmiths to plasterers and stonemasons, and each competed with the others for fame and honour. The great festivals provided the backdrop for this new commercial competitiveness and none more so than the summer festival of Corpus Christi.

On Corpus Christi 1400, York would have looked spectacular. During the festival it was traditional for the guilds to perform mystery plays, religious pieces telling Biblical stories that reflected the work of each guild. Each play was acted, costumed and set-dressed by the guild as a show of devotion and a lavish advertisement of their skills. On that day we might have joined the thousands of visitors to York, gathering at the various 'stations' around the city to await each of the wagons on which the plays were performed. In turn, each guild wagon would draw up and begin its play: the tinners would enact the creation of heaven, the plasterers the creation of Earth; the cardmakers dealt with God creating man, while it was the mariners and shipbuilders who, not surprisingly, told the story of Noah's Ark. The smiths had the job of nailing the body of Christ to the Cross, whilst only the goldsmiths could put on the story of the Three Kings – as they were the only ones with access to the necessary gold crowns. At any one station it would have been possible to watch around thirteen hours of plays on that day, accompanied by food, drink and not a little bawdiness, much to the disgust of local priests.

The guilds that proved so exuberant on Corpus Christi jealously guarded their rights and privileges, and their excessive secrecy could prove worrisome to the authorities. So concerned did the government become in the wake of the Peasants' Revolt that all guilds were required to send a copy of their ordinances to the Crown to prove that they were not simply a cover for plotting rebellion. Fraternities that were not officially sanctioned were frequently suppressed by the town authorities and the official guilds, proving that the freedoms for some were not necessarily available to all. Some groups, particularly journeymen, were not allowed to form groups as they threatened the privileges of the masters of established guilds. The journeyman spurrier Nicholas Symond seems to have been unaware of this when, in 1381, he attempted to bring a member of his illegal spurriers' fraternity to the Church courts for not attending meetings. Clearly he thought his group, which had been meeting for the past nine years in St Bartholomew's Church in London and even had its own ordinances and communal fund, was legitimate. The City authorities, and most particularly the spurriers, disagreed, particularly as the group was said to have set a minimum wage of twenty pence for twenty-five spurs. It was not, in the eyes of masters, for journeymen to set their own minimum wage. Symond's spurriers were ordered to disband.

For those guild members content to wait to become masters, there were numerous benefits, both in this life and the next. Had you walked into the guild hall of the merchant adventurers of York in the early fifteenth century (a building which still stands today) you would have found yourself in a self-help institution that cared for body and mind. In the comfortable upstairs hall of what was officially known as 'The Fraternity of the Lord Jesus Christ and the Blessed Virgin Mary' – the Trinity Guild for short – you might have discovered the members dining. The whole layout of this floor reflected the structure of the guild: at the entrance, near the 'service' end where the food and drink were brought in, the new apprentices sat, looking eagerly around at the valuable wall hangings, the trestle tables groaning under the weight of gold and silver cups and bowls, and the lustrous colours of the religious paintings that hung on the walls. The senior members of the guild would have worn their livery – fine robes made from rare imported fabrics and furs. The master and alderman of the Guild sat at the far end of the room on a raised platform. To the apprentices the latter looked almost like kings, but with a key difference: one day any apprentice might sit where they did.

Above the music of the minstrels playing in the gallery, the talk was probably of business: despite the religious name of their guild they met primarily to carry out a trade that had flourished in York since the Viking occupation: import and export. They were all relatively wealthy individuals – perhaps not landowners and certainly not aristocrats, but in some cases wealthier than either. They might not have had what a noble would have considered 'quality' but they had something that they knew was far more important in this new age: cash.

Walking downstairs you would have come upon an almost completely opposite scene, yet it was intimately related to the lives of the grandees above. This part of the guild hall was a hospital for thirteen poor men and women of the city, providing a valuable charitable service but also a unique benefit to members. Next to the hospital stood a small chapel where the poor incumbents were expected to pray for the good souls upstairs and also for the souls of former guild members as they navigated their way through the treacherous waters of Purgatory. This was after-life assurance, where the worthy poor's prayers, offered in exchange for food and shelter, helped ensure the eternal rest of guild members. This was also where the chantry priest employed by the guild prayed for the dead, funded by their subscriptions and the money raised from dinners. It was a new and practical solution to an old medieval problem.

Of course, guilds did not always behave charitably, and their commercial activities sometimes make them appear closer to the Mafia than a religious fraternity. Half a mile away from the merchant adventurers hall, and nearly a century away in time, the Red Tower gate in the city's walls would be the setting, not for a charitable dinner, but for murder. The Red Tower was the last of the gates in York's city walls to be completed, an out-of-the-way corner of town on the edge of a marsh, a place not much visited by the likes of guild masters. The gate being built here in 1490 was a modest affair in brick, its location not warranting the more expensive stone structure of other sites. While this had been good news for the guild of tilers, whose members had the contract to finish the work, it was the cause of increasing resentment among the stone masons who had built the rest of the wall. No doubt they worried that the increased use of brick, a light and relatively cheap material, would damage their business and their grumblings soon escalated into direct action.

In September 1490 two masons were sent to prison for wilfully damaging the tools of a tiler working on the Red Tower. If this was intimidation, it worked, and the tilers' guild petitioned the city council for protection during the work, claiming they were subject to threats of violence, mutilation and even murder. The council did nothing and October of the following year the tiler John Patrick paid the price for their inaction. What exactly happened on that autumn day the civic records do not show but at some point Patrick was ambushed at work and beaten, probably with his own tools. By the time his fellow tilers arrived the attackers were long gone and John Patrick himself was dead.

There was little doubt in the city about who was responsible and three days later two masons (including William Hindley, perhaps York's finest master mason) were arraigned in court charged with murder. They had worked nearby on the stonework for the wall and their guild's loss of the contract for the final gate had just pushed them too far. Their loyalty to their guild had driven them to murder. However although both men were convicted neither was hanged and their brief prison sentences suggest that their guild did an excellent job of lobbying the council for their early release. Hindley served just three days.

While some guilds worked for the protection of their members' jobs (at whatever cost) and others for the protection of their souls, another group took on the task of building many of the practical structures of this new world. In the late fourteenth century at Abingdon in Berkshire a guild was formed that wasn't specific to one craft but simply to that locality. It was a friendly society that brought together a disparate, denuded population and gave them common cause. The Guild of the Holy Cross was perhaps the Co-operative Society of its day.

Its purpose was to supply the social institutions once provided by the Church or their lords: schools for the children, alms-houses for the old and poor, chapels where their souls could be prayed for. Theoretically much of this work should have fallen to the local abbey, but this corporate religious body had little interest in furthering the aims of the people it dominated. In response the people of Abingdon ignored it and set up their guild in a chapel they built on the side of St Helen's Church. Above it in the 'chequer chamber', the guild met to plan the town's renaissance. If the abbey wouldn't run the town properly for them, they'd run it themselves.

A flavour of this entrepreneurial self-help can be gained from a poem found in the meeting room of one of the guild's alms-houses, written by the fifteenth-century guildsman and iron-monger Richard Forman. It tells of a day in the summer of 1416 when the guild met to build a bridge over the Thames at Culham:

> Upon the day of seynt Albon they began this game,
> And john Buchyns layne the first stoon in the kynges name...

Some three hundred local people answered the call to come bridge-building and they decided to make an event of it, enjoying a picnic of bread, cheese and roast chicken while the work was done. From the sound of it they certainly put their backs into it:

> The mattok was man handeled right wele a whyle.
> With spades and schovells they made such a noyse,
> That men myght here hem thens a myle...

And, no doubt, after quite a few of these 'working picnics', the bridge was finished. Its express purpose was to prevent people drowning in the river after storms had swollen it for

Dole [sad] it is to drawe a deed body oute of a lake.

But clearly there were financial advantages as well. The bridge brought new trade to Abingdon, which improved the town's fortunes and drastically reduced the profitability of competition from the nearby ancient town of Wallingford, originally built by Alfred the Great. As testament to the quality of the workmanship, the bridge still stands today.

The role of guilds in encouraging enterprise, promoting self-help, and providing physical and spiritual life assurance made them the new focus of town life and attracted considerable influence and wealth. In many towns guilds, particularly those without charters, were almost becoming a form of local government. Through them it was possible for people from relatively humble backgrounds to rise to prominence, and when they did they often let the guild share in their good fortune. Most famous of the guild members to 'make it good' at this time was Richard 'Dick' Whittington, perhaps the only businessman to become a much-loved pantomime character. His was one of the great success stories of the new system and his rise to prominence and its effects on those who heard about it explains the birth and perpetuation of the myth.

Richard Whittington was not from the poorest class – his father was a Gloucestershire knight – but as the third son there was little chance of him inheriting much land from his father's estate. Without land (and the social status and money it brought) the only other option open to Richard was to go to town and make his fortune. Before the Black Death the idea of moving away might have seemed dangerous, if not impossible, to many countryfolk, but with the aid of the guilds Richard did just that. Apprenticed in London, he went on to become one of the leading lights of the mercers' guild, which represented the cloth dealers. Having cornered the lucrative silk and velvet market, he rapidly rose to prominence by selling to the aristocracy who, thanks to the Sumptuary Law, were the only people, in theory, who could wear his goods. He went on to deal with the King himself, first selling Richard II two gold cloths for eleven pounds in 1389. When Richard was deposed ten years later he owed Whittington a thousand pounds, which the mercer immediately went about recouping by continuing to trade with the King's successor, Henry IV. Whittington's trade in luxury cloth and wool made him one of the richest merchants of his day; he was also three times master of the guild and four times Mayor of London. In fact he became so wealthy that it was necessary to invent a reason for his success in a world where aspiration was a wholly new concept – hence the legend of his magical cat. In the medieval mindset in which everyone was born into a station in life and died in it, magic still seemed the only possible way that Whittington could have been so successful.

Richard Whittington was grateful for the support the mercers' guild had given him and when he died, heirless, he left his huge estate not to the Church, as his ancestors might have done, but to the guild. At the time it was valued at five thousand pounds, well in excess of five million in today's terms. In return the mercers kept his name alive, building alms-houses, endowing the first guild hall library in London, funding a college of priests, making numerous bequests for church and hospital building, rebuilding Newgate gaol, and even commissioning a public lavatory. Today the mercers' guild still runs the alms-houses that bear Whittington's name.

It was not only entrepreneurial men who were gaining from the new opportunities that flowed in the wake of the Black Death. The chronic shortage of labour brought opportunities for work and trade to women that would not be seen again until the First World War. Many of these new opportunities sprang up in towns, to which young women had been coming in greater numbers than men since the days when Wharram Percy was a thriving Norman village. Towns had always offered an escape for women from the constraints of village life and a chance to earn independent wages, often in service, but the available work was often limited. Many a hopeful migrant found that the streets in medieval British towns were not always paved with gold, and begging and prostitution in the slum suburbs were ever-present. Indeed, the Latin word for the slum cottages inhabited by the suburban class, known as 'bordars', is *bordellus,* from which we take the modern word 'bordello'.

After the Black Death, however, women found themselves in demand to run the infrastructure of town life. For centuries they had been unofficially involved in business, often controlling many aspects of their husbands' trade, from hiring, managing and training apprentices to compiling accounts. Indeed, to become a master of his guild, a man had to be married – not to prove his respectability but to provide himself with the business partner who would ensure his workshop operated on a firm administrative footing. Now, with so many masters dead of plague, the women's role expanded. They now gained entry to many guilds that needed astute practitioners to keep their craft alive. They could join some as apprentices, either as single women (known as 'femme sole') or married ('femme couvert'), and might rise to become masters in their own right. In London, the customs of the City went as far as to state that on a master's death his wife would become responsible for continuing his business or finding someone to do so; in return, she would be made a full citizen of London with all the rights and privileges that afforded.

One woman who thrived in this atmosphere was Joanna Hill, who lived in a rented tenement building called the Three Nuns behind St Botolph's Church, then just outside the city walls of London in the 1420s and 1430s. As a young girl she had met a London bell-founder called Richard – perhaps when as an apprentice, he had come to her village to hang a new church bell. Bell-founding was a booming industry at the time as churches everywhere were being added to or rebuilt, and a successful founder was quite a catch. The match was made and Joanna came to London as Richard's wife. He seems to have been highly successful, running a major foundry from 1418 onwards, and twenty-three of his bells survive to this day, scattered across the country from Cornwall to Rutland.

In May 1440, however, Richard died, leaving Joanna as the sole executor of his will. But she did not intend to sit back and live off his money. Instead, she threw herself into the business, producing more than twenty bells in the following year, seven of which still ring in belfries today. Her pride in her work is clear: alongside the shield-shaped mark of her husband, on each bell she produced she added a diamond, the heraldic symbol for a woman. It was her mark, proof that she was now running the business.

When she, too, died, only a year after her husband, her will showed how successful she had been. In the last year she had taken on a new apprentice, so new in fact that she couldn't remember his name when it came to leaving him a few shillings. Worried about Purgatory, of course, she had left the huge sum of seventy marks for seven years of masses for her and

Richard's souls. Showing real affection for her late husband she also left twenty pounds for special requiem masses to be sung for him on the anniversary of his death for the next twenty years. Her best red gown, lined with fur – definitely not allowed by the Sumptuary Law – she left to her daughter Joanna, and she did not forget the poor and sick of her parish or the people of the Surrey village where she was born. She left her business in an excellent position, and she would have been proud to know that, twenty years after her death, another woman was running her foundry.

While women were now gaining entry into the business world, the road to success usually involved marriage. In the later Middle Ages marriage was as much about consolidating social and financial ties as about love and for most women had at least a degree of arrangement about it. From the Church's perspective, marriage was the next best thing to becoming a nun or hermit as it provided a framework in which the unpleasant business of procreation could legitimately be carried out – something that was in great need during the years after 1350.

The events that brought a woman to the church on her wedding day – or, rather, to the porch, where marriages were solemnised – might have begun many years before. For William Aungier and Joanna Malcake it had begun on the death of William's parents from plague. When he was eight his guardians had 'married' him to Joanna, who was two years his senior, probably for financial reasons. However, as William and Joanna were still children, in the eyes of the law they would not be officially married until William came of age and consented retrospectively to the marriage. Marriage meant mutual vows, which children could not make. And that was where William and Joanna's problems began. After three years in which the couple lived separately, he at school in Norfolk and she at home in Yorkshire, only seeing each other for two weeks in that time, William's guardian heard rumours that the sixteen-year-old Joanna had slept with several men and was now pregnant. William, not quite fourteen, was rushed to Joanna's house and ordered to consummate the marriage. He told a friend: 'It displeases me that I knew her once for she does not prize an affection that is upheld. And therefore, for sure, I intend never to consent to her that she be my wife, nor to cohabit with her.'

After a week of cajoling by Joanna's neighbours, William spent a night with his 'bride' but he kept his word to his friend. He refused to accept the marriage, moved away from the house and, in the spring of 1397, took the case to court. The financial concerns that made the match good enough for William's guardians were clearly not enough for William who, even in this mercenary marriage market, had hoped for at least a little love too.

Where the issue of money and land was less pressing, women had to protect their honour not only from the men of the village but from the vagaries of the law. In theory, the simple act of saying, 'I take you to be my husband/wife' was marriage in the eyes of the law, regardless of where the vow was taken, but sex provided the additional proof that a Church court might need to settle the matter. It was thus in the negotiation of marriage in return for sex that many village partnerships were brokered.

In 1358, when Robert Midleton asked Alice Welwyk to sleep with him she, quite naturally, said she would only consent if he married her. He replied that he could not vow to marry her as he didn't know if she could bear children, but if they had sex and she fell pregnant he would marry her. This was not a great deal for Alice, but she was persuaded when he agreed that while he couldn't promise her that he would marry her, he could promise her servant that he'd marry her if she became pregnant. In fact, he was simply trying to evade the law, and when a better match presented itself, to a woman from a wealthy local family, he dropped poor pregnant Alice. She was paid off, and did not dispute the reading of the banns for Robert and his new wife-to-be. It was only nine years later that she attempted to have his marriage annulled by the court on the grounds that she had married him first. But as the court pointed out, the manipulative Robert had made no vow to her, and she lost her case.

Other women were more cunning. On 17 October 1355, Maud Schipyn paid what might have been a costly visit to one Robert Smyth at his home in Bolton Percy. When she arrived she was a maiden but, thanks to her knowledge of the law, she was Robert's wife when she left some hours later. How she achieved it is, fortunately, recorded:

Margaret Thaker had been taken ill in the basement of Robert Smyth's house. And she saw through the door of the basement how Robert pushed and pulled Maud inside and there he tried to know her carnally. And Maud had said, 'Our god forbade that you should have the power to know me carnally unless you will marry me.' So Robert answered, 'Behold my oath that if I take anyone to be my wife, I shall take you if you will yield to me.' And Maud replied, 'Behold my oath that I will be at your disposal.' And so Robert took her in his arms and threw her to the ground and knew her carnally.

Of course, Robert had little intention of marriage and within a few weeks was strenuously denying what he had done. He didn't know that it was too late. Maud knew that legally she was married to Robert and to prove it she took him to court. On 22 December Maud and the now recovered Margaret

Thaker appeared confidently before the Church court which met in the south transept of York Minister. The court was used to such cases – it dealt with over two hundred contested marriages each year. The Church would even pay for those too poor to afford lawyers to bring cases – a form of medieval legal aid – and since 1362 access to the law had been increased when a statute had ordained that all pleas were to be made in English. People came to court to escape violent or otherwise unhappy marriages, using the only excuse the Church would accept for annulment: that they had been incorrectly entered into. This case, though, was the opposite. With a witness to the fact that Robert and Maud had both made vows and that consummation had quickly followed, Robert didn't have a leg to stand on. The vow alone was proof of marriage and the evidence of sex doubled it. Robert was married, whether he liked it or not.

Many of the advances made by women in the second half of the fourteenth century did not endure. By the mid-fifteenth century Britain's economy was in recession and, with less demand for workers, women were the first to suffer. In 1461 female weavers were told by their Bristol guild that they should give up their jobs in favour of the men who had been fighting for their country. (That sentiment almost exactly echoes the advertising campaigns at the end of the First World War, which encouraged women to 'go back to the kitchen' and leave their jobs to the men returning from the front.) Having learnt the trades and kept the economy going through the bad times, their competition was no longer wanted. By 1511 the men of the weavers' guild in Norwich were even claiming that women could not weave because they were not strong enough to operate the looms – which until then they had clearly proved was not the case.

Opportunity

While life for both men and women in the towns had been changing, it had not stood still in the countryside. New ways of working were emerging and, with them, new classes of people. Faced with a lack of labour and problems keeping up incomes in the ensuing Peasants' Revolt, many landlords had turned away from direct control of their estates in favour of leasing them in return for rent rather than making money from the sale of produce. The word they used to describe this was 'farming', which, of course, has survived although now it has come to mean the opposite. While farming allowed landowners to swap the instability of agriculture for a fixed income, it offered those with the money to rent these large parcels of land a host of opportunities.

One such family were the Pastons of Norfolk, who emerged from the Black Death as villeins, attached to the village of Paston and owing service to the lord there. But not for long. Thanks to the extraordinary survival of hundreds of letters between them in the fifteenth and sixteenth centuries, we can watch a family do what before had been impossible: rise through the ranks. In the Pastons we have Britain's first *nouveaux riches*.

The first Paston we can meet is Clement, probably still a tied labourer, described by an anonymous letter-writer, who was clearly no friend of the family, as

. . . a good plain husband[man], and lived upon his land that he had in Paston, and kept thereon a plough all times in the year, and sometimes in barlysell two ploughs. The saide Clement yede [went] at one plough both winter and summer, and he rode to mill on the bare horseback with his corn under him, and brought home meal again under him, and also drove his cart with divers corns to Wynterton to sell as a good husband[man] ought to do.

Faint praise indeed, but the Clement who wearily worked the fields founded a great dynasty. By educating his son at school, which was expensive and probably left him in debt, Clement showed that an ordinary rural family could aspire to greater things. And their son William proved worthy of their investment. He became a distinguished lawyer, a sergeant-at-law and finally a judge of the Common Pleas. As a man of some wealth he was able to make a judicious marriage to Agnes Berry, who brought with her what every aspiring gentleman needed: land. Installed in the manor of Oxnead, the Pastons had already gone from labourer to lord of the manor. From now on, marriage and land acquisition would become the main business of the family. It could be a dangerous game and the heads of the family brooked little or no resistance from the children they used as pawns. When Elizabeth Paston, William and Agnes's daughter, showed some reluctance to marry an ugly but wealthy widower of fifty, her mother quite literally took things into her own hands and Elizabeth, according to one letter: 'hath sin Easter the most part be beaten once in the week or twice, and sometimes twice on o day, and her head broken in two or three places'.

A generation later when Margery Paston married the family's bailiff, a match considered much beneath her, the family were left frankly apoplectic with rage. Having tried, and failed, to have the betrothal vows reversed, Margery's mother refused to have her daughter in the house. The Pastons were not fools, though, and the capable bailiff kept his job.

To illustrate how far the Pastons were prepared to go to achieve recognition, there is evidence to suggest that William and Agnes's son John, also a lawyer, might have counterfeited Sir John Fastolff's will, having worked his way into the dying knight's favour and become his personal lawyer. When the will of Fastolff, the model for Shakespeare's John Falstaff, was read and it became clear that John Paston was the main beneficiary, a long and bloody feud erupted between a number of powerful men who considered themselves his rightful heirs.

For the Pastons, land was the most important commodity as it brought with it both money and social standing. After 1413 new distinctions arose among these aspirational groups with the titles 'knight', 'squire' and 'gentleman' being defined in terms of landed income. Admission to one of these classes was essential for the Pastons and those like them, and even provoked fights in the street when proper protocols were seen to have been ignored. Memories of their days as serfs were forgotten as wealthy families bought 'class', which in the case of the Pastons went as far as paying the King to provide a patently false document claiming that the family had come over with the Conqueror.

All this social climbing cost money and making money from mixed farming in the years after 1350 had proved difficult. However, for those like the Pastons with the money to buy land, the answer was to change the economy of the landscape, and the life of the rural population. Sir Thomas More described the means by which they did this rather enigmatically:

your sheep that were wont to be so meek and tame, and so small eaters, now, as I hear say, be become so great devourers and so wild, that they eat up, and swallow down the very men themselves. They consume, destroy, and devour whole fields, houses, and cities. For . . . noblemen and gentlemen, yea and certain abbots . . . leave no ground for tillage, they inclose all into pastures; they throw down houses; they pluck down towns, and leave nothing standing, but only the church to be made a sheep-house.

The process he was talking about became known as enclosure. In a land with a labour shortage there were greater profits to be made from the wool trade than from growing cereals, and turning the open fields of wheat and barley over to pasture for sheep allowed landowners to employ fewer people while making more money. Furthermore, as British wool-growers began to process their wool, which they had previously sold raw, into cloth, the value of the crop increased further and the temptation to enclose grew. The old pattern of manorial demesne and open fields tilled by villagers was slipping away. In its place came open grassland and huge flocks of sheep. Soon wool-growers, like Thomas Paycocke of Coggeshall in Essex, were not just running an estate but effectively employing all the villagers, either directly as carders, spinners, fullers, shearmen and weavers, or in the trades that provided for them. Coggeshall was almost a rural factory.

For those on a manor that a landlord wished to turn over to pasture, and whose services were no longer needed, this was the end of a way of life. When the wealthy lawyer Thomas Pigott enclosed his land at Doddershall in Buckinghamshire on 11 August 1495, the 120 villagers were said to have left 'tearfully' and their twenty-four cottages fell into ruins. Such evictions must have been all the harder to bear when carried out by lords who, only a generation or two before, had been tied village labourers themselves, the friends and relatives of the people they were now evicting. When Cardinal Thomas Wolsey ordered an inquiry into the rapidly changing shape of the countryside in 1517, he noted grimly of one estate:

He held this land on the second of March 1489 when those messuages were laid waste and thrown down, and lands formerly used for arable he turned over to pasture for animals, so three ploughs are now out of use there, and eighteen people who used to work on that land and earn their living there and who dwelled in the houses have gone away to take to the roads in their misery, and to seek their bread elsewhere and so are led into idleness.

Not all those who remained in the countryside were as successful as the Pastons or as brutal as Thomas Pigott. Indeed, many minor gentry and wealthier peasants managed quite modestly, buying up parcels of land when they became available and only slowly changing the faces of the fields and villages around them. Once new families were established, and servile roots carefully covered over, the focus for their new-found wealth often turned back to the local church. While the great monasteries might have suffered a drop in bequests, a wave of religious fervour led to a surge in church building and augmentation in the soaring new Perpendicular style, with its 'four centred' arches, acres of window and fan vaulting. Most spectacular among these were the 'wool churches', built with the vast profits accruing to those who controlled the ever-expanding wool trade.

To walk into the church of St Peter and St Paul in Lavenham, Suffolk, is to walk into the minds of these aspirational builders. This church was not the work of a local aristocrat, although the Earl of Oxford suggested to the people of Lavenham that they might care to build it to celebrate the battle of Bosworth in 1485, but of the new classes of merchant and landowner. One of these, Thomas Spryng, described as a 'rich clothier' (he was the wealthiest man in the county after the Duke of Norfolk), donated three hundred marks just to build the tower. He was later buried with his wife in the church, having made the building into something resembling a personal mausoleum, filled with carvings of his recently acquired coat-of-arms and exhortations to pray for his soul. Most of the previous church, up to the chancel, was confidently swept away, the battered fourteenth-century font being just about all that was left of the former nave. The chancel, which was the financial responsibility of the Church, was pointedly left in its old style.

In the end the Earl of Oxford contributed to the building as well, both in the tower, where his arms can be seen, and the beautifully fan-vaulted south porch, but this was no longer simply an aristocratic undertaking. He and others like him had to share the glory with the Spryngs of this world – common but wealthy people without titles who, only a few generations before, might have been tied to his estates. Now the village of Lavenham (and it was still only a village) was the fifteenth wealthiest place in the country. To the Earl, and to the villagers who now looked up to Spryng, a former peasant, as their main benefactor, it must have seemed as though the world had been turned on its head. As the poet John Gower put it, in his 'Confessio Amantis' of around 1400:

> . . . What schal befalle hierafterward
> God wot, for now upon this tyde
> Men se the world on every syde
> In sondry wyse so diversed,
> That it welnyh stant al reversed,
> As forto speke of tyme ago . . .

In fact, the changes had barely begun.

The Perpendicular churches at Lavenham and elsewhere were a short-lived phenomenon, at least in the form that their builders knew them. Their brightly painted interiors, decorated statues, intricately carved rood screen, the reredos, candles, relics and plate – all the symbols of the medieval Christian world – were about to be swept away. New classes of people were bringing new ideas, which would change not just the interiors of churches but the face of society. For those peasants standing in silent awe in the recently completed nave at Lavenham in the early years of the sixteenth century so much had changed, but it must have seemed that at least the Church remained solid, with its rituals and festivals and its careful marking out of the agricultural and social year. But they were wrong. The stone body of Lavenham church would survive, but the rich medieval clothes in which it was now dressed would soon be torn away. With them would go the certainties of the religious calendar, the power of the saints, the doleful statue of the Virgin Mary that now stared out from Spryng's new Lady Chapel and, in the end, the medieval world itself. A new age was being born, one marked by opulence and glamour at the top of society but riven with rebellion and riot beneath. It would prove a difficult birth but it would be the birth of the modern world.

7
Leaving the Land

The stars move still, time runs, the clock will strike,
The devil will come and Faustus must be damned.
Christopher Marlowe

On the morning of 18 May 1539, the scene in the little church
at Morebath in Devon was as it had been the day, week,
year, perhaps even century before. The light shone through the
coloured glass in the windows, the high cross looked down
from the rood beam across the chancel arch and the statues of
the saints, most particularly St Sidwell, the priest's favourite,
gazed out across the empty nave. Before the high altar a candle
was burning, as it always did, and as for centuries it always
had done. Keeping this candle alight was a matter of some
concern for the village. Each year they appointed a warden to
administer a small fund that paid for the beeswax and wicks,
and each year its accounts were meticulously recorded by Sir
Christopher Trychay, their priest, in his account book.

The candle in question was known as the Alms Light, and
it burned before the high altar in memory of all the dead of the
parish, but particularly for those who had no other memorial.
Morebath was a small place, and a poor one, and for the vast
majority of parishioners who had prayed for centuries beneath
its church roof, prayers were their only epitaph. The stone
grave slabs in the floor and the brass and stone monuments
on the wall were for the rich landowners, be they old blood
or new money. For the poor, a single candle burned.

But 18 May would not end like all those days that had gone

before. That day Joan Goodman, warden of the Alms Light, had paid a visit to the priest. Together they had gone through the accounts, and the nineteen pence for the previous year's wax and wicks had been paid out. There was now two shillings and eightpence left in the fund, which would normally have been handed over to the new warden. But not this year. Instead, the money was handed back to the priest to go into other, less contentious projects. In return he dismissed Joan from her job – the last of the Alms Light wardens. In the church, the candle guttered and died, and in the pencil-line of smoke that rose from the smouldering wick was written the epitaph of the medieval world.

The events that led to the extinguishing of the candle in Morebath are known today as the Reformation. It was a time in which the old Catholic order was challenged across Europe as new ways of experiencing Christianity spread across the continent. In countries where these 'Protestant' ideologies took root, wholesale change in the nature of religion followed and, in a world where religion sat at the centre of everyday life, a wholesale change in lifestyle as well.

The Reformation arrived in Britain not on the lips of radical preachers but in the court bundles of lawyers. Henry VIII was experiencing problems with his heir supply, which he blamed squarely on his wife, the Spanish Katherine of Aragon. She had provided him with an heir of last resort – a girl, Mary – but Henry wanted a boy and to get one he believed he needed a new wife. There was a candidate in the background, Anne Boleyn, the hugely ambitious daughter of the aspirational merchant Thomas Bullen – she had changed her name to the more French-seeming 'Boleyn' to increase her romantic allure. But a problem was lurking in the shadows. Henry, Katherine, Anne and England were all Catholic and all, at least in matters of marriage, under the authority of the Pope. The Pope would not allow Henry to divorce Katherine, so Henry determined to divorce England from the Pope.

The political machinations that led to the English Church splitting from Rome probably seemed distant to the villagers of late medieval Britain, but their effects would be seen everywhere. In the first instance, those who lived on or near monastic land would hear about the changes as Henry helped himself to a useful windfall from the break in the Dissolution of the Monasteries. For a long time, the wealth, and hence power, of the monasteries had been a thorn in the side of the monarchy. Secular landowners always did the decent thing and died, sometimes with heirs to inherit but otherwise leaving their estate to revert to the Crown. Monasteries and other religious houses were immortal however; their abbots might die, but the institution lived on. When a pious landowner left them land, or money to buy land, they kept it for ever. By the beginning of the sixteenth century, the religious houses of Britain owned well over a quarter of all cultivated land in England, which made them nearly as powerful a force in the land as the King himself. And unlike all of the other people in the country, they gave their ultimate allegiance to a foreigner, the Pope, and not to the King. With the Church separated from Rome's control, they had to go and, by a stroke of luck, that also meant that the King would get their lands and wealth.

The degree to which people who lived on monastery land believed the logic of the dissolution probably varied. To some, the monasteries were cruel landlords, parasitically living off the labour of their tenants, but to others they were a source of work, alms and faith. With the minor, and later the major, houses dissolved, their tenants lost either good or bad landlords, but outside the immediate circle of the King, everyone saw those spiritual landlords quickly replaced with a secular equivalent. The King did not intend to keep all this land – he couldn't afford to if he was to keep his nobility happy – so the satisfaction that some perhaps felt as their monastic land-lord was expelled would have been tempered by the arrival of a new, secular lord of the manor, who had been given by, or purchased the estate from, the King. For some, life would then continue much as before, with the abbey church perhaps retained as the new parish church or simply quarried away for cheap building stone. For others, such as the tenants at Malmesbury in Wiltshire, it would mark the beginning of a whole new way of life: the abbey was bought by a business tycoon and turned into a clothing factory, with apparently little local complaint. Either way, while some might have cared, few dared to raise their voices against the change.

While few monasteries were defended to the death by their tenants, there were protests, and violent ones at that, in a century where the glamour of royal Tudor court life barely concealed an atmosphere of seething rebellion. The first erup-tion to affect the rural population of England began in the autumn of 1536 and would become the largest rebellion against Henry's changes in the Church to affect the north of England. There, the monasteries were major employers and the nobility, always more powerful away from the centre of royal authority in London, clung more doggedly to their Catholic beliefs. But beyond that, the people of the north were now seeing other effects of the dissolution, which looked like affecting their daily lives as well as impinging on their beliefs, and that mattered. The dissolution was justified in terms of abolishing idolatry, disruptive religious festivals and pilgrimages, and controlling the influence of priests, but new taxes, such as the 'first fruits and tenths', required every priest to pay a tenth of his income to the state, taking money out of the parish. More importantly still, the Protestant railings against idolatry and festivals threatened to strip the churches bare and reduce village life to a soulless monotony, without pageant or festival. These fears brought together an unlikely group of allies, including peasants, lords and abbots, under the banner of the 'Five Wounds of Christ', in a major protest movement that threatened Henry's crown: the Pilgrimage of Grace.

At the Cistercian abbey of Meaux, where the monks were still heavily involved in the wool trade, news of forthcoming 'visitations' by commissioners (a prelude to dissolution) reached them in 1535. The men dispatched by the Crown were Doctors Legh and Leyton, famed for their 'surprise' tactics – arriving at monasteries unannounced and making probing inquiries into the moral rectitude of the inhabitants, even going so far as to ask the monks if they slept with boys or women. The results, recorded in the 'Black Book', formed the basis for a justifiable dissolution. The monks at Meaux must have thought they had little opportunity to escape the clutches of the commissioners until news reached them of the uprising in Lincolnshire, which, by 1536, was spreading to Yorkshire and even to the monasteries themselves. Some monks had willingly joined the insurgents; others, like the Cistercian Abbot Sedbar of Jervaulx, had been literally dragged off to join them.

The Cistercians had already suffered a blow when their house at Sawley, in Lancashire, was dissolved in May of that year with other smaller monasteries, but their spirits lifted when news came in October that Pilgrimage rebels had accompanied the monks back to Sawley, where they reoccupied the site, throwing out the royal agents. These Cistercians at least were going to fight for their beliefs, and their livelihood, and it is likely that the hymn of the Pilgrimage was written here by one of the newly radical monks, who complained:

> Alack, alack,
> For the church's sack
> Poor common wake
> And no marvel
> For clear it is
> The decay of this
> How the poor shall miss
> No tongue can tell.

But the Pilgrimage of Grace was not to succeed. No doubt the Meaux chapter was sombre in 1536 when news arrived that Abbot William Thirsk of their mother-house, Fountains, had been deposed and had retired to Jervaulx. How much darker the mood then when, following the Cistercian involvement in the Pilgrimage, a message arrived that he had been arrested for treason and hanged. With the ringleaders of the rebellion rounded up and executed – clerics and laymen alike – all that the surviving Cistercians could do was wait. That wait came to an end at Meaux on 11 December 1539 when the commissioners of the King arrived to take possession of the site. While the abbot signed the deed of surrender, the monks were already being turned out and contractors brought in to strip the lead from the roofs. The King had plans for the buildings themselves. The church, refectory, chapterhouse and dormitory were all dismantled and the stones sent to Hull to build new fortifications. The stones of Meaux would end their days, perhaps appropriately, still defending the town that her monks had built.

The Reformation did not stop in the monasteries. If the

statues, relics, paintings and furniture of abbeys were idolatrous, then so were their counterparts in every parish church. For centuries these buildings had been the focus of the community, explaining the place of villagers in the wider world and in the life they hoped for beyond death. They were where the piety of the congregation was displayed in bequests, from a penny for a candle to hundreds of pounds for new aisles and altars. It was also where they came to ask saints to intercede for them in the daily struggle for life, and to remember and pray for those who had gone before and now awaited final judgement in Purgatory.

In the Reformation all of this changed, leaving many confused and resentful. There had been much wrong with the old Church, but it was familiar and everyone had invested their lives in it. Across England and Wales the first signs of the coming change were already visible in 1538. Had we walked into even a simple medieval church before the Reformation we would have found a place that bore little resemblance to our modern image of a parish church. It was a lively, even gaudy place, the walls painted with colourful portrayals of stories and characters from the Bible. On entering a typical church through the south porch, where many generations of villagers had been married, we might perhaps have seen on the north wall a huge painting of St Christopher carrying the infant Jesus – a reminder to the visiting traveller of their patron saint and to the congregation of the road all Christians travelled. Looking to the east (on our right) we would have seen the main nave and perhaps one or two side aisles – open and empty in the days before pews. There might have been a Lady Chapel at the end of the south aisle, with a painted and jewelled wooden, or perhaps stone, image of the Virgin on its altar, and candles surrounding it. Across in the north aisle there was perhaps another chapel, dedicated to the patron saint of the church, with another small statue, and at its foot, a Limoges enamel box with a rock-crystal cover containing a precious relic – perhaps a bone – of the saint. Looking down the main nave, the chancel arch might loom over the congregation with a 'doom' painting surrounding it, acting as both promise and warning. Across it, leading into the chancel, stood a wooden screen, elaborately carved, painted, perhaps even gilded. From its many niches, a host of carved saints peered out. To the north side, a small stone spiral staircase in the wall wound up to a gallery above the screen from where the priest often addressed his flock. Above this a single massive oak beam – the rood beam – stretched across the void, supporting a cross with a carving of the crucified Christ.

Beyond the screen lay the chancel, the province of the priest, and the part of the church for which authorities, not the congregation, were responsible. As such it might have been plainer, perhaps even still built in an older style, with thicker walls and small, mean windows. On the right, looking towards the altar, we could have seen three stone seats set into the wall – the sedilia – for the priest and his canons, each with a richly embroidered cushion. Beside them a little locked cupboard, the aumbrey, held the consecrated Host. Across on the north wall another much larger cupboard, the banner stave locker, would have been filled with the pennants, flags, ribbons and silk streamers that were paraded through the village on holidays. At the far east end the high altar would have been resplendent with its embroidered velvet cloth. On this stood a gilded cross and the main beeswax altar candles, while behind, a carved screen, the reredos, might have featured a painting of the Passion.

In the coming century much of this would change – although

it would take the Puritan zeal of the Civil War to finally erase the traces of medieval Christianity from most churches. Return to that same church a century later and you enter a different world. Successive injunctions from central government had banned the statues, and those that could be removed had been. Locals, perhaps even the priest, bought them and either kept them in their houses or hid them from the Church commissioners in the hope that the old ways would return. The stone carvings still attached to the body of the walls, which could not be removed, were instead defaced, leaving rows of decapitated saints. On the side altars, the statues and candles had gone. The reliquary had been secretly walled up in a forgotten corner of the tower. Looking through the chancel arch, only the scars of the great screen and rood beam survived on the walls, the banner stave locker beyond hung open, its pennants and flags sold to the highest bidder. In the north wall, the little spiral staircase that once led to the rood loft now opened out into thin air and only a tiny pulley, far above on the ceilings, remained as a reminder of the sombre cloth that was once lowered over the great cross during Lent. The paintings were still on the walls, but there was talk of whitewashing over them.

If there had been time to talk about the changes to the Church in England there was little opportunity for discussion in Scotland where the Reformation came to some areas quite literally overnight, packaged in John Knox's sermons rather Henry VIII's divorce papers. From the great cathedrals such as St Andrew's, which was stripped of its Catholic furnishing in less than twenty-four hours, to the little churches at places like Inverary, where the locals doggedly chipped away the now 'idolatrous' figure of Christ from its beautiful stone cross, the Reformation swept across Scotland with even greater ferocity than it had in England and Wales. It may have arrived a little later, but its effects were every bit as profound.

By 1560 Scottish churches were becoming more like their English counterparts: altar rails, icons and images had all been removed and wall paintings whitewashed. But this was not simply religious vandalism. Clearly there were places in which Protestantism offered people something new and popular. Conservatism meant that many objected to change, but change could bring benefits. From the new pulpits in the churches of Scotland, preachers spread the word of God in the native language of the inhabitants, including Gaelic, and the congregations were encouraged to take part in what had previously been a 'spectator sport'. As they fought their way through the Metrical Psalms of Geneva for the first time in the 1560s, the rhythmic chanting helped them store away vast tracts of a book that had previously been kept distant from them, the Bible, and began to set the scene for Sunday services of hymns and sermons that would still be familiar across the country in centuries to come.

But even in this brave new world, not all of the old ways were forgotten. When the parishioners of Burntisland on the east coast of Scotland built themselves a new church at the end of the sixteenth century they incorporated echoes of the old Catholic order. Now that their optional appearance at mass had been replaced with compulsory attendance at Sunday service, which might last for hours, the local fishermen had taken the practical step of building a back door to the church through which they could slip unnoticed during the service when the tide was high and the sea beckoned. Above the door an inscription talked of 'God's Providence', the force that had replaced the saints and the Virgin in protecting them from the awaiting sea.

Inside the church the fishermen had their own gallery, as did the other craft and trade guilds, with inscriptions directly invoking the protection of God (where the medieval guilds had once asked for the protection of their patron saints). After some initial resistance, the guilds were adapting to the new order and, having dropped their overtly Catholic rituals, were making a claim for prominence in the new church, as the careful arrangement of their pews shows. Now that attendance at church was compulsory – with failure punished by fines and public condemnation – the permanent pew was replacing the old style walk-in service. It provided a little comfort during the hours of sermonising and made a clear statement as to who was who in the community. Not surprisingly, the pew in the centre of the church, opposite the pulpit, was built by, and reserved for, the local laird, Lord Melville.

The interests of the new Protestant Church also went far beyond the pews. Protestantism wasn't just about a new form of service, a new language of prayer or even new doctrines, it was about a whole new way of life. In Burntisland the kirk elders had taken to prowling the streets looking for sinners to haul before the kirk sessions court. Sins such as 'fornication', 'drunkenness' and 'Sabbath breach' could all bring a hefty fine as well as an appearance on the 'penitent stool' in the centre of the church the following Sunday – a very public humiliation. But the reach of the Reformation spread further than the moral values of the people. The medieval church had been at the centre of community life: its festivals marked out the rhythms of the agricultural year, its courts administered the laws of marriage and inheritance, and its bequests paid for the care of the poor and elderly. In the Reformation all these things went too. Back at Morebath, the strain was showing.

The village 'funds' – religious bequests that provided much

of the church income – had been abolished and the priest's much-loved statue of St Sidwell had been banished. The church candles were extinguished forever, and the high altar on which they had once stood had been replaced with a communion table. Many of the church holy days had also been abolished and people had been ordered to work on them. During the reign of the devoutly Protestant Edward VI, new injunctions were published, pushing the Reformation further: rosary beads were banned and processions forbidden (with the banners and flags that accompanied them). All remaining images in churches were removed and the chantries, in which so many had found comfort from their fears of Purgatory, were dissolved along with the concept of Purgatory itself.

One result of all these changes was that, by the Easter of 1549, rebellion was brewing in the West Country. The abolition of the centuries-old Palm Sunday procession rankled, but in towns like Ashburton in Devon it was the dissolution of the chantries that really hurt. Many guilds in the later Middle Ages had founded chantries, and townspeople had invested heavily in them. In Ashburton, as in Abingdon, the guild that ran the chantry also effectively ran the town, managing its market, hospital and water supply. When this was suppressed and all its assets confiscated, the future of the town itself was in peril. The townsmen, and a few local farmers, responded by beating up the servants of the commissioners sent to confiscate the chantry's property. In Cornwall some even resorted to murder. While the guilds suffered, there were rumours that the government intended to go further still and demand that every church compiled an inventory of all its goods, which many felt was a prelude to confiscating all parish assets. But, strangely, it was not money that proved the final straw in the far west that Easter, but the introduction of the Book of Common Prayer to replace the Latin service book, which was promptly banned.

While many in the south-east of England might have welcomed a prayer book in their own language, that was not the case in Cornwall – where, of course, Cornish was still widely spoken. Reports reached London in early June that there was trouble in Bodmin and that it was spreading. When the priest at Sampford Courtney in Devon began reading to his congregation from the new prayer book on 10 June, there were loud protests and he was forced to begin again, this time using the old Latin missal. With tempers flaring, mobs were soon on the streets. As news of the rising spread, groups from villages across the West Country answered the call to rebellion. The local landowner in Sampford Courtney, who was unwise enough to try to reason with the mob, was murdered on the steps of his own house. Adding insult to injury they buried his body north–south instead of the Christian east–west – the mark of a heretic. At Clyst St Mary, an attempt by an over-zealous Protestant gentleman to relieve an old woman of her banned rosary beads brought the whole village out in open revolt when she protested, 'sayinge she was threatened by the gentleman, that except shee woulde leave her beades and geve over holie breade and water the gentleman woulde burne theyme out of theire howses and spoyle theim'.

By the beginning of July a 'peasant army', of a kind unseen since the Peasants' Revolt, had gathered on the outskirts of Exeter and laid siege to the city, with the banner of the 'Five Wounds of Christ', which had signalled the Pilgrimage of Grace, again fluttering in the breeze. The demands of the rebels give us an insight into the concerns of the people of rural Cornwall and Devon: the ancient ceremonies of the Church were to be restored, the statues brought back, the much-hated English prayer book and Bibles recalled. Perhaps more strangely to modern eyes, they demanded that Purgatory be reinstated. The response of the government was to instruct the nobility and gentry of the counties to order their peasants to return home – a move that would probably have had little effect even if the gentry hadn't been in passive agreement with the rebels. As it was, the changes in the Church and villages brought about by the Reformation and a series of punitive new taxes on sheep and cloth, designed to pay for a futile war with France, had made many landowners at least tacit supporters of the rebellion.

The government's next course of action went to the other extreme. Lord Russell, a major beneficiary of the dissolution, with an army of mercenary troops, was sent west. At Fenney Bridges by Clyst Heath on 5 August this professional army annihilated the gathered peasants. Most of the rebels were massacred, and those who escaped were hunted down and killed. The worst treatment was reserved for those clergy who had obstinately refused to adopt the new liturgy and had, in the eyes of the government, incited the rebellion. Their leader, a Cornishman called Robert Welshe, was hung in chains from his own church tower, with the symbols of the old faith, his robes, rosary and other such 'popyshe trash', hung about him. There he was left to die of exposure, which he duly did – 'verie patientlie', as one witness put it.

Retribution for the rising was swift and brutal. Sir Anthony Kingston, the provost marshal, was sent west with the power to judge, condemn and execute any rebels he found, and the savage eagerness with which he took up the commission is still remembered in Devon and Cornwall today. The contemporary historian Richard Carew, although a devote Protestant himself, recorded Kingstone's excesses with some distaste, claiming, in one instance, that he: 'left his name more memorable than commendable amongst the Bodmin townsmen, for causing the Mayor to erect a gallows before his own door, upon which, after he had feasted Sir Anthony, he himself was hanged'.

In St Ives, in Cornwall, he is remembered as having played the same trick on the portreeve, John Payne. Having asked Payne to build a gallows, Sir Anthony asked if it was strong enough. Legend has it that the portreeve replied that he was sure it was, which prompted Sir Anthony to reply: 'Then get up speedily, for they are prepared for you.'

When Payne protested, Sir Anthony riposted, 'In faith, there is no remedy, for you have been a busy rebel.'

And, indeed, there *was* no remedy – no trial, no right of appeal and no pardon. It is estimated that in the initial fight and the subsequent retribution the West Country lost as many lives as it did in both world wars.

It may seem strange today that so large a proportion of the population of the West Country should rise up against moves to make their faith more accessible, but the speed and totality of the changes threatened, as many saw it, the very fabric of their world. Nor did the Reformation stop at the lychgate of the church: it was also visible in the daily life of the village. 'Church houses' were attached to many churches – effectively village halls – where celebrations and festivals of the ritual year were held. At different times in the year they were also the venue for riotous wakes following funerals, harvest feasts, Christmas revels, which might include the often frowned-upon appointment of a Lord of Misrule, and the frequent 'church ales'. From the Church's perspective, the latter was just another way to raise money for the church, but it was more than that: church ales brought the community together for a party, at which the church provided both the venue and the drinks.

Just like the processions and church festivals, though, most of the fun and games were heavily criticised by the Protestant reformers, and in 1548 the Church authorities banned them, citing them as the cause of 'disorder' – which was then becoming endemic in the area. Without the funds or ales, churches like Morebath were virtually bankrupt.

The interest the authorities had developed in the festivals and games of rural life was not strictly concerned with saving souls. Protestant bishops and reformers might have talked piously about the problems of drunkenness and the redundant idolatry of Catholic celebrations but beneath the surface lay another, more recent concern.

Since the beginning of the enclosures the attitude of the landed classes towards the general population had been changing, and in response to this the attitudes of the population had changed too. For all the ferocity of its suppression, the Prayerbook Rebellion would not be the last uprising of the century. Elsewhere that same year others were also camped around towns and cities in silent, but sometimes violent, protest at the changes taking place.

In East Anglia Robert Kett, a middle-aged yeoman and tanner, had become the figurehead of another rising following the gathering of a large crowd at Wymondham in Norfolk. They were determined to put on the old plays and summer games that had previously been associated with the now dissolved monastery there. The focus of discontent seems to have shifted quickly from the direct effects of the Reformation and on to a more pressing economic issue: the enclosure of once common lands by the ever-aspiring gentry and aristocracy. Strangely, it was after the crowd had attacked enclosure fences belonging to Robert Kett that he offered to lead them against the enclosers in marching on Norwich. There, the swelling band was joined by many of the city's poor. At Mousehold, to the south of the city, the protesters set up a defended camp and issued their demands. Among their long list they ask for the abolition of several corrupt and unfair practices by landlords, restrictions on enclosing land and, in the knowledge that the Duke of Norfolk was imprisoned in the Tower of London, they made a bold bid for universal freedom in clause 16, which states: 'We pray thatt all bonde men may be made ffre for god made all ffre with his precious blode sheddyng.'

John Ball and Wat Tyler would have been proud of them, but the government's response was no different from what it had been in Exeter. The Crown dispatched not a negotiator but an army. After a short-lived initial success, which saw the rebels take the city of Norwich, the rebellion was put down and Kett, like poor Robert Welshe in Cornwall, died hanging in chains.

It had been a turbulent summer for the government, the religious reformers and the enclosers, and the growing rebelliousness of a people once considered so passive was leading the authorities to develop a new and not necessarily healthy interest in their morals and values. A second Reformation was taking place: a Reformation of Manners. The main beneficiaries of the huge changes taking place in the country – the religious reformers and the wealthy gentry (who were often one and the same) – were beginning to see their workforce in a new light. They were becoming a dangerous nuisance, all too ready to fight for what they believed were their rights, and obsessed with antiquated, divisive revels and festivals. For the zealous Protestant, such drunken revels were a hangover from the 'popish' festivals that had to be eradicated, while for the enclosing landowners they represented dangerous gatherings of workers, who might use an occasion of traditional games to raise rebellion against those who were changing this ancient world.

Protestant clerics in particular began to publish and preach against the supposedly banned but clearly surviving games and festivals, including John Northbrooke of Bristol who, in 1579, wrote a particularly saucy denunciation of plays and games, which he considered to be devices of the heathen Romans. Others joined in the clamour, calling for the abolition of church ales, and a reduction in the number of Church holidays on which games could be organised. It was perhaps no coincidence that many of these pious men were in the pay of the wealthiest landowning families of the day, who were growing to fear all rural gatherings as cauldrons of seething discontent.

Foremost among those recording what they hoped was the death of this lewd, medieval world was Philip Stubbes who, in his *Anatomie of Abuses* of 1583, recorded village festivals and games with a rarely matched disdain. Although his intention was simply to point out the profanity and vulgarity of such events he was in fact recording the swansong of the rites and rituals of the medieval village.

. . . the chiefest jewel they bring from thence is their May-Pole, which they bring home with great veneration, and thus. They have twenty or forty yoke of oxen, every ox having a sweet nosegay of flowers placed on the tip of his horns and these oxen draw home this May-Pole (this stinking idol rather), which is covered all over with flowers and herbs, bound roundabout with strings, from the top to the bottom, and sometimes painted with variable colours, with two or three hundred men, women and children following it with great devotion. And thus being reared up, with handkerchiefs and flags hovering o the top, they strew the ground round about, bind green boughs around it, set up summer halls, bowers and arbours hard by it. And then they fall to dance about it.

In recording the May Day events Stubbes does his best to portray the scene in as bad a light as possible but it is difficult, from his description, not to want to join in. Of course Stubbes would have been furious to learn that he has had a part in preserving the memory of such 'revels'. His audience at the time were good Protestants, who would have been 'shocked' by the profanity he described, and landowners, who would shiver at the thought of two or three hundred villagers riotously gathering together. His message was aimed at these classes, who clearly thought themselves different from, and certainly 'above', those he described. Both groups probably enjoyed, with a combination of righteous indignation and prurient titillation, his descriptions of rural dancing: 'For what clipping, what culling, what kissing and bussing, what smooching and slabbering one of another, what filthy groping and unclean handling is not practised every where in these dancings?'

But his readers among the gentry might have thought he had gone too far when he turned his puritanical attentions to the vices of their class, most particularly their vanity as he saw it expressed in their lavish Elizabethan hats, which he likened to 'fluttering sails and feathered flags of defiance to virtue'.

Attempts to suppress the 'common' festivals of the ritual year were having another effect on both towns and villages, which would further distance the rich from the poor. The medieval Church, through its emphasis on charity, had provided, in a small way, a form of welfare state. In the late Middle Ages the rich had been encouraged to give money to the Church, which it would spend on the poor. This might have taken the form of running a hospital for the sick, as the merchant adventurers had done in York, doling out bread and ale at the monastery gate to those in need, or simply providing employment for the poor on monastic estates. The system might have been haphazard but it provided a way for the rich to subsidise the poor while believing they were gaining spiritually from it.

And there were poor, in ever-increasing numbers. Every village had them: those who had fallen on hard times; the invalids and sick, whose illness prevented them working; and the generational poor, those too young or too old, or perhaps with young families and whose resources were spread just that bit too thin. All of those people required help at some time in the form of food, shelter or care, and traditionally the Church had raised money for this through its festivals, ales and charitable donations. When eventually the question of who would provide for the poor reached the ears of the Tudor government, the reply came back, 'You all will,' and the Tudor Poor Laws were born.

The Poor Laws were designed to take up the slack in provision for the poor that the changes in the Church had created. Instead of relying on ecclesiastical charity, levies were now to be locally raised on the whole population to provide for the poor and the sick. But the sixteenth century was not like the previous one: enclosure had forced many rural workers off the land, and the combination of a rapidly rising population and huge inflation had put the bare necessities of life beyond the reach of increasing numbers of people. In each parish an 'overseer of the poor' was appointed to raise local taxes and to decide who among the unfortunates should receive the money and how much. Should the overseer deem you indolent or criminal, one of the 'pilferers and bastard-bearers' that were believed to plague Britain, that might mean you would receive nothing. The new poor were no longer seen as a necessary vehicle by which the rich could demonstrate their piety: they were simply a threat.

The response in cities like Norwich was to measure and categorise them, separating the deserving from those considered unworthy and the 'local poor' from 'undesirable aliens'. In 1570 the burghers of Norwich organised a census to discover what their requirements under the Poor Laws were, and the picture it painted was bleak. The Norwich of the census describes a town where the poor are everywhere, living on the streets, in hovels on the outskirts of town and squatting in the disused towers of the medieval walls. One family living in an old tower is recorded as 'Agnes Longworth of 40 yere, wedowe, that work nott; & 2 children of 9, 6 yer, that begge, & have dwelt here ever.' and their situation as, 'No allms. Myserable pore.'

Normally the burghers might have expected about five per cent of the population to need serious help, with another 10 per cent occasionally requiring aid to avoid starvation. In Norwich that year the census found 20 per cent in immediate need. No doubt many had come to town from the surrounding countryside, having lost their rural livelihood to the enclosers.

In a town with too many people and not enough work, even the able-bodied were in trouble. Peter Browne and his family are described as:

... porter, a cobler of 50 yeris, hath lyttle worke, and Agnes his wyfe, of 60 yeris, that worketh nott but hav ben syk syns Christmas, but in helth she spyn white warpe; 3 daughters of 18, 16, of 14 yeris which all spyn when they can get yt, but nowe they ar withoute worke. They have dwelt here above 20 yeris, & they have one daughter, Elizabeth, is idle & sent from cervis with William Naught of Thorp, wher she dwelt 3 quarters of a yer.

Many in the town must have looked bitterly to the wealthy wool farmers of East Anglia, who had displaced these people and were now taking the profits while the townsfolk were forced to pay for them. Their response was not to attack the farmers however, but just to eject their poor from the city.

The poor were now divided into the worthy and unworthy, and the difference was clearly marked out for all to see. After 1586 in Scotland, towns took to labelling their poor with the town's mark, to show they were justifiable 'charges' on the town's purse. Those without the mark were turned out.

Just south of the border in Cumbria even the right to be poor was becoming hard-fought. Anne Bowman spent fifteen years petitioning the local authorities in her village of Kirkoswald to grant her a pension after her husband's was revoked on his death. Despite her age, sixty-two, and her position as mother of five children, one of whom was mentally ill, the parish deemed her 'fit to work'. In response Anne continued to petition it, and these documents survive, giving us a fleeting echo of one voice of the normally silent poor: 'I being old feeble and infirm desire that I may not be confined to an old ruinous house which is without the cry of any neighbours ... for that unmerciful and savage behaviour would confine me to a dismal corner where none might relieve me or help me in my hunger-bitten condition.'

Despite her infirmities, Anne clearly had a good knowledge of the law and drew on powerful local support from the minister to defend herself from the accusations of the overseer of the poor, but she continued to divide the community. While the local gentry provided some charitable support, as their medieval ancestors had, the much poorer boatman refused to let her travel in his boat – allegedly under pressure from the overseer of the poor – forcing her to walk many extra miles to cross the river Eden by bridge. He, more than his wealthy neighbours, had reason to resent Anne's finally being granted a pension. The wealthy had always provided charity for people like her, but now he had to as well. There was nothing he could do about the law, but he must have approved of the decision to force her to wear a pauper's badge – an appropriate humiliation.

As the numbers of poor increased, however, humiliation would not be enough. Those who followed in Anne Bowman's footsteps found that the new remedy in towns across Britain was to put the poor to work. Within a century those found traipsing between towns without work were liable first to find themselves in 'houses of correction' and, after 1676, in the workhouse.

In London, where the population quadrupled between 1500 and 1600, the increasing desperation of those at the bottom of society was matched by an increasing intolerance at the top. Among the many women who moved to the city to escape rural poverty, not all found work in the great houses and many ended up in more dangerous professions, particularly prostitution. Now that there were no great monastic houses to provide for destitute newcomers, procurers and pimps encouraged young rural women into the 'oldest profession' as, so 'Mrs Green' told a young Alice Sharpe, 'It is better to do so than to steal.'

Before the Reformation there had at least been a licensing system of sorts in parts of London to control this trade, but with a new puritanical wind blowing through government, brothels were banned. Of course, that didn't mean they went away, and in places like Turnmill Street, in East London, the road was still lined with 'bawdy howses' and filled with 'night-walkers', all just living in a more dangerous and unregulated world. The judges, before whom they made frequent appearances, seemed unable to turn away this tide of vice and, other than impose prison sentences and fines, could do little more than splutter impotently about the 'many lewd and loose persons who keepe comon and notorious brothell howses and harboure and entertaine divers impudent and infamous queanes and whores . . .'

In an increasingly polarised society, it was not only an unregulated sex trade, unemployment and abject poverty that threatened the poor. In the religious confusion left by the Reformation a new threat was emerging, for poor women in particular. An age of 'witch crazes' was dawning, when personal and family vendettas were cruelly settled in the fires of puritanical zeal. In an increasingly fundamentalist atmosphere, the old Catholic fear of Purgatory after death had been replaced by a very real fear of demons invading the world of the living. One concerned bishop wrote to Elizabeth I in 1562 claiming that 'Witches and Sorcerers within these last few years are marvellously increased within your grace's realm. These eyes have seen most evident and manifest marks of their wickedness. Your grace's subjects pine away even unto death; their color fadeth, their flesh rotteth, their speech is benumbed, their senses are bereft.' But this could also be used as an excuse, and as the gap between rich and poor in the village grew, the accusations increased.

In the late sixteenth century Warboys, in Cambridgeshire, was just such a village, and when the Throckmorton family accused the Samuels of witchcraft, more than supernatural demons were at work. Warboys, like so many other villages, had been suffering the effects of the Poor Laws, which required it to take charge of its poor. For the Samuels, this must have been good news as they should have been on the receiving end, but the Throckmortons ensured that it wasn't.

The fight between the Throckmortons and the Samuels must have been typical of what was happening in many towns and villages, although not all chose accusations of witchcraft as a means of settlement. The Throckmortons arrived in Warboys in 1589 as the new tenants of the manor. They were a successful, well-connected Puritan family, with five daughters aged between nine and fifteen – a typical family 'on the up'. The Samuels were equally typical of a less fortunate class. Alice Samuel, known as 'Mother Samuel', her husband and daughter were poor tenant farmers, renting lands and generally getting in the way. They were certainly not Puritans – indeed, they were not even regular churchgoers.

When Jane, the young daughter of Robert Throckmorton, began to have seizures (possibly due to epilepsy) in November 1589, it was Alice who found herself in the firing line. When she visited Jane, the girl accused her of witchcraft. Then the other children began to fall ill and made similar accusations. Alice stayed away from the house, but the allegations continued. With doctors unable to diagnose the problem, the increasingly desperate family blamed Alice for sending a familiar to bewitch the children in the form of a demon chicken that sucked blood from Mother Samuel's chin! A contemporary pamphlet claimed later that she not only admitted to the bird's existence but was well aware of its evil intent: 'Being asked whether it was a naturall chicken, she saith it was not, she knoweth it was no naturall chicken.'

The family's fate was sealed when Lady Cromwell, step-grandmother of Oliver, visited the Throckmortons, her husband's tenants, and repeated the claim. Allegedly she asked to cut and burn some of Alice's hair – a standard procedure to stop a bewitching – but Alice would not let her. That night Lady Cromwell fell sick with a 'mystery illness' and dreamed about Alice Samuel's cat. A year and a half later when she died it seemed to the Puritanical Cromwells and the Throckmortons that Alice must be to blame. Under great pressure Alice eventually confessed to witchcraft and, under orders from Robert Throckmorton, 'banished' the evil spirits she was accused of sending to plague them. Apparently the children made a sudden and complete recovery. Alice, aware of the danger in what she had admitted, tried to retract her confession. The girls' fits returned. Alice, her husband and daughter were arrested and put on trial. While Alice claimed to be pregnant – which was highly unlikely in someone of over sixty – to avoid the death penalty her daughter Agnes in a proud but ultimately futile gesture refused to do so, saying: 'I will not be both held witch and strumpet!'

Whatever other mitigating circumstances might have been found, the court was not in a mood to hear them and, on 4 April 1593, the entire family was hanged. The troublesome Samuels had been removed and another family name could be struck off the Warboys poor list. As Sir Walter Scott later put it: '. . . the purposes of justice were never so perverted, nor her sword turned to a more flagrant murder'.

The full cause of the Warboys accusations will probably never be known. In part some might have believed the witchcraft claims, and certainly if anyone was going to be blamed for such a thing it would have been the 'undesirable' Samuels. No doubt once the claim had been made the Throckmortons felt they had to 'keep up appearances' and couldn't let the matter drop, even if it meant someone's death.

The gulf between rich and poor in Warboys continued to grow against a backdrop of increasing social tension. The 1590s were some of the worst years since those just before the Black Death. The population across Europe was booming but a series of terrible harvests had put the price of grain beyond many and hunger heightened the divisions set in place by the reformations of religion and manners. In other parts of Europe full-scale peasants' revolts were breaking out, but in Oxfordshire a peculiarly 'British' uprising was under way.

Had we stood on top of Enslow Hill near Bletchingdon on a cold evening in 1596 we might have seen a line of people wind their way up the hill from the villages of Hampton Gay and Hampton Poyle. It was an unlikely army of ten men and boys, armed with rusty pikes and antique swords, led by a lad called Bartholomew Steere. At the top of the hill the little band lit a fire and waited. As the night drew in they huddled closer, peering from time to time towards the villages around them, looking for lights heading their way. It proved a long, cold, and lonely night on Enslow Hill however. Come the morning, there were still just ten men here, shivering in the icy air. With a shrug they rose to their feet, stamped out the embers of the fire and began to shuffle back down the hill towards their villages. The Oxfordshire Rising was over.

Today we would know nothing of this 'revolt' and the people who instigated it were it not for the knee-jerk reaction of the local gentry. The rebels who had called the villagers to take up arms against the landlords the previous night might have slipped back to their houses and continued their lives if Roger Symonds, a carpenter in Hampton Gay, had not mentioned it to the local priest while he was mending his bookcase. News that the local peasantry had banded together and threatened to cut the throats of the gentry spread like wildfire: from vicar to local landlord to aristocrat and so to government.

Their response was swift. Roger was interviewed in the village where he claimed he had heard Bartholomew Steere call:

'Care not for work, for we shall have a merrier world shortly; there be lusty fellows abroad, and I will get more, and I will work

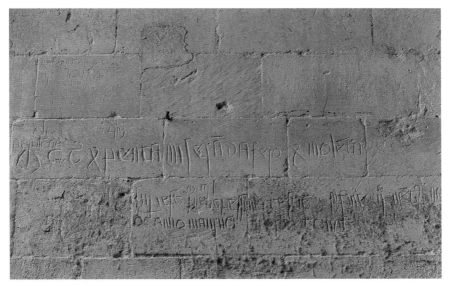

43. *Last testament. This graffiti was scratched on the tower wall of Ashwell church in Hertfordshire on 22nd September 1350 by one of the villagers while Black Death raged around them. It reads:* '1350. The people who remain are driven wild and miserable. They are wretched witnesses to the end.'

44. *The ghost of Mediaeval Britain. The village of Wharram Percy in Yorkshire was largely abandoned in the century after the Black Death and was never repopulated. Today the cottages, fields, gardens and even the line of the high street can still be made out as humps in the fields. The only building to survive above ground is the ruined church, top centre, around which the mediaeval inhabitants of this little village lie buried.*

45. *When Adam delved . . .*
The radical preacher John
Ball addressing a crowd at
Smithfield during the
Peasants' Revolt. Despite
being characterised by the
aristocracy as a rebellion
amongst the lower orders of
society it was actually led by
well educated people like Ball
and attracted many of the
clergy to its cause.

46. *Closer to God. This mediaeval illumination from the Ancrene*
Wisse - a rule book for anchoresses - shows an anchoress being
blessed. After the Black Death many parishes were keen to attract
these holy women who voluntarily had themselves walled into small
cells attached to local churches. In return for food they provided the
parish with what they hoped was a closer link to God, and one
which might protect them better than the established church had
done during the Black Death.

47. *Turn again. The rise of Dick Whittington from the minor gentry to become one of the wealthiest and most influential men in Britain was considered extraordinary in a time when social ambition simply did not exist. To explain his meteoric rise to prominence the story was circulated that he possessed a magical cat and so the pantomime tale was born.*

48. *In guild we trust. The guilds of late mediaeval Britain provided an essential introduction to town life. The craft guilds managed the apprentice system and operated a closed shop to squeeze out non-guild opposition. Many also served a religious function, providing a focus for charity and managing funds to pray for dead guild members. The magnificent Corpus Christi guildhall at Lavenham in Suffolk had only been in use thirty years when Henry VIII dissolved the guild – he disapproved of its religious associations.*

49. *The mediaeval welfare state. The hospital of St. Cross in Hampshire was founded in 1132 to provide for thirteen poor men. So well managed was its endowment that it still operates to this day, offering board and lodging to 25 'brothers' and even providing a 'wayfarer's dole' of bread and ale to those who ask at the porter's lodge. A last vestige of mediaeval Britain.*

50. *A hospital ward. Mediaeval hospitals offered food, shelter and prayer but could do little to help most of their patients medically. The services of hospitals were generally provided by charity; the presence of a chapel on the ward was not simply for the souls of patients but to ensure that they prayed for the benefactors who paid for their treatment.*

51. *New money. The later mediaeval period had brought opportunity to those who could seize it. The Wealden house 'Bayleaf' at the Weald and Downland Museum in Sussex allows us to step into the world of one of this 'better sort' of yeoman farmers, in a building restored to how it may have looked at the very end of this period.*

52. *Privacy. The owner of Bayleaf didn't intend to live the communal life his predecessors had. While his house still had a hall for eating and entertaining in, it also had a relative novelty – private rooms. Upstairs in the chamber the master and his family could escape from the household and enjoy the comforts their wealth had brought them from the oak bed (with truckle for the children) to the fine linens and painted cloths kept in the coffer at its foot.*

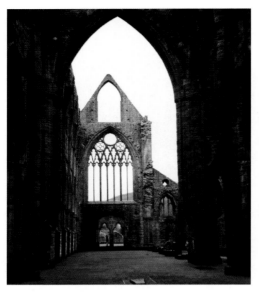

53. 'The church be made a sheephouse . . .' *The great Cistercian monastery at Tintern in Monmouthshire was dissolved on the third of September 1536. With its roof, windows and floors stripped, grass returned to the nave, and this once powerful wool-producing house became sheep pasture itself.*

54. 'It is but lyke a Christmas game . . .' *The Prayer Book rebels' demands of 1549 rejected the new English language service and bible and declared, 'we wyll have olde service of Mattens, masse, Evensong and procession in Latten as it was before.' The government was not impressed and the rebellion was ruthlessly put down.*

Articles,

and all other auncient olde Ce-
temonyes vſed heretofoʒe , by
our mother the holy Church.
❡ Item we wil not recevue the
newe ſcruyce becauſe it is but
lyke a Chʒiſtmas gāme,but we
wyll haue oure olde ſeruice of
Mattens,maſſe, Euenſong and
pʒoceſſion in Latten as it was
befoʒe. And ſo we the Coʒnyſhe
men(wherof certen of vs vnder
ſtādeno Englyſh)vtterly refuſe
thys newe Englyſh.
❡ Item we wyll haue euerye
pʒeacher in his ſermon, & euery
Pʒyeſt at hys maſſe , pʒaye ſpe-
cially by name foʒ the ſoules in
purgatoʒy,as oure foʒefathers
dyd.
❡ Item we wyll haue the By-
ble and al bokes of ſcripture in
Englyſh to be called in agayn,
foʒ

55. *The end of merrie England. Philip Stubbes' 'Anatomie of Abuses' carefully documented the festivals and feasts which still survived in the countryside from before the Reformation as examples of evil and lewd practices he hoped to see eradicated.*

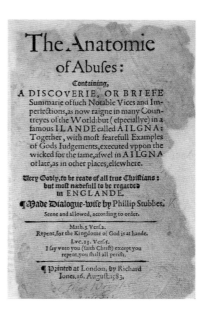

56. *Mayday. Philip Stubbes would no doubt have been horrified to learn that his detailed descriptions of village festivals and holidays actually helped to preserve many aspects of mediaeval life that were dying out. Since his death, his book has been used many times to help revive practices such as dancing around the maypole.*

57. *First outlines of a revolution. In the coal mines of Wales, shown here in a sketch of the lead and coal mines of Mostyn drawn in 1684, new technologies and a new deal between employers and employees were mapping out the path to an industrial revolution.*

58. *The end of the old. This last look at mediaeval London shows a city already in the process of change. The river is beginning to fill with ships taking British colonists across the globe and returning with the exotic goods Londoners craved. The insatiable growth of London in the following 50 years would drive Britain to the edge of the Industrial Revolution, and when, three years after this scene was painted, the centre of the city was burnt to the ground, it rose from the ashes as the first modern city on earth.*

one day and play the other,' adding, that there was once a rising at Enslow Hill, when they were entreated to go down, and after were hanged like dogs, but now they would never yield, but go through with it . . .

The result was mayhem. While many Oxfordshire gentry took to their beds, feigning illness to avoid having to travel what they believed were roads now filled with murderous peasants, the government dispatched officers to arrest the culprits. Five men were taken into custody and sent to London for trial. So fearful were the authorities that the country stood on the brink of a carefully organised revolt, that specific instructions were sent on how the prisoners should be bound and tied to horses so that they could not communicate with each other and hence effect their rescue. In fact, there was no one to rescue them and in London they were racked – it was one of the last times in British history that torture was authorised – interrogated and tried.

As the five were brought out for execution we might have recognised the now broken and haunted face of Bartholomew Steere, who had shivered that night on Enslow Hill. He was an unlikely rebel in an unlikely army, but perhaps typical of a new breed of reluctant insurgent. He was a local man, still young, and had the same expectations of life as his parents and the older generations he knew. But what had been available to them was no longer available to him. He was of an age when he would have been expected to marry and settle down, but he couldn't: his parents had no land to give him as the fields they rented and the common lands they tended were being enclosed by the local landlord. Land that, only a generation before, would have passed unquestionably to him was now set aside for lucrative sheep pasture. Without land

Bartholomew could not raise money and without money he could not build or buy a house. Thus he could not marry and take his place in the village. Nor did the enclosing lord have wage labour for him: sheep are low-maintenance and a few shepherds could tend areas that many tens of labourers would previously have been needed to plough. Bartholomew Steere wanted to be a normal villager but instead found himself unemployed and without a future. It was that which had brought him to Enslow Hill and his untimely death. But he did not die in vain.

The Oxfordshire Rising had a greater effect on people's lives than many of the more bloody rebellions. A government acutely aware of the disorder across Europe and fearful of a much larger revolt at home passed the Tillage Act in 1597, restoring land in Oxfordshire to the plough that had been pasture since the beginning of Elizabeth's reign. What had come out in interrogation was that the rebels had laid their plans carefully: they knew about the disturbances in distant Spain, they knew how to communicate their message through the village churches and the servants' quarters of the great houses, and they knew where the important centres of power were. They had even planned to join up with the apprentices in London, who were also fomenting discontent. This revolution had failed, but the government was well aware that it might have succeeded. If the rebels had a weakness, it was their painfully simple demands: a 'heavenly' world where there was enough to eat and everyone got an occasional day off. It was a vision of paradise blinkered by their own grinding poverty.

While the immediate concerns of some facing eviction from their villages might have been eased, the growing population and food shortages continued to affect many into the turbulent years of the seventeenth century. A population under pressure

256

produced new champions and victims – in the form of women.

Ann Carter was no more a rebel than Bartholomew Steere, but in looking out from her window across the little harbour of Maldon, in Essex, where she had lived all her life, she could see that the world was changing and in ways that were not to her liking. Life had been hard for Ann since she married a poor butcher. At one time they had had a servant but she had fallen pregnant and left and now it seemed unlikely that they could afford to replace her. To supplement her husband's income, Ann was working in the black economy, buying and reselling fish without a licence.

These were times of political tension: the Stuart dynasty had been on the throne since the death of Elizabeth I in 1603, ruling both Scotland and England, two countries that had accepted Protestantism. There were rumours, though, that the Stuarts, and King Charles I, were secretly Catholic. Perhaps as galling to Ann were the clear signs that those who were benefiting from the rapidly expanding economy were the King's favourites, who controlled the legal trade and suppressed her own enterprises.

Events came to a head for Ann in 1629 when famine struck not just Britain but the whole of Europe. At first Maldon was in no real trouble: it was a port with reasonable grain supplies, and certainly enough to feed its population. But the country's economy was changing. In what was rapidly becoming 'capitalist' Britain, supplies went to the highest bidder wherever they might be, and food that would once have been sold in the local market was now just as likely to find its way to the rich centres like London. That was exactly what Ann saw as she looked out of her window. As the grain supply dried up, foreign merchants, sanctioned by the King, speculatively bought up all the local supply to export to the capital – which the King knew would present him with far more of a danger than a small country town if its population went unfed. The people of Maldon on the other hand could starve, and they did.

It was this that turned Ann Carter and some other Maldon women into rebels. As the people gathered on the hill above the town they could see the empty market below and, beyond, the remaining grain being loaded on to Flemish ships. They decided to rebel, but carefully: only women would involve themselves, perhaps because in law they, as chattels of their husbands or fathers, could not be legally accused of riot. From their vantage-point over the town, word went out and soon a band of Essex wives had gathered. They marched the two miles down to the harbour, boarded the ships, held out their bonnets and aprons and demanded that the bemused sailors fill them with grain. Then, with full bonnets and aprons, they marched home.

This simple act had a profound effect on the local authorities. An investigation was soon mounted to inquire of the women, 'What man moved you to this event?' The women of Maldon replied, 'We are women without the law,' and when they were asked the cause of their protest, they replied, 'The cry of the country and my own want.' Such sophisticated tactics had clearly required some central planning and it rapidly emerged that Ann Carter lay at the heart of the matter. She, like the pauper Anne Bowman, had a good working knowledge of the law and her surviving statement is filled with her annotation and corrections. Every time the office taking the statement used the loaded word 'riotous' she had it carefully struck out.

But Ann hadn't finished, and her brush with the law doesn't seem to have made her any less bold. Just two months later she was again fomenting rebellion, this time on horseback and calling herself 'Captain'. She sent letters to the clothworkers, whose business was in crisis, offering to lead them in a rebellion against their masters and, in particular, against the merchant accused of selling off the town's grain supply. The clothworkers found the merchant and placed him under 'arrest', 'tried' and fined him, then broke into his storehouse to help themselves to the grain.

The authorities were compelled to act. The town's sergeant was sent to arrest Ann. This was in itself a dangerous undertaking. When the sergeant had been sent to arrest her husband for debt he received a riposte from his belligerent wife, when she 'stroked his head with a cudgel'. When the bailiff arrived on another occasion to ask why she no longer attended church on Sunday, he too received short shrift: although he only felt the lash of her tongue she told him she would attend church when he provided someone to do her Sunday work for her. This time, however, the sergeant got his woman.

In other times the troublesome Ann Carter might have been seen as little more than a local eccentric but in a time of crisis, with nation-wide food shortages and Parliament recently suspended by the King, the authorities of Maldon viewed her differently. Ann had touched many raw nerves: she had questioned why she would work for so little, why she should be left to starve, and why she, as a woman, could not have the rights that even poor men enjoyed. Her questions were answered with one simple act. After trial as an accomplice to theft, Ann Carter was hanged.

With the Civil War looming it was perhaps not surprising that town and village authorities were becoming concerned about social unrest. The Civil War is usually seen as a battle between two forces, that of the Catholic-leaning monarchy with the old aristocracy, and the Parliamentary Protestant gentry. But for many, perhaps most of the people, the niceties of religious observance or the private practices of the King were of small consequence.

In August 1645, Hambledon Hill still stood guard over the Dorset countryside, its summit still scarred with the ghosts of ditches and banks built nearly five and a half thousand years before when this had been a meeting place and religious site for some of Britain's first farmers. In 1645 however we might have witnessed another meeting there. The Civil War had already dragged on for three years, and while it might have driven political fault lines through and between the wealthy families of England, its main effects on those in town and country had been felt in the repeated predations of both armies. Now the people of Dorset had decided to fight back. They had dug in on the summit of this old meeting-place to challenge any army that came their way. As their motto proudly said:

> If you offer to plunder or take our cattle,
> be assured we will bid you battle.

The call to battle had come at the end of a concerted campaign to rescue press-ganged army recruits from the Royalist and Parliamentary armies and disrupt the tax collectors, who were bleeding the countryside dry in their attempts to fund the two factions. Now, in a formal stand against both sides, between two and four thousand people, who were tired of war and political or religious intrigue, were gathered there, waving the white flags that had got them the local name 'Whiteboys'. But these were not flags of surrender. Although armed with only the agricultural tools from their farms and the wooden cudgels that gave them their other name, 'Clubmen', they intended to fight.

In truth they were not a formidable army, being so poorly equipped and with clergymen, not generals, as their leaders and tacticians. Oliver Cromwell and his New Model Army knew this as they marched towards Hambledon – they had recently captured fifty leaders of the Clubmen with little difficulty as they met in Shaftesbury. In a swift attack from the rear the majority of the Whiteboys were routed and ran for cover. The final stand, some four hundred die-hards under the command of the Reverend Braval of Compton Abbas, were then dragged off the hill by fifty of Cromwell's dragoons. They were unceremoniously dumped in the village church for the night, and then Cromwell himself came to lecture them on their folly. They were, he said: 'poor silly creatures, whom if you please to let me send home, they promise to be very dutiful'. And sent home they were.

In the Peak District another group, perhaps more a product of this new world than their country cousins in the west, were faring better. Lead-mining was a boom industry in the seventeenth century, providing the main ingredient of pewter for tableware, sheeting for roofs and, of course, the main constituent of ammunition. As such the miners had something to offer either side and something that even a king would bargain for. For centuries the relative independence of the lead miners had been a fact of Peak District life. They created their own villages, had their own court to decide ownership disputes over mines, and their own internal politics. Their fundamental interest was not 'King' or 'Parliament' but 'lead-miners', so when the King wrote to them in 1642 asking for support, his letter was the talk of both pulpit and alehouse. He was prepared to make the mines an offer: in return for their support on the battlefield he promised to waive some taxes he had levied on them. The miners responded with a more pertinent demand: that the King should abolish the 'lead tithe'. This tax was based on the assumption that lead ore, like a vegetable, 'grew back' after mining so a tithe could be charged on it as with agricultural produce. Lead-miners, of course, knew that this was rubbish and considered the tax most unjust. The King agreed.

The miners, however, proved less than wholehearted in their support. At Haddon Hall in Derbyshire the Earl of Rutland had only recently expelled miners from his estate and as such they had little love for the aristocratic and royal faction. Some might have gone to fight for Parliament, others certainly refused to fight for the King, but most took the opportunity when the Earl of Rutland fled his estate to move back there and mine lead for the highest bidder. After all, both sides needed ammunition.

When the Civil War ended and the Earl of Rutland – who had in fact remained neutral throughout – returned, he found his estate filled with miners. It took him eleven years and one enormous fist-fight to evict them. In the Peaks it seems that the winner of the Civil War was not Parliament or Royalty but industry.

By the end of the Civil War it was not only the horizons of industry that were expanding. Whole new modes of living and thinking were emerging. London, as the most rapidly expanding city on earth, was bringing together not just more and more people but many new ideas. A revolution in thinking, which had begun in the Reformation with the humanist movement, was emphasising the role of human reason, as opposed to divine revelation, in understanding the world. For those with access to education and the willingness to think outside the old boundaries of that religious world, it was to be a period of 'Enlightenment', in which the medieval acceptance of the divine order of the world was to be replaced by the search for scientific and mathematical order. When Isaac Newton used mathematical formulae to describe everything from the fall of an apple to the motion of a planet, he was not just rewriting the laws of physics:

the revelation that the vast complexity of the world, which had previously been attributed to an almighty and unknowable God, could be described in a few lines of mathematics was stunning. The universe was no longer a work of magic, it was a machine that could be understood and predicted.

The effects of the search for rational explanations of the world reacted far beyond the halls of the newly formed Royal Society or the corridors of academe. If knowledge of physics was attainable through experiment and observation, the logic ran, then perhaps the same was true of business, economics – everything. Newton began his academic career describing physical laws in Cambridge, but he ended it by putting his love of exactitude into practice as warden and then master of the Royal Mint at the Tower of London. Under his supervision the old British coinage was collected and reissued in a new, machine-made and standardised form, of uniform weights and purity, and with an innovative 'milled' edge and inscription to prevent silver being clipped from the edges. It might not seem as revolutionary as the 'apple-falling-on-his-head' story, but it allowed everyone across the world to know and trust the value of a British coin.

Rational ideas were put to use in trade, which was rapidly expanding in the light of the new scientific improvements in cartography, navigation and ship-building. Measurement was the order of the day: the quantification of anything and every-thing in standardised units. From the casual business meetings at the coffee-house opened by Edward Lloyd in 1687 the world's largest insurance brokerage grew up where even risk – or what the medieval mind might have called 'fate' – was measured.

Of course, the talk of the coffee-house and Newton's coinage were of little immediate concern to those still losing their land and livelihood in the country. However, the Enlightenment would offer some alternative to the old, medieval ways of life. The Reformation had torn down many of the structures of the medieval world but offered little by way of replacement. In an age of reason, when the world and everything in it could be seen as a machine, new opportunities were emerging. This – at least in the minds of some intellectuals – was a world that could be understood and improved, a world in which there was even a place for some of those displaced from their old lives in the countryside. The new British colonies that were stimulating London trade required new colonial workforces, and offered new lands to a people who had for centuries been restricted by the sea that surrounded them. The demands of the rapidly swelling cities – particularly London, where by the end of the century one in nine of the population of England would live – also required the development of larger-scale industries to feed, clothe and provide for their inhabitants. The people of the city were not subsistence farmers – they didn't grow their own food or make their own clothes – but they needed someone to fulfil those role for them. Cottage industries boomed, doing everything from weaving to soap-boiling, while manufacturers scrambled to produce the new essentials, such as guns, clocks and books. This fed the desires of a new breed, the consumer, and fuelled the novel obsession with 'shopping'. It was the birth of the high street. Those who could afford them enjoyed luxuries from around the world, brought to their doorstep through the Port of London. In return London had to have goods to export to pay for them. London was a ravenous beast, and if it was to keep growing it had to be fed on an ever-increasing scale. In response by 1700 only 40 per cent of the population of Britain was still involved in agriculture against 60 per cent on the continent. For the rest, the opportunities and constraints of new businesses awaited.

One of the new businesses that answered London's call was the coal-mining industry of the north of England and Wales, which was drawing the once-surplus population into wage labour in a bid to provide for this remarkable expansion. Coal-mining, unlike lead-mining, was a capitalist industry, run not by the miners but by wealthy investors who, still in an age before steam, provided coal to heat the burgeoning towns and cities. They looked beyond the local market to trade with the whole country and the world beyond, and needed to produce goods on a scale that made them affordable. Coal-mining was a business that benefited from size, and small operations were rapidly bought up by the large producers. By 1700 these 'economies of scale' enabled an area such as Tyneside to produce five times as much coal as the whole of the rest of Europe.

Competition between the mining operations and the mining areas was also growing. After 1650 the population was stabilising, and following the Great Plague of 1665, it had even fallen back, increasing the demand for skilled labour. In the drift mines of Neath in South Wales the hewers, skilled miners who cut the coal, were most in demand. They were in a position to bargain, as the lead-miners had, and in doing so would take the first steps on the tricky road of industrial relations.

Coal-mining was about volume, but industrial working practices were new to the working population, and not everyone shared the capitalist coal-owners' obsession with profit. The previous hundred years had seen high levels of unemployment and many had become used to taking time off, which had led to a decidedly relaxed attitude to work. Hewers were used to fulfilling their weekly coal quota in about three and a half days, after which they would retire to the alehouse for food and drink. The next day they might be joined by the putters or watermen, who transported the coal – a less skilled job, which took a little longer – who worked a four-day week.

Trying to control and motivate this workforce was a perennial problem for the owners. Skilled workmen could not be sacked as they were needed, so corporal punishment was often invoked. One owner, however, took a different approach at his colliery in Neath. He was Humphrey Mackworth.

Mackworth had bought his colliery in 1695 and showed from the beginning that he was keen to invest in the long-term. The horse-drawn carts on tracks that took his coal from the face to the loading area were an early step in the development of the railway. He also dug a canal to take his coal across the country, signalling the birth of Britain's first integrated transport system. But his greatest investment was in people. He had manned his mine by tempting skilled miners to join him from Tyneside and Shropshire, and was keen to ensure that others didn't poach them. As a rational man in a rational age he consulted his adviser, William Waller, about the practicalities of running the mine and keeping his workers. He knew he needed the miners more than they needed him, so out went the whips and in came the perks. On turning up for work in Mackworth's colliery in the late seventeenth century we would have been in for a shock: to begin with, the working week was longer and quotas were higher, but in return Mackworth offered motivation rather than punishment. A hewer enjoyed such novel privileges as higher basic pay than that offered by other mine-owners, sick pay, and even a pension for his wife. He also offered hope to those apparently beyond it: he granted condemned prisoners their freedom in return for five years' hard labour at his coal face.

Mackworth was a new breed of 'lord of the manor', offering to care for a population from cradle to grave in return for their absolute dedication to his business. Everything they did was for him, and in return he provided almost everything they needed. In Mackworth's mine in 1699 we are standing on the edge of the Industrial Revolution. Far below we might just make out the blackened figures of the miners, breaking the coal free from the face. As the rhythmic sound of pickaxe on rock rises up, we might, for a moment, let the years fall away and think back to the not dissimilar sound of tool on stone drifting out across the Yorkshire hills nine thousand years before as one of these miners' Mesolithic forebears prepared his tools for the hunt.

Epilogue

The dawning of the year 1700 saw many rural farmers packing up their few possessions and heading off to start a new life. They were no longer tied by manorial courts to the land, they were free to go where they pleased. Free to become a success, perhaps even an aristocrat, but also free to starve unless 'saved' by the Poor Laws. As they walked for the last time down the village street they were not walking through a ghost town – there were still farmers, vicars and blacksmiths – but the old communal fields were beginning to be fenced in: they belonged now to the gentleman farmer, not the village. The church that had stood since shortly after William the Conqueror's invasion was still in use each Sunday, but it was no longer the vividly painted home of Catholic festivals, or the stage for Anglo-Saxon justice. Outside the village bounds our farmer might have walked down a Roman road on his journey to find work in the descendant of a Roman town. On the hills he might have seen sheep grazing on the grassy ramparts of the Iron Age hillfort that once guarded this same farmland. Perhaps he climbed an unimposing mound – the remnants of the grave of one of his Bronze Age ancestors – to view the road ahead. A road that ran past a line of stones from a time that no one could remember, put there by the descendants of the people who had first cleared this region of trees. And there at his foot, unnoticed, lay a small flint flake, left on that spot by the men and women who watched the English Channel and the North Sea slowly fill, and the island we call Britain, form.

Over nine thousand years had passed since then, nine thousand years in which men and women lived off – and imposed themselves on – the land. Now that intimate bond was breaking.

Acknowledgements

Listing the people I need to thank for their help in this project is somewhat daunting and not a little humbling as television series are always the work of a large group of people and both it and this book are based on the research of a still larger band of academics.

I should begin with Bettany who is the perfect companion for a stroll through nine thousand years of British history. On the production side I would like to thank Philip Clarke and all those at Wildfire TV and Ralph Lee and all at Channel Four who made the series possible in the first place and for giving me the chance to play a part in the making of it.

The process of reading all the material and contacting and interviewing the hundreds of academics whom we consulted would have been impossible without all the production staff: Paul and Polly the directors; the superb research staff, Anna, Adrian and Matilda; and the production team, Mel, Sandra, Esi, Jane and Liz, who made the series happen. That's before I've even started to consider the film crew, editors and technical folk who made it all look so good.

The writing of this book has been a pleasure, made all the more enjoyable by the support and help of Julian Alexander at Lucas Alexander Whitley, and Rupert Lancaster and Juliet Brightmore at Hodder and Stoughton. The book would also have been very dull indeed without Emily Hedges' wonderful picture research and rather eccentric without Hazel Orme's copy editing.

Acknowledgements

Most of all, however, I want to thank all the academics and specialists who have given so freely of their time and expertise. Throughout the academic establishment I have found nothing but enthusiasm for the idea behind this book and generosity in giving both the time and knowledge to help me realise it. Over the last year the research team and I have been privileged to speak to many of the finest minds studying the history and archaeology of Britain in what has been, in a way, a year-long tutorial and certainly an unparalleled education. I suppose this book might then be considered the final examination in which I have tried to reflect what I have learnt from those who know far more than I but which, no doubt, also reflects my own misinterpretations and misunderstandings. I now await the results with some trepidation. The list below covers, I hope, all those who have helped in this tutorial, some extensively, some briefly, but all of whom deserve credit. They are, in alphabetical order:

Lindsay Allason-Jones, Ian Armit, Gavin Aycliffe, Brian Ayres, Mike Baille, Tristan Bareham, John Barrett, Caroline Barron, Nick Barton, Cordelia Beattie, Tom Beaumont-James, Guy de la Bedoyère, Lee Beier, Anthony Birley, John Blair, Peter Borsay, Alan Bowman, Keith Brannigan, David Breeze, Don Brothwell, Aubrey Burl, Jesse Byock, Neil Campling, Helen Castor, Chris Chippindale, Sally Crawford, Amanda Clarke, David Clarke, John Collis, Robert Colls, Chantal Conneller, Glyn Coppack, Margaret Cox, Rosemary Cramp, John Crichton, Barry Cunliffe, Andy Currant, Jane Dawson, Pat Dennison, Barry Dobson, Thomas Dowson, Eamon Duffy, Alistair Dunn, Christopher Dyer, Ben Edwards, Kevin Edwards, Geoff Egan, Dave Evans, Richard Evershed, Neil Faulkner, Jon Finch, Noel Fojut, David Gaimster, Jane Geddes, Richard Gem, Roberta Gilchrist, Kate Giles, Mirriam Gill, Kate

Acknowledgements

Gilliver, Jeremy Goldberg, Damian Goodburn, Miranda Green, Jane Grenville, Richard Hall, Steve Hartgroves, Mark Hassall, John Hatcher, Maria Hayward, Francis Healy, Martin Henig, JD Hill, Catherine Hills, Richard Hingley, Jerry Hooker, Michael Hoskin, Pat Hudson, Ronald Hutton, Liz Hallam, Vanessa Harding, Heinrich Härke, Richard Harris, Steve Hindle, John Hines, Ralph Houlbrooke, Richard Hoyle, Maurice Howard, Simon James, Matthew Johnson, Katherine Keats-Rohan, Chris Kelly, John Lewis, Keith Lilley, John Lord, Sam Lucy, Michael Lynch, Diarmaid MacCulloch, Colin Martin, Anne Marwick, Simon Mays, Gordon Maxwell, Jackie Mc.Kinley, Chris Meiklejohn, Paul Mellars, Roger Mercer, David Miles, Martin Millet, Gustav Milne, Steve Minnitt, Richard Morris, Deirdre O'Sullivan, Mark Overton, Olwyn Owen, David Palliser, Mike Parker-Pearson, Frederik Pedersen, Tim Pestell, Mike Pitts, Andrew Prescott, Francis Pryor, Richard Reece, Andrew Reynolds, Colin Richards, Julian Richards, Mike Richards, Steve Rigby, Gordon Roberts, Paul Robinson, Warwick Rodwell, David Roffe, Gervase Rosser, Peter Rowley-Conway, Miri Ruben, Miles Russell, Philip Schofield, Tim Shadla-Hall, Jim Sharpe, Niall Sharples, Harvey Sheldon, Ian Simmons, Paul Slack, Terry Slater, Marie-Louise Sørensen, Douglas Speirs, John Spurr, Kay Staniland, Jo Storey, Mark Stoyle, John Styles, Barrold Taylor, Masie Taylor, Elaine Treharne, Mark Thomas, Margo Todd, Roger Tomlin, Garthine Walker, John Walter, Diane Watt, Mike Weale, Jonathon West, Alasdair Whittle, Jane Whittle, Caroline Wickham-Jones, Tom Williamson, Tony Wilmott, Andy Wood, Patrick Wormald, Becky Wright, Keith Wrightson, Derek Yalden.

For permission to use translations and quotations from their published works I would like to thank Roger Tomlin and the

Acknowledgements

Oxford Committee for Archaeology for permission to quote his curse translations in *Tabellae Sulis: Roman Inscribed Tablets of Tin and Lead from the Spring at Bath*, 1989; Kevin Crossley-Holland and the Boydell Press for translations of Anglo-Saxon poetry in *The Anglo-Saxon World*, 1982; Chris Dyer, Yale University Press and Penguin Books for quotations and case studies from *Making a Living in the Middle Ages: The People of Britain 850–1520*, 2002; Richard Vaughan and Alan Sutton Publishing for translations of Matthew Paris' *Chronica Majora* in *The Illustrated Chronicles of Matthew Paris*, 1983; Michael Swanton and Alan Sutton Publishing for translations of the *Gesta Herewardi* in Ohlgren, T. *Mediaeval Outlaws* (1998).

Every reasonable effort has been made to acknowledge the ownership of the copyright material included in this volume. Any errors that may have occurred are inadvertent and will be corrected in subsequent editions provided notification is sent to the author.

More personally I also want to thank my family, without whom I would never have developed a love for history, and most of all, my wife Steph, who has not only read and corrected every draft of this book and compiled the bibliography but also bravely maintains that she enjoyed the process.

Picture Acknowledgements

Bibliography

Below is a somewhat eclectic bibliography of sources used in making both the television series and this book. I have tried to divide the material up into a general section and then by book chapter although many books were useful in more than one.

General

Briggs, Asa, *Social History of England*, Weidenfeld & Nicholson, 1994.

Cunliffe, Barry (ed.), *The Oxford Illustrated History of Prehistoric Europe*, Oxford Paperbacks, 2002.

Davies, John, *The Making of Wales*, Sutton Publishing, 1999.

Davies, John (trs.), *A History of Wales*, Penguin, 1994.

Gillingham, John, *et al.*, *The Oxford History of Britain: The Middle Ages*, Oxford Paperbacks, 1992.

Hallam, Elizabeth, and Prescott, Andrew (eds), *The British Inheritance: A Treasury of Historic Documents*, British Library Publishing, 1999.

Lynch, Michael (ed.), *The Oxford Companion to Scottish History*, Oxford University Press, 2001.

Mercer, Roger (ed.), *The Archaeology of Scotland*, Edinburgh University Press, 2004.

Morgan, Kenneth O. (ed.), *The Oxford Illustrated History of Britain*, Oxford University Press, 1984.

Salway, Peter, *et al.*, *The Oxford History of Britain: Roman and Anglo-Saxon Britain*, Oxford Paperbacks, 1992.

Simmons, Ian G., *An Environmental History of Great Britain: From 10,000 Years Ago to the Present*, Edinburgh University Press, 2001.

1: Making the Land

Bradley, Richard, *An Archaeology of Natural Places*, Routledge, 2000.

Bradley, Richard, *The Significance of Monuments: On the Shaping of Human Experience in Neolithic and Bronze Age Europe*, Routledge, 1998.

Brothwell, Don R., and Brothwell, Patricia, *Food in Antiquity: A Survey of the Diet of Early Peoples*, Johns Hopkins University Press, 1998.

Brothwell, Don, *Diseases in Antiquity: A Survey of the Diseases, Injuries, and Surgery of Early Populations*, Charles C. Thomas Publishing, 1967.

Burl, Aubrey, *The Stone Circles of Britain, Ireland and Britanny*, Yale University Press, 2000.

Burl, Aubrey, *From Carnac to Callanish: The Prehistoric Stone Rows of Britain, Ireland, and Brittany*, Yale University Press, 1993.

Burl, Aubrey, *The Stonehenge People*, Everyman, 1987.

Burl, Aubrey, *Prehistoric Stone Circles*, Shire Publications, 1979.

Chippindale, Christopher, *Stonehenge Complete*, Thames & Hudson, 1983.

Cox, Margaret, and Mays, Simon, *Human Osteology: In Archaeology and Forensic Science*, Greenwich Medical Media, 2000.

Bibliography

Dowson, Thomas, *The Archaeology of Art*, Routledge, 2002.

Edwards, Kevin J., and Ralston, Ian B. M. (eds.), *Scotland After the Ice Age: Environment, Archaeology and History 8000 BC–AD 1000*, Polygon, 2003.

Gibson, Alex, *Stonehenge and Timber Circles*, Tempus Publishing Ltd, 1998.

Gosden, Chris, *Prehistory: a Very Short Introduction*, Oxford University Press, 2003.

Mellars, Paul, and Dark, Petra, *Star Carr in Context: New Archaeological and Palaeoecological Investigations at the Early Mesolithic Site of Star Carr, North Yorkshire*, MacDonald Institute for Archaeological Research, 1998.

Mellars, Paul, and Andrews, M. V., *Excavations on Oronsay: Prehistoric Human Ecology on a Small Island*, Edinburgh University Press, 1987.

Mercer, Roger, *Farming Practice in British Prehistory*, Edinburgh University Press, 1981.

Mercer, Roger, *Hambledon Hill: A Neolithic Landscape*, Edinburgh University Press, 1980.

Mercer, Roger (ed.), *Beakers in Britain and Europe: Symposium Proceedings*, British Archaeological Reports, 1977.

Parker-Pearson, Michael, and Richards, Colin, *Architecture and Order: Approaches to Social Space (Material Cultures)*, Routledge, 1997.

Parker-Pearson, Michael, and Schadla-Hall, R. J., *Looking at the Land: Archaeological Landscapes in Eastern England*, Leicestershire Museums, Arts and Records Service, 1994.

Pitts, Michael, *Hengeworld: Why Was Stonehenge Built?*, Arrow, 2001.

Pitts, Mike, *Hengeworld: The Discoveries at Stanton Drew and the Reconstruction of the Ancient Civilisations of Wessex*, Century, 2000.

Richards, Colin, *Dwelling Among the Monuments: An Examination of the Neolithic Village of Barnhouse, Maeshowe Passage Grave and Surrounding Monuments at Stenness*, MacDonald Institute for Archaeological Research, 2003.

Russell, Miles, *The Early Neolithic Architecture of the South Downs*, Archaeopress, British Archaeological Reports, 2001.

Russell, Miles, *Flint Mines in Neolithic Britain*, Tempus Publishing, 2000.

Simmons, Ian G., *The Environmental Impact of Later Mesolithic Cultures: On the Moorlands of Britain*, Edinburgh University Press, 1996.

Simmons, Ian, and Tooley, Michael, *The Environment in British Prehistory*, Cornell University Press, 1981.

Sørensen, Marie-Louise, *Gender Archaeology*, Polity Press, 2000.

Whittle, Alasdair W. R., *Europe in the Neolithic: The Creation of New Worlds*, Cambridge University Press, 1996.

Whittle, Alasdair, *Sacred Mound, Holy Rings: Silbury Hill and the West Kennet Palisade Enclosures: a Later Neolithic Complex in Wiltshire*, Oxbow Books, 1997.

Wickham-Jones, Caroline, *Orkney: A Historical Guide*, Birlinn, 1998.

Wickham-Jones, Caroline, *Historic Scotland Book of Scotland's First Settlers*, B. T. Batsford, 1994.

2: *Home*

Armit, Ian, *Historic Scotland: Celtic Scotland*, B. T. Batsford, 1997.

Armit, Ian, *The Later Prehistory of the Western Isles of Scotland*, Archaeopress, British Archaeological Reports, 1992.

Armit, Ian (ed.), *Beyond the Brochs: The Changing Perspectives on the Atlantic Scottish Iron Age*, Edinburgh University Press, 1991.

Chamberlain, Andrew T., and Parker Pearson, Michael, *Earthly Remains: The History and Science of Preserved Human Bodies*, British Museum Press, 2001.

Cunliffe, Barry, *The Extraordinary Voyage of Pytheas the Greek: The Man Who Discovered Britain*, Penguin, 2002.

Cunliffe, Barry, *Facing the Ocean: The Atlantic and Its Peoples, 8000 BC to AD 1500*, Oxford University Press, 2001.

Cunliffe, Barry, *The Ancient Celts*, Oxford University Press, 1997.

Cunliffe, Barry, *English Heritage Book of Iron Age Britain*, B. T. Batsford, 1994.

Cunliffe, Barry, *Wessex to AD 1000 (A Regional History of England)*, Longman, 1993.

Cunliffe, Barry, *English Heritage Book of Danebury*, B. T. Batsford, 1993.

Cunliffe, Barry, *Danebury: Anatomy of an Iron Age Hillfort*, B. T. Batsford, 1983.

Cunliffe, Barry (ed.), *The Danebury Environs Programme: the Prehistory of a Wessex Landscape*, Oxford University School of Archaeology, 2000.

Green, Miranda J., *Celtic World*, Routledge, 1995.

Green, Miranda, *Symbol and Image in Celtic Religious Art*, Routledge, 1992.

Green, Miranda J., *The Gods of Roman Britain*, Shire Publications, 1983.

Haselgrove, C., *et al.*, *Understanding the British Iron Age: an Agenda for Action: A Report for the Iron Age Research Seminar and the Council of the Prehistoric Society*, Trust for Wessex Archaeology, 2001.

Hill, J. D., *Ritual and Rubbish in the Iron Age of Wessex*, Archaeopress, British Archaeological Reports, 1995.

Hill, J. D., and Cumberpatch, C. G. (eds.), *Different Iron Ages*, Archaeopress, British Archaeological Reports, 1995.

Hutton, Ronald, *The Pagan Religions of the Ancient British Isles: Their Nature and Legacy*, Blackwell, 1991.

James, Simon, *The Atlantic Celts: Ancient People or Modern Invention?*, British Museum Press, 1999.

James, Simon, *Exploring the World of the Celts*, Thames and Hudson, 1993.

James, Simon, and Rigby, Valery, *Britain and the Celtic Iron Age*, British Museum Press, 1997.

Miles, David (ed.), *Romano-British Countryside: Studies in Rural Settlement and Economy*, British Archaeological Reports 103, 1982.

Parker Pearson, Michael, *The Archaeology of Death and Burial*, Sutton Publishing, 2001.

Parker Pearson, Michael, *English Heritage Book of Bronze Age Britain*, B. T. Batsford, 1993.

Pryor, Francis, *Seahenge: New Discoveries in Prehistoric Britain*, HarperCollins, 2001.

Pryor, Francis, *Archaeology and Environment of a Fenland Landscape*, English Heritage Publications, 2001.

Pryor, Francis, *Farmers in Prehistoric Britain*, Tempus Publishing, 1998.

Pryor, Francis, *Etton: Excavations at a Neolithic Causewayed Enclosure Near Maxey, Cambridgeshire, 1982–97*, English Heritage Publications, 1998.

Pryor, Francis, *Flag Fen: Prehistoric Fenland Centre*, B. T. Batsford, 1991.

Pryor, Francis, *Excavation at Fengate, Peterborough, England: The Fourth Report*, University of Toronto Press, 1982.

Sharples, Niall M., *Scalloway: a Broch, Late Iron Age Settlement and Medieval Cemetery in Shetland*, Oxbow Books, 1998.

Sharples, Niall M., *Maiden Castle*, B. T. Batsford, 1991.
Stead, I. M., *et al.*, *Lindow Man: The Body in the Bog*, Cornell University Press, 1986.

3: *Under the Eagle*

Allason-Jones, Lindsay, *Roman Woman: Everyday Life in Hadrian's England*, Michael O'Mara, 2000.
Allason-Jones, Lindsay, *Women in Roman Britain*, British Museum Press, 1989.
Allason-Jones, Lindsay, and McKay, Bruce, *Coventina's Well: A Shrine on Hadrian's Wall*, Trustees of the Clayton Collection, 1985.
Bennett, Julian, *Towns in Roman Britain*, Shire Publications, 1984.
Birley, Anthony, *Garrison Life at Vindolanda: A Band of Brothers*, Tempus Publishing, 2002.
Birley, Anthony, *The People of Roman Britain*, B. T. Batsford, 1979.
Bowman, Alan, *Life & Letters Roman Frontier*, Routledge, 1994.
Bowman, Alan K., *Life and Letters on the Roman Frontier*, British Museum Press, 1998.
Bowman, Alan K., and Thomas, J. David, *Vindolanda: The Latin Writing-tablets*, Society for the Promotion of Roman Studies, 1983.
Brannigan, Keith, *Roman Britain – Life In An Imperial Province*, Readers Digest Association, 1980.
Breeze, David J., *Roman Forts in Britain*, Shire Publications, 2002.
Breeze, David J., *Historic Scotland: 5000 Years of Scotland's Heritage*, B. T. Batsford, 1998.
Breeze, David J., *Roman Scotland*, B. T. Batsford, 1996.

Bibliography

Breeze, David J., *Roman Forts in Britain*, Shire Publications, 1983.

Breeze, David J., *Northern Frontiers of Roman Britain*, Batsford, 1982.

Handford, S. A. (trs.), Caesar, Julius, *The Conquest of Gaul*, Penguin, 1951.

Casey, P. J., *Roman Coinage in Britain*, Shire Publications Ltd, 1980.

Cunliffe, Barry, *English Heritage: Roman Bath*, B. T. Batsford, 1996.

Cunliffe, Barry, *Fishbourne: A Roman Palace and Its Garden*, Thames & Hudson, 1971.

De la Bédoyère, Guy, *Roman Towns in Britain*, Tempus Publishing, 2003.

De la Bédoyère, Guy, *Eagles Over Britannia: The Roman Army in Britain*, Tempus Publishing, 2001.

De la Bédoyère, Guy, *The Golden Age of Roman Britain*, Tempus Publishing, 1999.

De la Bédoyère, Guy, *English Heritage Book of Villas and the Roman Countryside*, B. T. Batsford, 1993.

De la Bédoyère, Guy, *Roman Towns in Britain*, Batsford, 1992.

Faulkner, Neil, *The Decline and Fall of Roman Britain*, Tempus Publishing, 2001.

Fojut, Noel, *et al.*, *The Ancient Monuments of the Western Isles*, Mercat Press, 1994.

Gilliver, Kate, *The Roman Art of War*, Tempus Publishing, 1999.

Hanson, W. S., and Maxwell, Gordon S., *Rome's North West Frontier: the Antonine Wall*, Edinburgh University Press, 1984.

Henig, Martin, *The Art of Roman Britain*, University of Michigan Press, 1995.

Henig, Martin, *Religion in Roman Britain*, Routledge, 1988.

Hingley, Richard, *Roman Officers and English Gentlemen: The Imperial Origins of Roman Archaeology*, Routledge, 2000.

Bibliography

Hingley, Richard, *Rural Settlement in Roman Britain*, B. T. Batsford, 1990.

Hutton, Ronald, *The Stations of the Sun: A History of the Ritual Year in Britain*, Oxford University Press, 1996.

Johnston, David E., *Roman Villas*, Shire Publications, 1979.

Millet, Martin, *English Heritage Book of Roman Britain*, B. T. Batsford, 1995.

Millett, Martin, *The Romanization of Britain: An Essay in Archaeological Interpretation*, Cambridge University Press, 1990.

Milne, Gustav, *Roman London*, B. T. Batsford, 1995.

Milne, Gustav, *The Port of Roman London*, B. T. Batsford, 1993.

Potter, T. W., *Roman Britain*, British Museum Press, 1983.

Reece, Richard, *The Coinage of Roman Britain: Life and Landscape*, Tempus Publishing, 2002.

Reece, Richard, *The Later Roman Empire*, Tempus Publishing, 1999.

Reece, Richard, *My Roman Britain*, Oxbow Books, 1989.

Salway, Peter, *Roman Britain: a Very Short Introduction*, Oxford Paperbacks, 2000.

Swan, Vivien G., *Pottery in Roman Britain*, Shire Publications, 1988.

Tomlin, Roger, *Tabellae Sulis: Roman Inscribed Tablets of Tin and Lead from the Spring at Bath*, University of Oxford Committee for Archaeology, 1989.

Willmott, Tony, *Birdoswald Roman Fort: 1800 Years on Hadrian's Wall*, Tempus Publishing, 2001.

Wilmott, Tony, *Birdoswald: Excavations of a Roman Fort on Hadrian's Wall and Its Success*, English Heritage Publications, 1999.

Wilmott, Tony, and Wilson, Pete, *The Late Roman Transition in the North*, Archaeopress, British Archaeology Reports, 2000.

4: *Land of the Wolf*

Alexander, Michael (trs.), *The Earliest English Poems*, Penguin Books, 1977.

Alexander, Michael (trs.), *Beowulf*, Penguin, 1973.

Sherley-Price, L. (trs.), Bede, *A History of the English Church and People*, Penguin, 1968.

Blair, John, *The Anglo-Saxon Age: a Very Short Introduction*, Oxford Paperbacks, 2000.

Byock, Jesse L., *Viking Age Iceland*, Penguin, 2001.

Campbell, James (ed.), *The Anglo-Saxons*, Phaidon Press, 1982.

Cramp, Rosemary, *Studies in Anglo-Saxon Sculpture*, Pindar Press, 1999.

Crawford, Sally, *Childhood in Anglo-Saxon England*, Sutton Publishing, 1999.

Crossley-Holland, Kevin (ed., trs.), *The Anglo-Saxon World*, Boydell Press, 1982.

Crossley-Holland, Kevin (trs.), *The Exeter Riddle Book*, Folio Society, 1978.

Edwards, Ben, *Vikings in North West England*, Lancaster University Press, 1998.

Graham-Campbell, James (ed.), *et al.*, *Vikings and the Danelaw: Papers from the Proceedings of the Thirteenth Viking Congress, Nottingham and York, 21st–30th August 1997*, Oxbow Books, 2001.

Graham-Campbell, James (ed.), *et al.*, *Cultural Atlas of the Viking World*, Andromeda, 1994.

Hall, Richard, *English Heritage: York*, B. T. Batsford, 1996.

Hall, Richard, *English Heritage Book of Viking York*, B. T. Batsford, 1994.

Hall, Richard, *The Viking Dig*, Bodley Head, 1984.

Bibliography

Hallam, Elizabeth (ed.), and Savage, A. (trs.), *Anglo-Saxon Chronicles*, Papermac, 1988.

Hamerow, Helena, and MacGregor, Arthur (eds), *Image and Power in the Archaeology of Early Medieval Britain: Essays in Honour of Rosemary Cramp*, Oxbow Books, 2001.

Härke, Heinrich, *Archaeology, Ideology, and Society: The German Experience*, Peter Lang Publishing, 2002.

Hill, David, *At Atlas of Anglo-Saxon England*, Basil Blackwell, 1984.

Hills, Catherine, *Blood of the British, From Ice Age to Norman Conquest*, George Phillip, 1986.

Hills, Catherine, *The Origins of the English*, Duckworth, 2002.

Hines, John (ed.), *The Anglo-Saxons from the Migration Period to the Eighth Century: An Ethnographic Perspective*, Boydell Press, 1997.

Hines, John, *The Scandinavian Character of Anglian England in the Pre-Viking Period*, Archaeopress, British Archaeological Reports, 1984.

Lee, M., and Trelawny, E., *The Mackerel Destroyers*, Tean Press, 1999.

Lucy, Sam, *Early Anglo-Saxon Cemeteries of East Yorkshire*, Archaeopress, British Archaeological Reports, 1998.

Lucy, Sam, and Reynolds, Andrew (eds), *Burial in Early Medieval England and Wales*, Society for Mediaeval Archaeology Monograph Series, 2002.

Morris, Richard, *Churches in the Landscape*, Phoenix Press, 1997.

O'Sullivan, Deirdre, and Young, Robert, *English Heritage Book of Lindisfarne*, Batsford, 1995.

Owen, Olwyn, *The Making of Scotland: The Sea Road: A Voyage Through Viking Scotland*, Birlinn, 1999.

Pulsiano, Philip, and Treharne, Elaine (eds), *A Companion to Anglo-Saxon Literature and Culture*, Blackwell, 2001.

Raffel, Burton (trs., ed.), and Olsen, Alexandra H. (ed.), *Poems and Prose from the Old English*, Yale University Press, 1998.

Reynolds, Andrew, *Later Anglo-Saxon England*, Tempus Publishing, 2002.

Reynolds, Andrew, *Life and Landscape in Later Anglo-Saxon England*, Tempus Publishing, 1999.

Richards, Julian, *Blood of the Vikings*, Hodder & Stoughton, 2002.

Richards, Julian D., *Viking Age England*, Tempus Publishing, 2000.

Richards, Julian D., *English Heritage Book of Viking Age England*, B. T. Batsford, 1991.

Treharne, Elaine M. (ed.), *Old and Middle English: An Anthology*, Blackwell, 2000.

Winterbottom, Michael (ed., trs.), *Gildas, The Ruin of Britain and Other Works*, Phillimore, 1978.

Wood, Michael, *In Search of England, Journeys into the English Past*, Penguin, 2000.

5: Free and Unfree

Aston, Michael (ed.), *et al.*, *The Rural Settlements of Medieval England*, Blackwell, 1989.

Beaumont James, Tom, *English Heritage: Winchester*, B. T. Batsford, 1997.

Beresford, Maurice, *The Lost Villages of England*, Sutton Publishing, 1998.

Brooke, Christopher, *et al.*, *English Romanesque Art, 1066–1200*, Weidenfeld and Nicolson, 1984.

Coppack, Glyn, *Fountains Abbey: The Cistercians in Northern England*, Tempus Publishing, 2003.

Bibliography

Coppack, Glyn, *The White Monks: The Cistercians in Britain*, Tempus Publishing, 1998.

Coppack, Glyn, and Fergusson, Peter, *Rievaulx Abbey*, English Heritage Publications, 1994.

Douglas, David C., and Greenaway, George W. (eds), *English Historical Documents, Volume II, 1042–1189*, Eyre Methuen, 1981.

Dyer, Christopher, *Making a Living in the Middle Ages: The People of Britain 850–1520*, Penguin Books, 2003.

Dyer, Christopher, *Everyday Life in Medieval England*, Hambledon and London, 1994.

Dyer, Christopher, *Standards of Living in the Later Middle Ages: Social Change in England c.1200–1520*, Cambridge University Press, 1989.

Gilchrist, Roberta, *Gender and Archaeology: Contesting the Past*, Routledge, 1999.

Gilchrist, Roberta, *Contemplation and Action: The Other Monasticism*, Leicester University Press, 1995.

Gilchrist, Roberta, *Gender and Material Culture: The Archaeology of Religious Women*, Routledge, 1993.

Gilchrist, Roberta, and Oliva, Marilyn, *Religious Women in Medieval East Anglia: History and Archaeology c.1100–1540*, University of East Anglia Press, 1993.

Gillingham, John, and Griffiths, Ralph A., *Medieval Britain: a Very Short Introduction*, Oxford Paperbacks, 2000.

Hallam, Elizabeth (ed.), *The Plantagenet Encyclopedia: An Alphabetical Guide to 400 Years of English History*, Weidenfeld & Nicholson, 1990.

Hallam, Elizabeth (ed.), *The Plantagenet Chronicles*, Weidenfeld & Nicholson, 1986.

Harris, Richard, *Discovering Timber-framed Buildings*, Shire Publications, 1998.

Bibliography

Hinde, Thomas (ed.), *The Domesday Book: England's Heritage, Then and Now*, Hutchinson, 1985.

Keats-Rohan, K. S. B., *Domesday People: a Prosopography of Persons Occurring in English Documents, 1066–1166: Domesday Book*, Boydell Press, 1999.

Koenigsberger, H. G., *Medieval Europe 400–1500*, Longman, 1987.

Allen, R. (trs.), Lawman, *Brut*, Orion, 1992.

Lewis, Carenza, *et al.*, *Village, Hamlet and Field: Changing Medieval Settlements in Central England*, Manchester University Press, 1997.

Lilley, Keith D., *Urban Life in the Middle Ages: 1000–1450*, Palgrave, 2001.

Maddicott, John, and Palliser, David (eds), *The Medieval State: Essays Presented to James Campbell*, Hambledon and London, 2000.

Ohlgren, Thomas H., *Medieval Outlaws, Ten Tales in Modern English*, Sutton Publishing, 1998.

Orme, Nicholas, *Medieval Children*, Yale University Press, 2001.

Pestell, Tim, and Ulmschneider, Katharina (eds), *Markets in Early Medieval Europe: Trading and Productive Sites, 650–850*, Windgather Press, 2003.

Prescott, Andrew, *English Historical Documents*, British Library Publishing, 1988.

Pounds, N. J. G., *The Medieval Castle in England and Wales, A Social and Political History*, Cambridge University Press, 1990.

Ravensdale, Jack, *The Domesday Inheritance*, Souvenir Press, 1986.

Robinson, David (ed.), *et al.*, *Cistercian Abbeys of Britain: Far from the Concourse of Men*, B. T. Batsford, 1998.

Rodwell, Warwick, *English Heritage Book of Church Archaeology*, B. T. Batsford, 1989.

Rodwell, Warwick, *The Archaeology of the English Church: The Study of Historic Churches and Churchyards*, B. T. Batsford, 1981.

Rodwell, Warwick, and Rodwell, Kirsty, *Rivenhall: Investigations of a Villa, Church and Village, 1950–77*, Council for British Archaeology, 1985.

Roffe, David, *Domesday: The Inquest and Book*, Oxford University Press, 2000.

Saul, Nigel, *A Companion to Medieval England, 1066–1485*, Tempus Publishing, 2000.

Slater, Terry, *Warwickshire: a History*, Phillimore, 1997.

Soulsby, Ian, *The Towns of Medieval Wales: A Study of Their History, Archaeology and Early Topography*, Phillmore, 1983.

Vaughan, Richard (ed., trs.), *The Illustrated Chronicles of Matthew Paris, Observations of Thirteenth-Century Life*, Sutton Publishing, 1993.

Warren, W. L., *Henry II*, Eyre Methuen, 1973.

Wilkinson, Donald, and Cantrell, John, *The Normans in Britain*, Macmillan Education, 1987.

Zeigler, Philip, *The Black Death*, Penguin, 1982.

6: *Opportunity*

Barron, Caroline, and Sutton, Anne (eds), *Medieval London Widows, 1300–1500*, Hambledon and London, 1994.

Barron, Caroline, and Stratford, Jenny (eds), *The Church and Learning in Late Medieval Society: Studies in Honour of R. B. Dobson*, Shaun Tyas, 2002.

Beresford, Maurice, *History on the Ground*, Sutton Publishing, 1998.

Britnell, Richard (ed.), *Daily Life in the Middle Ages*, Sutton Publishing, 1998.

Bibliography

Castor, Helen, *The King, the Crown, and the Duchy of Lancaster: Public Authority and Private Power, 1399–1461*, Oxford University Press, 2000.

Coppack, Glyn, *Mount Grace Priory*, English Heritage Publications, 1991.

Coppack, Glyn, and Aston, Mick, *Christ's Poor Men: The Carthusians in Britain*, Tempus Publishing, 2002.

Crowfoot, Elisabeth, *et al.*, *Textiles and clothing c.1150–c.1450: Medieval Finds from Excavations in London*, Boydell Press, 2002.

Egan, Geoff, *Archaeology of Modern London*, Sutton Publishing, 2002.

Gaimster, David R. M., and Stamper, Paul (eds), *Age of Transition: Archaeology of English Culture 1400–1600*, Oxbow Books, 1998.

Gimpel, Jean, *The Cathedral Builders*, Pimlico, 1983.

Goldberg, P. J. P., *Medieval England: a Social History 1250–1550*, Hodder & Stoughton Educational, 2000.

Goldberg, P. J. P. (ed.), *Women in Medieval English Society*, Sutton Publishing, 1997.

Goldberg, P. J. P., *Women, Work and Life-cycle in a Medieval Economy: Women in York and Yorkshire c.1300–1520*, Clarendon Press, 1992.

Grenville, Jane, *Medieval Housing*, Leicester University Press, 1998.

Hallam, Elizabeth M. (ed.), *Chronicles of the Age of Chivalry*, Bramley Books, 1998.

Harding, Vanessa, *The Dead and the Living in Paris and London, 1500–1670*, Cambridge University Press, 2002.

Haydon, Peter, *The English Pub, A History*, Robert Hale, 1994.

Herrin, Judith (ed.), *A Medieval Miscellany*, Weidenfeld & Nicolson, 1999.

Bibliography

Holt, Richard, and Rosser, Gervase (eds), *The English Medieval Town: A Reader in English Urban History 1200–1540*, Longman, 1990.

Keen, Maurice, *Origins of the English Gentleman*, Tempus Publishing, 2002.

Keen, Maurice, *The Penguin Social History of Britain: English Society in the Later Middle Ages 1350–1500*, Penguin Press, 1990.

Keen, Maurice, *The Pelican History of Medieval Europe*, Penguin, 1969.

Langland, William, *The Vision of Piers Plowman, A Complete Edition of the B-Text*, Orion, 1987.

Lynch, Michael, *Edinburgh and the Reformation*, J. Donald, 1981.

Lynch, Michael, *et al.*, *The Scottish Medieval Town*, John Donald Publishers, 1988.

Lynch, Michael (ed.), *Early Modern Town in Scotland*, Croom Helm, 1986.

MacDonald, A. A. (ed.), *et al.*, *The Renaissance in Scotland: Studies in Literature, Religion, History and Culture Offered to John Durkan*, Brill, 1994.

Menuge, Noel James (ed.), *Medieval Women and the Law*, Boydell Press, 2000.

Pedersen, Frederik, *Marriage Disputes in Medieval England*, Hambledon and London, 2000.

Pedersen, Frederik, *'Romeo and Juliet of Stonegate': a Medieval Marriage in Crisis*, Borthwick Institute Publications, 1995.

Rigby, Steve, *A Companion to Britain in the Later Middle Ages*, Blackwell, 2002.

Rodwell, Warwick, *English Heritage Book of Church Archaeology*, B. T. Batsford, 1989.

Slater, T. R., and Rosser, Gervase (eds), *The Church in the Medieval Town*, Ashgate Publishing, 1998.

Virgoe, Roger, *Private Life in the Fifteenth Century: Illustrated Letters of the Paston Family*, Weidenfeld & Nicholson, 1989.

7: Leaving the Land

Beier, A. L., *Masterless Men: Vagrancy Problem in Britain, 1560–1640*, Methuen, 1985.

Beier, A. L., and Finlay, Roger, *Making of the Metropolis: London, 1500–1700*, Longman, 1986.

Borsay, Peter, *The English Urban Renaissance: Culture and Society in the Provincial Town 1660–1770*, Clarendon Press, 1989.

Clark, Peter, and Slack, Paul, *Crisis and Order in English Towns, 1500–1700: Essays in Urban History*, Routledge, 1972.

Clifford, D. J. H. (ed.), *The Diaries of Lady Anne Clifford*, Sutton Publishing, 1992.

Davis, Norman (ed.), *The Paston Letters*, Oxford University Press, 1983.

Duffy, Eamon, *The Voices of Morebath: Reformation and Rebellion in an English Village*, Yale University Press, 2001.

Duffy, Eamon, *The Stripping of the Altars: Traditional Religion in England 1400–1580*, Yale University Press, 1992.

Fletcher, Anthony, and MacCulloch, Diarmaid, *Tudor Rebellions*, Longman, 1997.

Geddes, Jane (ed.), *King's College Chapel, Aberdeen, 1500–2000*, Northern University Press, 2000.

Guy, John, *The Tudors: a Very Short Introduction*, Oxford Paperbacks, 2000.

Guy, John, *et al.*, *The Oxford History of Britain: The Tudors and Stuarts*, Oxford Paperbacks, 1992.

Hatcher, John, *The History of the British Coal Industry: Before 1700: Towards the Age of Coal*, Clarendon Press, 1993.

Bibliography

Hatcher, John, *Plague, Population and the English Economy, 1348–1530*, Palgrave, 1977.

Hill, Christopher, *The World Turned Upside Down*, Penguin, 1991.

Hindle, Steve, *The State and Social Change in Early Modern England, c.1550–1640*, Palgrave, 2000.

Hindle, Steve, *The Birthpangs of Welfare: Poor Relief and Parish Governance in Seventeenth-century Warwickshire*, Dugdale Society, 2000.

Houlbrooke, Ralph, *Death, Religion, and the Family in England, 1480–1750*, Oxford University Press, 1998.

Houlbrooke, Ralph, *English Family Life 1576–1716*, Blackwell, 1988.

Hoyle, R. W., *The Pilgrimage of Grace and the Politics of the 1530s*, Oxford University Press, 2001.

Hutton, Ronald, *The Rise and Fall of Merry England: The Ritual Year 1400–1700*, Oxford University Press, 1994.

Johnson, Matthew, *An Archaeology of Capitalism*, Blackwell, 1995.

Kermode, Jennifer, and Walker, Garthine (eds), *Women, Crime and the Courts in Early Modern England*, University College London Press, 1994.

MacCulloch, Diarmaid, *The Later Reformation in England, 1547–1603*, Palgrave, 1990.

Miller, Edward, and Hatcher, John, *Medieval England: Towns, Commerce and Crafts, 1086–1348*, Longman, 1995.

Morrill, John, *Stuart Britain: a Very Short Introduction*, Oxford Paperbacks, 2000.

Overton, Mark (ed.), *et al.*, *Capitalism at Home: Production and Consumption in English Households, 1600–1750*, Routledge, 2003.

Overton, Mark, *Agricultural Revolution in England: The*

Transformation of the Agrarian Economy 1500–1850, Cambridge University Press, 1996.

Overton, Mark, *Population Growth and Agrarian Change in Early Modern England*, University of Newcastle Press, 1985.

Pullar, Philippa, *Consuming Passions, A History of English Food and Appetite*, Penguin, 2001.

Sharpe, James, *Witchcraft in Early Modern England*, Longman, 2001.

Sharpe, James, *The Bewitching of Anne Gunter*, Profile Books, 1999.

Sharpe, James, *Instruments of Darkness: Witchcraft in England 1550–1750*, Hamish Hamilton, 1996.

Slack, Paul, *From Reformation to Improvement: Public Welfare in Early Modern England*, Clarendon Press, 1998.

Slack, Paul, *The English Poor Law, 1531–1782*, Cambridge University Press, 1995.

Slack, Paul, and Ward, Ryk (eds), *The Peopling of Britain: The Shaping of a Human Landscape*, Oxford University Press, 2002.

Snodin, Michael, and Howard, Maurice, *Ornament: A Social History Since 1450*, Yale University Press, 1996.

Spurr, John, *England in the 1670s*, Blackwell, 2000.

Spurr, John, *English Puritanism*, Palgrave, 1998.

Stone, Lawrence, *Family, Sex and Marriage in England 1500–1800*, Penguin, 1990.

Stoyle, Mark, *West Britons: Cornish Identities and the Early Modern British State*, University of Exeter Press, 2002.

Stoyle, Mark, *Loyalty and Locality: Popular Allegiance in Devon During the English Civil War*, University of Exeter Press, 1994.

Todd, Margo, *The Culture of Protestantism in Early Modern Scotland*, Yale University Press, 2002.

Todd, Margo (ed.), *Reformation to Revolution*, Routledge, 1995.

Walter, John, *Understanding Popular Violence in the English*

Revolution: The Colchester Plunderers, Cambridge University Press, 1999.

Walter, John, and Schofield, Roger (eds), *Famine, Disease and the Social Order in Early Modern Society*, Cambridge University Press, 1991.

Watt, Diane (ed.), *Medieval Women in Their Communities*, University of Wales Press, 1997.

Watt, Diane, *Secretaries of God: Women Prophets in Late Medieval and Early Modern England*, D. S. Brewer, 1997.

Williams, C. H., *English Historical Documents, Volume V, 1485– 1558*, Eyre & Spottiswoode, 1967.

Williamson, Tom, *The Transformation of Rural England: Farming and the Landscape*, University of Exeter Press, 2002.

Williamson, Tom, *Shaping Medieval Landscapes: Settlement, Society, Environment*, Windgather Press, 2002.

Whittle, Jane, *The Development of Agrarian Capitalism: Land and Labour in Norfolk 1440–1580*, Clarendon Press, 2000.

Wood, Andy, *The Politics of Social Conflict: The Peak Country, 1520–1770*, Cambridge University Press, 1999.

Wrightson, Keith, *Earthly Necessities: Economic Lives in Early Modern Britain*, Yale University Press, 2000.

Wrightson, Keith, *English Society, 1580–1680*, Hutchinson, 1982.

Youings, Joyce, *The Penguin Social History of Britain: Sixteenth-century England*, Penguin, 1991.

Index